Schweppes®

THE FIRST 200 YEARS

Portrait from a description of Jacob Schweppe during his stay in London 1792–1799

Douglas A. Simmons

Schweppes®

The First 200 Years

ACROPOLIS BOOKS LTD.

Washington, D.C.

ACROPOLIS BOOKS
Colortone Building, 2400 17th St., N.W.
Washington, D. C. 2009

ISBN 0 87491 536 8

Contents

Foreword

It comes to few people to write the official history of a commercial entity on the occasion of its bicentenary. Douglas Simmons, formerly Company Secretary, retired in 1981 after 49 years of dedicated service with Schweppes and Cadbury Schweppes. He then turned historian, found a new métier and this book is the result. A fascinating story has found a worthy teller.

In his investigations he has, like all fine historians, discovered new facts and eliminated some myths. He has brought us closer to the real Jacob Schweppe and his daughter Colette, to his partners and to his successors in the business he created.

It is perhaps a reflection of the ethos of Schweppes that this book is not so much about organisations and systems as about people – a series of remarkable people who followed Jacob Schweppe and progressively transformed his personal legacy into an international enterprise. It is no exaggeration to say that in starting his business in Geneva in 1783, Jacob Schweppe also founded an industry which his successors and competitors have developed. His imagination and determination, his courage in risking his fortune – within a decade of the French Revolution – set an entrepreneurial standard for his successors: indeed, enterprise has been the hallmark of subsequent progress.

Jacob Schweppe's first profession was that of bijoutier, a jeweller and a craftsman in precious metal – a man committed to fine and precise workmanship who created for himself the standards for his artefacts. The range of drinks subsequently sold under his name followed his precepts as to the definition and observance of unique standards of excellence: hence, their international reputation.

What a splendid paradox that this German-born, naturalised-Swiss should come to England to create products which in time, bearing his name as a brand, would gain international regard as being essentially British! The paradox goes further: Schweppes Tonic, par excellence an immediately acceptable drink in this age of mass consumption, retains its patrician image – 'Le drink des Gens Raffinés' – as so precisely defined in Schweppes advertising of the 1970s in France.

Anthony Thorncroft in his closing chapter on advertising comments on the lasting identity of Schweppes and its advertising and on the remarkable Schweppes campaigns which have been an integral part of the history and art of advertising.

The best of those campaigns combined the wit and elegance of eighteenth-century European society with their twentieth-century equivalent. Indeed, the felicitous title of this book – 'Schweppes – The First 200 Years' – epitomises the allusive character of the text of so many of the memorable advertisements.

The Schweppervescence of which Jacob Schweppe was the inventor has lasted for two hundred years adding, in Dr Johnson's words, to 'the public stock of harmless pleasure'. Now Schweppes, in alliance with another famous name, Cadbury – unique, too, in its field – is on the point of entering upon its third century.

May it continue, lightly Schwepping its way, giving a lift to the spirits and joy to the heart of an ever increasing number of consumers, nicely defined nearly two hundred years ago as . . .

'the Nobility, Gentry, the Faculty and the Public in general.'

Nunc est Schweppendum.

BASIL E. S. COLLINS
Deputy Chairman and Chief Executive
of Cadbury Schweppes p.l.c.

Acknowledgments

My grateful thanks are due to all those persons and institutions who have helped me in my research. Especially to W. Zurbuchen, State Archivist of Geneva (now retired) and his staff for their sustained interest over several years and from whom I received many records of Jacob Schweppe's life in Geneva; Ph. Monnier, Conservator of the Department of Manuscripts, Bibliothèque Publique et Universitaire, Geneva, for kindly giving permission to quote from H. A. Gosse's manuscripts in his care; the relevant papers may be found in bundles Ms. fr. 2633, 2649 and 2651. To M. R. Winwood for his kind permission on behalf of the Trustees of the Matthew Boulton Trust to reproduce extracts from the Matthew Boulton Papers. Extracts from the diary of the 2nd Earl of Minto are quoted by courtesy of the Trustees of the National Library of Scotland. To Christoph Bachmann, Deacon of the Kirchenkreises, Witzenhausen and to Hans Koch, Mayor and Walter Dietrich, Archivist, of Witzenhausen. To Mrs V. E. Ainsworth and Miss Marguerite Syvret for their research into the history of the families Brohier and Lauzun details of which are quoted by courtesy of the Lord Coutanche Library, Société Jersiaise, St. Helier. To Lt Col. A. R. Evill, and Henry C. S. Evill for information generously provided from their family archives and to Mrs Betty Kenward for her remembrances of the Kemp-Welch family. To Maître Jean Dutoit, Advocate of Geneva and Dr F. E. Ducommun, Pharmacist of Nyon for their courtesy and advice. To Stephen Ballard of Colwall for recalling details of Malvern springs from the days of his grandfather and for encouragement and help received from Dr H. S. Torrens of Keele University, Dr D. J. Jeremy of the Business History Unit, London School of Economics and from Dr Pierre Bertrand and Paul Schulé of Geneva. I am grateful to the Birmingham Reference Library for permission to refer to correspondence between W. Henry and J. Watt junr. in the Boulton and Watt Collection and to the following librarians and archivists: M. Y. Ashcroft, County Archivist, the North Yorkshire County Archives; The County Archivist, Royal County of Berkshire; A. Henstock, Principal Archivist, Nottinghamshire Record Office; Miss Jean M. Kennedy, County Archivist, Norfolk Record Office; R. G. Hughes, Principal Keeper, City of Derby Museums and Art Gallery; E. J. Chapman, Chief Librarian, Doncaster Central Library; G. G. Hand, Assistant County Librarian, North Yorkshire County Library and The Public Record Office, London. I record my special thanks to all past and present directors and staff of Schweppes at home and abroad who have contributed to the story and to Mrs Joan Conrad for typing my manuscripts. Finally, I owe much to my wife for her support and patience during my extended preoccupation with all things Schweppes.

I have also derived information from the following sources:

W. Kirkby: *The Evolution of Artificial Mineral Waters*, Manchester, 1902.

C. Ainsworth Mitchell: *Mineral and Aerated Waters*, London, 1913.

J. J. Riley: *A History of the American Soft Drink Industry*, Washington, D.C., 1958.

G. B. Beattie: 'A Brief History of Soft Drinks', *The Soft Drinks Trade Journal*, 1953.

J. R. Partington: *A History of Chemistry*, Vol. 3, London, 1962.

A. E. Musson and E. Robinson: *Science and Technology in the Industrial Revolution*, Manchester University Press, 1969.

S. D. I.: *An account of the Soft Drinks Industry in Britain during the emergency years 1942–1948*, compiled by Kenneth Penn.

'*The Marble Archer*', House journal of Schweppes 1946 to 1969.

Bibliothèque Britannique, Geneva, 1798–1809.

Barbara Hutton: *Clifton and its People in the Nineteenth Century*. Yorkshire Philosophical Society, 1969.

Essai sur les eaux minérales naturelles et artificielles, Paris 1821. (Henri Brohier's thesis for his degree of Doctor of Medicine.)

Th. Heyer: 'Notice sur Jaques et Nicolas Paul', extrait

du *Bulletin de la Classe d'Industrie et de Commerce de la Société des Arts,* No. 85.

'Rapport sur La Fabrique d'Eaux Minérales de M. Louis Gerbel', extrait du *Bulletin de la Classe d'Industrie et de Commerce* de la Société des Arts de Geneve. Séance du 12.4.1858.

Hooley – Man of Millions, by Gerald Bowman. Edinburgh Evening Dispatch, 29th June 1956.

The Story of Schweppes (South Africa) Ltd., by Eric Rosenthal and Charles Morrison.

DOUGLAS SIMMONS

Anthony Thorncroft wishes to express his appreciation to all those who contributed to the creation of the many advertisements which made the advertising chapter such an enjoyable one to write and, in particular, to thank those upon whose memories he drew in interviews – namely William Franklyn, Leonard Garland, David Ogilvy, A. E. (Tubby) Pitcher, Royston Taylor and Douglas Simmons.

The publisher thanks the following for permission to use certain photographs: Barnaby's Picture Library, Press Association, Evening Standard, London Express Pictures, Mansell Collection, London Transport.

Introduction: The Birth of an Industry

The first soda water, marvellously effervescent though not then 'Schweppervescent', was known as Mr Bewley's Julep. For it is to Richard Bewley of Great Massingham, Norfolk, that credit is given for creating this beverage, in 1767. 'Dissolve three drams of fossil alkali in each quart of water and throw in streams of fixed air ....' said his recipe in the language used by the chemists of the day in this evolving branch of science. Centuries of speculation and experimentation on the nature of natural mineral waters and their special curative properties had preceded the publication of Richard Bewley's recipe.

The first successes had come in the seventeenth century when, with improving methods of chemical analysis, the solid contents of natural mineral waters had begun to be identified. A German chemist discovered and gave his name to 'Glauber's salt'. In 1697 Dr Nehemiah Grew showed that Epsom Water contained magnesium carbonate and a few years later Friderick Hoffman found the same bitter salt in the water of Seidlitz. The other field of research concerned the mysterious spirit that inhabited natural sparkling waters which, at first, seemed almost beyond investigation. This was the 'fixed air' of Richard Bewley's recipe, so called because of its capacity to be absorbed or 'fixed' in alkaline solutions, and variously designated the 'wild spirit', 'the soul of the waters', or 'spiritus mineralis' – our now familiar carbon dioxide or CO_2

The mineral springs of Europe had been used by the Romans, mainly for bathing, and enjoyed for their beneficial effects. The hot mineral springs of Bath caused them to build their own city of Aquae Sulis there, with extensive baths and temples. The practice of drinking spa waters became firmly established during the Middle Ages. Many springs with curative powers were identified and because of their seemingly miraculous properties were frequently called holy wells or given the names of saints. Among the springs of the Malvern district are St Ann's Well, St John's Well and a Holy Well. Once there was also an Eye Well which was believed to heal optical disorders.

Although J. B. van Helmont of Belgium had shown, in the first half of the seventeenth century, that gas from burning wood, his 'gas sylvestre', was identical with the 'wild spirit' of the sparkling waters, it was not until the latter part of the eighteenth century that its properties had been largely clarified and means discovered of generating and collecting the gas for subsequent solution in water. Dr Joseph Priestley, the English clergyman-scientist, sometimes described as the father of our industry, had conducted experiments in methods of impregnating water with fixed air, first using carbon dioxide collected over fermenting vats of beer and later liberating the gas from chalk by means of sulphuric acid. Priestley was not working in a novel field, water having already been carbonated using a separate source of gas, but his genius enabled him to draw several significant conclusions vital to successful carbonation. He recognised that atmospheric air must be excluded and in particular he foresaw the value of using a pump to saturate the water with greater quantities of CO_2 by compressing the gas, and continuing the process of absorption by agitation under pressure.

Following Priestley's experiments, and with the growing awareness of the medicinal value of artificially carbonated waters, the stage was set for commercial developments. In 1775 Dr John Mervin Nooth communicated to the Royal Society details of his ingenious 'gazogene' which could conveniently be kept on the sideboard in the home and which, with some improvements, remained in use for making small quantities of carbonated water far into the nineteenth century. To Thomas Henry, chemist and apothecary of Manchester, is attributed the honour of being the first to manufacture artificial mineral waters for sale commercially. Henry improved upon Nooth's gazogene, devising an apparatus which could aerate ten or twelve gallons at one operation, and which was suitable for use on the larger scale required by apothecaries and hospitals. In 1781 he published a paper describing the apparatus, which may, however, have been in use some years before. By this time also, reliable analyses had been made of the chief British and Continental spa waters which could therefore be prescribed by physicians and made up by apothecaries. The apparatus available for executing these prescriptions, however, was still quite rudimentary. The waters were classified according to the salts included in them. Most in demand were those with alkaline salts which were used in the treatment of digestive troubles, rheumatism and gout. There were also aperient waters, waters containing iron, lithium or barium salts, and sulphurous and arsenical waters.

The approbation of physicians was a factor in the rise of the cult of drinking the waters at resorts blessed with a natural supply of mineral waters. The heyday of these spas came in the eighteenth and early nineteenth centuries, Bath becoming the most fashionable watering place in England under the rule of the indefatigable master of ceremonies, Beau Nash. But such places were for the rich and famous. Artificial mineral waters, formulated according to need and available in the principal towns in the country, grew in popularity with a wider public. Indeed, because the salts contained in natural waters were not always present in the most desirable combination, the fashion for exact copies of them gradually changed in favour of formulations of aerated waters containing those salts which could most usefully be taken for medicinal purposes, generally comprising soda, potass and lithia waters. Jacob Schweppe established his business in England with a range of soda water and artificial Rochelle, Seltzer, Spa and Pyrmont waters. Magnesia water

appears to have been added in about 1820 and Potass water about 1835, though the artificial waters of Rochelle, Spa and Pyrmont had by then been discontinued.

The transition from medicinal to sweetened and flavoured aerated waters extended over a long period. It had been a common practice for some soda water or seltzer water to be mixed, if desired, with syrups, wines or spirits, but the manufacture of prepared flavoured drinks for consumption purely as refreshing beverages seems not to have begun until the early 1800s. The trend progressed slowly, though more rapidly in America than in Britain, but was fairly well established in both countries in the 1830s. Nevertheless Seltzer, Potass and Lithia waters continued to be sold by Schweppes, alongside a widening range of sweetened drinks, until the second world war.

This is the story of Jacob Schweppe, the jeweller of Geneva who began in 1780 to develop a system for the manufacture of artificial mineral waters; of his success and the events which caused him to move to London and start production there; and of the growth over two centuries of the first small factory, in Drury Lane, into the world-spanning organization which is Schweppes today. It is, too, the story of a resolute adherence to the highest standards of quality and business practice, laid down by Jacob Schweppe, on the part of successive generations of management and workers in the firm which he founded.

Schweppes®

The First 200 Years

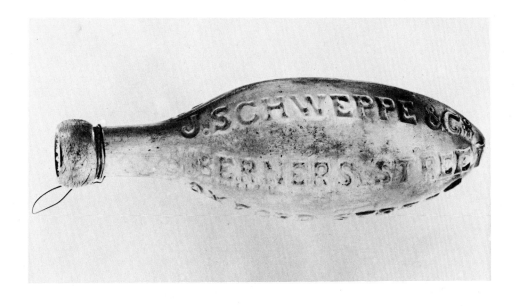

Chapter I

Jacob Schweppe in Germany and Geneva
1740–1791

An old engraving of Witzenhausen and the Werra valley

Jean Jacob Schweppe, son of Conrad Schweppe, was born in 1740 in Witzenhausen, in the district of Hesse, in West Germany. This picturesque town of some 20,000 inhabitants lies beautifully situated among the wooded slopes of the lower Werra valley. The census of 1731 named only 1460 people living in the old town then, among whom there were four families with the name of Schweppe. In the inner town there is a wealth of ancient buildings, mostly of the sixteenth century but also of earlier date. Here in the Liebfrauenkirche Jacob Schweppe was baptised on 16 March 1740. The extraordinary course of his early life, which eventually led him from Witzenhausen to Geneva, has a magical quality reminiscent of the stories told by those other Hessians, the brothers Jacob and William Grimm from nearby Cassel. It is not too difficult to imagine that the brothers may even have heard his strange history when they journeyed among the country-folk collecting their fairy stories.

When Jacob was eleven or twelve years old his parents, considering him to be too delicate for a life in agriculture, allowed a travelling tinker to take charge of him. After a short time the tinker was so much surprised by the boy's dexterity in mending pots that he took him back to his parents, saying that although he might make his fortune if he kept their son, he could not think of confining him to a calling so much below his talents; that they should lose no time in placing him under a silversmith where his success and fortune were certain. This was done and at the silversmith's the same thing occurred. Jacob's talents and skill were so evidently suited for a more difficult branch of the profession that the silversmith recommended his removal to a bijouterie. Here his success and his fortunes continued to increase.

Eventually he was drawn to the city of Geneva, attracted no doubt by its fame as a centre for watch-making and jewellery. The year of his arrival is not known but he was certainly in Geneva late in 1765. His name appeared in the records on the occasion of his marriage on 4 October 1767 at the Temple of the Madeleine to Eléonore Roget, daughter of Antoine Roget and of Susanne Bertrand. On 19 September 1768 he was formally received as *habitant* of Geneva, the first step in the progressive accession of rights of citizenship of Geneva, and can thereby be considered to have been granted Genevese nationality. It would have been a prerequisite of the granting of the status of *habitant* that Jacob was of the Protestant faith.

In Geneva Jacob was probably first in the employment of Jean Louis Dunant, bijoutier, but in May 1777 he entered into a partnership contract with Dunant's son, also Jean Louis, in a similar business to be conducted under the name of Dunant and Schweppe. His partner provided the major portion of the capital but as he was in poor health Jacob agreed to carry the main burden of the business, the expenses and profits of which were shared equally. Three months after this Jacob was admitted as a maître-bijoutier by the Guild of his craft in Geneva, submitting as his chef-d'oeuvre a *nécessaire* which was praised for its good workmanship, and paying a fee of one hundred florins. The partnership of Dunant and Schweppe was wound up in 1786 at the expiry of the contracted period of nine years, during which time the capital of the business had about doubled. It is clear that Jacob was quite soon in comfortable circumstances since in 1783 he became the proprietor of a country house at Bouchet, a hamlet in the district of Petit-Saconnex on the outskirts of Geneva. The house exists to this day although modified by additions during the nineteenth century.

Jacob and his wife Eléonore had nine children, of whom eight died either at birth or in early childhood. One child only, their daughter Nicolarde, called Colette, born on 27 January 1777 and baptised four days later in the Church of St Gervais, survived and outlived her parents. Louise, born in 1779, was the only one of her brothers and sisters Colette was ever to know; she died in a smallpox epidemic in 1787 aged eight, when Colette was nearly eleven. To Jacob and Eléonore, therefore, Colette was a very precious daughter.

No portrait of the family, or any member of it, is known, though it is certain that such existed. Two descriptions of Jacob and one of Colette, contained in passports issued in 1798 and 1814, give details of their general appearance. In 1798 Jacob, then aged fifty-eight, was described as five feet three inches in height, grey-haired and partly bald, with grey eyes, a large nose, average mouth, the lower lip slightly prominent, a long face with high forehead, full cheeks and pointed chin. Colette, then aged twenty-one, was of small stature, rather plump, brightly coloured, hair and eyebrows of chestnut brown and with black eyes. Like her father, she had a large nose, average mouth and pointed chin; she had however a round full face

and moderate forehead. Jacob's passport of 1814 gave fewer details. His hair by then was white and he had a greying beard. His eyes were said to be brown instead of grey!

Jacob described himself as an enthusiastic amateur scientist. Whilst earning his living with his gems and trinkets of precious metal, he diverted himself in the study of science and by reproducing various experiments which he was able to read about in the current journals of physics. After the discoveries of Joseph Priestley of England and of chemists of other nations on gases and their combination with water, he reproduced their experiments with equal success by dint of application and regardless of any expense. But he concluded that the methods employed in their laboratories were too feeble in comparison with those of nature in the production of natural mineral waters.

Jacob's awareness of the works of Joseph Priestley on gases gives an indication of when his own interest in the subject was born. Priestley began his experiments with fixed air in 1767–8 and published his pamphlet entitled *Directions for Impregnating Water with Fixed Air* in London in 1772, which included the remark 'I do not doubt but that, by the help of a condensing engine, water might be much more highly impregnated with the virtues of the Pyrmont spring'. Lavoisier followed with a similar suggestion in 1773. It seems reasonable to conclude therefore that from about this time Jacob was not only well acquainted with the theory and practice of carbonation but was awaiting further developments with increasing impatience. Since the constituent parts of mineral waters were known, why should it not be possible to combine them to the degree desired? This thought put him on his mettle and at last he struck out on his own, making such a determined attempt that he gave up all his other occupations in order to succeed.

At last he reached a stage superior to anything which had been achieved at that time, but still not as good as he was aiming for, and he pressed on, frequently correcting and modifying his experiments and his apparatus. Meanwhile the artificial mineral waters he was producing were of good quality and he regretted letting them go to waste. Therefore he proposed to the doctors of the town that any of their poorer patients who might benefit from them could have them free, and the offer was accepted and acted upon. Soon Jacob reached the degree of perfection he desired. The demand for the waters grew and extended to people in easier circumstances, and then to the rich, but still free of charge as Jacob's only interest in his researches had been the satisfaction of his curiosity and his 'amour propre'. Many people however were reluctant to take the waters free and eventually he was obliged, though unwillingly, to place a nominal price on them to cover his outgoings. Therefore it was by 1783, or even earlier, that the focus of Jacob's activities had moved from progressive experimentation to commercial development. Indeed, it would be reasonable to say that Jacob Schweppe was thus the founder of the soft drinks industry as we know it today since he was the first to invent an apparatus capable of aerating water to equal or exceed the aeration of natural mineral waters in quantities sufficient to support a widespread trade.

Jacob's absorption in the new technology of producing mineral waters was jolted by family worries in 1788. Colette was a musical child and, clearly with the encouragement of her parents, was developing into an accomplished harpist. A young Frenchman, Jean Claude Elouis, who had been persuaded the previous summer to stay in Geneva to teach the harp, was introduced to the Schweppe family, found Jacob and Eléonore extremely courteous, and as an act of friendship gave lessons to Colette. Later, he boarded with the family while occupying a room in the same apartment block in the Rue de Cornavin – a proposal of Eléonore's which enabled the Schweppes to make him some recompense for the lessons.

Elouis was so impressed with Colette's gifts and aptitude that he cut down his other engagements (which had included teaching the harp to Prince Edward of Kent) to spend four or five hours a day with her, practising and making music with her in houses all over Geneva. Colette was only twelve, and her parents liked and admired Elouis without conceiving that he was becoming deeply attached to their daughter; it must have been a profound shock when Colette told them that Elouis wanted to marry her when she was old enough. Jacob told her she was far too young even to think of marriage, and when Elouis himself asked for Colette's hand, he refused his consent. Elouis won her mother's agreement to a marriage in six years' time, but Jacob was adamant; in any case, neither Elouis nor Colette wanted to wait so long.

The couple were now naturally given much less freedom, and Elouis persuaded Colette that the restrictions imposed by her parents were tyrannical and that they should elope – though he was later to claim that she had first broached the scheme. Elope they did, Colette setting off to the tryst on her own volition, and changing with alacrity into boy's clothing in the coach in which she fled from Geneva. Elouis' plan, a desperate one, was to reach Strasbourg where Colette would enter a convent for two or three years, after which he would marry her.

Colette of course was quickly missed in Geneva, and Jacob guessed at once what had happened; he had been given a warning by Colette herself that Elouis might press her to elope. Two of Jacob's friends and a coachman went off in pursuit and found the couple at Liestal. There were violent upbraidings on Elouis' part, and even an attempt at an escape; but Colette was taken back to her parents, who met her at Aubonne. Elouis accompanied her for part of the homeward journey, finding time to write a long note in which he described Jacob as the man he cared for most in the world and who he hoped would one day again be his friend: his farewell glimpse of Colette was in her coach, on the homeward road, where from his horse he threw her kisses, calling repeatedly as he galloped by 'Adieu Colette!'

Colette had always occupied her own room at the inns where they had stayed, and Elouis had acted honourably to her. The Schweppes had clearly held the young man in high regard, and Jacob brought no formal charges against him: but the law could not overlook the crime of what was in fact abduction of a child. Elouis, in addition to being banished from Geneva forever, was condemned to make honourable amends throughout the town, clad in a white shift, with bare head and feet, bearing a flaming torch in his hand, on pain of death. Elouis did not appear to answer the charges, and the sentence was accordingly ordered to be executed in effigy.

Colette was contrite and apparently quite content to be home again with her parents. The curious episode of her elopement made no difference, as we shall see, to her father's trust in her, nor to her future happy marriage. Let us hope that the harp was soon heard again in the Rue de Cornavin.

The sale of Jacob's waters became general, and in the space of ten years from its beginning, the little business had become firmly established and had even extended into foreign parts. At that stage Jacob transferred the charge of sales to a friend, someone in whom he had such confidence that he did not hesitate to allow him to assist in the operation of his machine; but his faith was misplaced. This friend and employee conceived the idea of obtaining another machine like Jacob's and making mineral waters for himself, which he could sell among Jacob's. Not understanding the principles of the machine, which he had only seen in operation, he approached a well-known engineer in

Geneva, Nicolas Paul, to make one for him. Paul turned this opportunity to his own advantage. He threw together a poor machine for Jacob's friend but at the same time made a good one for himself. With this he lost no time in boldly announcing himself as a competitor in business. Jacob took the view that Paul's rivalry could only be to the detriment of his business and its reputation, and he preferred therefore to join him.

The partnership which Jacob Schweppe formed with Nicolas Paul in April 1790 also included his father Jaques Paul, born in 1733 and a descendant of a French family. He was an especially skilful mechanic and inventor. In 1776 the Government took the unusual step of freely according him bourgeois status in recognition of his talents, and in 1788 nominated him director of *La Machine Hydraulique*. This was the machine, constructed in 1708, which raised water from the Rhône to the upper levels of the town to supply the fountains and provide drinking water. The massive water-wheel was situated at the tip of the island facing the lake and is commemorated in the name of the Pont de la Machine. In addition, Jaques Paul was engaged on such public works as the improvement of fire pumps and means of escape from burning buildings. A serious fire in Geneva in 1789 caused much concern over such matters; the Society of Arts, of which Jaques Paul was a member, became involved and enquired about methods in use in England. Jacob Schweppe was named, with Jaques Paul and others, as one who contributed significantly to the adaptation of the English ideas for use in Geneva. Jaques Paul was also entrusted with the supervision of weights and measures to which he brought new standards of exactitude. Examples of his work as a maker of mathematical and scientific instruments can be seen in the museums in Geneva today. He was held in high esteem by the eminent physicists of Geneva, De Luc and H. B. de Saussure. De Saussure wrote of him 'M. Paul is one of the most distinguished artists of our town and is capable not only of constructing the most delicate instruments but also even of perfecting the ideas of the physicist who has ordered them to be made'. Due to poor health in his latter years, however, Jaques Paul played little part in the partnership. He died in 1796.

Rather less is known of his younger son Nicolas, though it seems that he was hardly less brilliant than his father. Born in 1763, he had been included with his father in the grant of bourgeois status. Like his father, he became a skilled mechanic. Together they presided over the complete overhaul of *La Machine Hydraulique* and Nicolas eventually succeeded his

father as its director. Father and son were therefore both experts in pumps. Nicolas is also known to have demonstrated to the Society of Arts certain steelyards that he had constructed which offered notable improvements in operation. At the time he became a partner of Jacob Schweppe, he had for several years past been a friend of Henry Albert Gosse, a pharmacist, and a highly respected man in Geneva; they had once been involved together in ballooning. Nicolas had been anxious to escape from the constraints of his position in Geneva. He had sought advice from Gosse, a man twenty years his senior and one whom he admired for his achievements, on whether he should take up an offer from Paris to buy the business of a mathematical instrument maker. In pursuit of this scheme he went to Paris late in 1785 with introductions to a number of people who received him with much kindness, but also with flattery which went to his head. The business failed to prosper and he wrote to Gosse chastened and dejected. He begged Gosse, who still remained his example, not to lose faith in him. He moved on to London, where he stayed for a time with Dudley Adams, an optician and mathematical instrument maker of Charing Cross. By 1788 he had rejoined his father in Geneva. It may have been because of his lack of success in Paris and London that Nicolas Paul grasped at Jacob's secret, when it came his way, as an opportunity to embark on a new undertaking in which he could play a leading role.

No sooner had Jaques and Nicolas Paul joined with Jacob Schweppe in partnership than the partners, with Nicolas as spokesman, opened discussions with Gosse to persuade him to throw in his lot with them. As a young man Gosse had left his father's business of bookseller in Geneva and gone to Paris to study chemistry, botany and pharmacy. It was therefore said of him that he was born among books and lived among bottles. Returning to Geneva as Master of Pharmacy, he established a laboratory in Place Longemalle. As well as being a celebrated pharmacist he became one of the founders of the Swiss Natural Sciences Society. He was a highly professional man, described as of a lively and authoritarian character, with strong commitments to public affairs, a man of action, devoted citizen and filled with libertarian principles. He was a philosopher, a disciple of J. J. Rousseau and imbued with a deep love of nature from the time of his childhood. In his dispensary he kept, in a chest, the mummy of a saint (or so it was rumoured) which he had acquired during his stay in Paris from a sacristan who had wished to make a little money. It was kept in an attic and his employees would not go near it. After his death

Geneva in the 18th Century. In the foreground is 'La Machine Hydraulique' where Schweppe, Paul and Gosse sometimes met

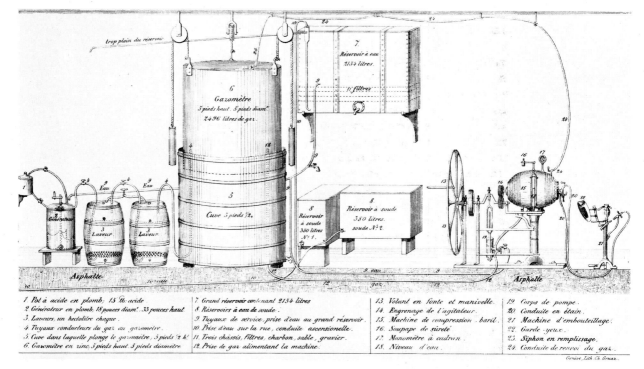

An aerated water apparatus in use in 1858 illustrating the principles of the system devised by Jacob Schweppe, c. 1780–1783

the mummy was returned to the care of the church.

Gosse himself had been experimenting with the manufacture of artificial mineral waters but admitted that he could not match the levels of carbonation produced on the apparatus in use by Schweppe and Paul. He would be a valuable man to work with them. His skills in chemistry and pharmacy were required for the determination of the nature, quantity and purity of the salts introduced into the waters; where they were to be obtained; and on questions relating to the generation of carbonic acid gas. Gosse reacted cautiously to the terms proposed, and pointed out that he might compete with Schweppe and Paul by undercutting their prices. He also complained that the partners would not at that stage reveal to him their system of carbonation. To this Paul blandly replied that he should understand that when Monsieur Schweppe communicated his methods to him and his father it was only after the legal agreements had been signed by all parties! Paul's persuasion was successful however and Gosse agreed to join the partnership.

The method or system of production invented by Jacob Schweppe passed into history under the name of the Geneva System or the Geneva apparatus. There

were probably variations in the layout of this apparatus but in principle it consisted of a container, enclosing an agitator, for the generation of carbon dioxide from chalk and sulphuric acid, from which the gas was passed through water in one or more purification vessels and thence into a gasometer; the gas was then conveyed with the aid of a pump into a closed wooden carbonating vessel, bound with strong iron hoops, where it was dissolved in water under pressure with the assistance of an agitator. The apparatus was the first to make practical and efficient use of a compression pump, as had been suggested by Priestley and Lavoisier, and its principles were still in use in Europe a century later.

Most writers on the subject have credited the first use of the compression pump in the carbonation process, and therefore the invention of the Geneva System, to Nicolas Paul. This assumption has been based on conjecture, having regard to the reputation of Nicolas Paul and his father as expert mechanics and inventors, and to their practical experience with pumps. Moreover Nicolas Paul in 1797, when he was no longer in partnership with either Schweppe or Gosse, registered a patent for the use of a pump to increase carbonation. Also he allowed ambiguous statements to be published, focusing praise upon himself for the excellence of his apparatus, which tended to mislead. As a result for the greater part of two centuries the credit for the first use of the force pump and the creation of the Geneva Apparatus has been denied to the one to whom it truly belongs, that is to Jacob Schweppe.

Paul was always careful to keep his method of carbonation secret, even from the representatives of the Society of Arts in Geneva and the National Institute of France in Paris, who reported his process. Jacob Schweppe left no description of his apparatus though discussions on the plant between the partners in 1790, recorded by Gosse, with some rough sketches of his, have left impressions. Jacob did, however, leave a personal statement of his involvement with artificial mineral waters and how his invention came into the hands of Nicolas Paul. It is in his own distinctive handwriting and its authenticity is unquestionable. He makes it clear that he had been following the work of Priestley, who in 1772 had suggested the use of a 'condensing engine' for more efficient carbonation. He had almost certainly read of the same suggestion by Lavoisier in 1773. Jacob was devoting the whole of his creative energies and practical skill to the achievement of his object; he was a perfectionist, and ultimately succeeded to the degree he desired, well beyond that which had been achieved by anyone else. This does not prove that he adopted the pump, but the conjunction of these facts with other contemporary evidence forces one to the conclusion that he did. Jacob asserted that the quality of his waters was as perfect before as after his partnership with Paul, and that all Paul did, in his capacity of mechanic, was to perfect parts of the apparatus in ease of operation. Paul himself, when inviting Gosse to join the partnership, indicated that the methods which could not as yet be revealed to Gosse were the same as those withheld by Jacob Schweppe until he and his father had signed the agreement. Gosse left written corroboration that Jacob was the sole inventor of the first means employed in Geneva for the manufacture on a large scale of artificial aerated mineral waters – in other words, the Geneva System of which the pump became a known component. Gosse also confirmed the appropriation of Jacob's invention by Paul. His words have the ring of authenticity that one would expect from such a highly professional and high principled man. They are totally convincing.

When Jacob in due course returned to Geneva after his retirement from business in England, he was astonished and indignant to see statements in a number of journals implying that the credit for the system he had invented belonged to Nicolas Paul. It was for this reason that he drew up his account of the true facts. The last word that appears to have been written on the matter is in the form of a letter from Jacob, dated 1 January 1809, from his country home outside Geneva, to the editor of the *Bibliothèque Britannique*. This begins,

When an invention has been of some usefulness, its author may no doubt be forgiven for wishing not to be forgotten. Your review, so justly esteemed, contains in several articles an account of my rights to the invention of the art of manufacturing artificial mineral waters on a large scale; in others the impression is given that the late Mr Paul, my former associate, had some part in that invention. I attach some importance to having the facts in this regard clearly established; and your impartiality, which I fully acknowledge, makes me hope that you will insert my claim in one of your future editions.

Jacob then referred to the articles which he considered

Extract of a memorandum written by Jacob Schweppe describing the birth of his idea

Signatures to the partnership agreement of 12 June 1790

had been misleading and disposed of these by quoting an article of 1802 by Professor Odier, one of Geneva's best known doctors of medicine, in which he said, 'Mr Schweppe, first inventor of the machine by means of which Mr Paul, his former associate, prepares in quantity all kinds of aerated waters, has taken this art from Geneva to London'.

The terms of the Schweppe, Paul and Gosse partnership, which was for a period of nine years from 1 July 1790, were agreed before a notary in Geneva on 12 June 1790. The Notarial Act acknowledged that Jacob Schweppe had already dedicated ten years to manufacturing artificial mineral waters. It specified that the firm's name should be 'Schweppe, Paul and Gosse'. On 4 September there appeared in the *Journal de Genève* a prospectus announcing the establishment of the partnership and its proposed activities. The prospectus explained the disadvantages associated with the use of imported natural mineral waters, the loss of quality and efficacy as a result of transport and long periods of storage, and emphasised the advantages of the firm's products which often surpassed the natural waters in purity and aeration. Reference was made to the ailments in which use of the waters was beneficial and doctors and sick persons were invited to ask for any mineral waters which they needed, of which, they were assured, exact copies would promptly be made. Attached to the prospectus was a commendation signed by ten leading doctors in Geneva which again stated that it was about ten years since Schweppe had the idea of imitating natural mineral waters and furthermore that for seven or eight years, he had manufactured Seltzer water and Spa water which had enjoyed such a high reputation in the town that their sales had greatly surpassed those of natural mineral

waters. The prospectus revealed considerable changes in the business, resulting from the partnership. Jacob's trade had probably been confined mainly to Seltzer water and Spa water manufactured from non-distilled water. The new firm proposed to use distilled water as a base for all their products and to manufacture in addition to Seltzer and Spa the waters of Pyrmont, Bussang, Courmayeur, Vals, Seidschutz, Balaruc, Passy and indeed any reputable mineral waters. Distilled water was also offered for sale at a low price for drinking in preference to the water from local sources.

Just as the range of products had been widely extended, it was soon decided by the partners to enlarge the scope of the business by establishing a factory in London. For this purpose it would have been inconvenient for Gosse to have left his pharmacy for a lengthy period. Nicolas Paul, then twenty-seven, might have seemed the obvious choice to be sent to England but he had already failed abroad, as Gosse knew better than anyone. Also, his father's increasing infirmities no doubt required Nicolas to give him additional support in regard to *La Machine Hydraulique* and in his atelier. Jacob, in his fiftieth year, was chosen for the task.

In Geneva at that time was an English doctor, William Belcombe, who had been living there for the past two years; two of his children had been born there. He was soon to return to England. Dr Belcombe would have known many of the local people interested in scientific developments, among them being Jacob Schweppe, the two Pauls and Gosse. The partners agreed to include him in a separate establishment for Great Britain, in which his part would be to publicise the business by all possible means, in particular to the medical profession. Again it was Paul who was the spokesman in recruiting Dr Belcombe, as previously with Gosse. Dr Belcombe showed great enthusiasm for the project during his remaining weeks in Geneva. How much he was able to achieve in the early days after the opening of the London factory is unfortunately unknown. (Belcombe became an eminent doctor in York; he seems to have made mental illness his chief though not his only interest.)

For the space of a month during October and November 1790, until Dr Belcombe's departure,

---

A page from the Prospectus published in the Journal de Genève on 4 September 1790

PROSPECTUS

D'une Société établie à Genève par MM. Schweppe, N. Paul, Mécanicien, & H. A. Gosse, Maître en Pharmacie, pour la compofition des Eaux minérales artificielles.

L'EFFICACITÉ des Eaux minérales, & la facilité avec laquelle elles paffent, leur ont donné une telle célébrité que leur commerce s'étend jufqu'aux Indes Orientales.

Mais ces Eaux ne peuvent conferver toujours le même degré de pureté & de force : le changement dans leur température, les pluies abondantes, une fécherefle fuivie, la perte qu'elles font ordinairement de leurs principes volatils par leur tranfport & leur long emmagafinage, les fraudes enfin dont elles font fufceptibles, font varier leurs propriétés médicales, & peuvent même les anéantir. De plus, l'éloignement de leur fource, & la cherté qui en eft la fuite, en rendent l'ufage impoffible aux perfonnes qui ne font pas dans l'aifance.

Tous ces inconvéniens ont été fentis depuis long-tems. De très-habiles Chymiftes, tels que MM. Venel, Bergmann, de Fourcroy, &c. &c. ont cherché à y remédier en analyfant & en recompofant, avec beaucoup de foin, diverfes Eaux minérales.

Aidés par les travaux de tant d'Hommes célèbres, éclairés par les nombreufes découvertes de la chymie moderne & par les analyfes les plus exactes, poffédant nous-mêmes quelques moyens, nous nous fommes réunis en fociété pour imiter les Eaux minérales les plus utiles.

Toute Eau douce contenant plus ou moins de principes fixes, nuifibles à l'économie animale, ne nous a point paru propre à fervir de bafe à nos compofitions; nous avons penfé que nous ne pourrions remplir notre but que par une diftillation très-foignée de cette même Eau.

Les Eaux minérales préparées avec cette Eau diftillée, qui eft d'une pureté parfaite, ne préfentent aucun des inconvéniens indiqués ci-deffus. Il n'y a plus à craindre de variations dans leurs propriétés médicales par l'alternative de la pluie & de la fécherefle, du froid & du chaud, & leur prix fe trouve à la portée de tous les malades.

Ce n'eft pas d'aujourd'hui que les Eaux minérales artificielles font connues dans Genève ; M. Schweppe compofoit depuis fept à huit ans avec de l'eau non-diftillée des Eaux de *Seltz* & de *Spa*, qui ont joûi dans cette Ville d'une telle réputation, que leur débit y furpaffoit beaucoup celui des Eaux minérales naturelles.

Sans vouloir entrer dans le détail des propriétés de chacune des Eaux minérales, nous ferons obferver, qu'en général les Eaux de *Seltz* font un remède fouvent employé dans les cas de bile, de putridité, d'acreté, de catharre, de toux & d'affection de poitrine, foit qu'on les prenne pures, foit qu'on les tempère, felon les cas, avec un peu de firop ou de lait ; & prifes feules, ou mêlées avec du vin, ou un firop aromatique, elles font même devenues une boiffon d'agrément : que les Eaux de *Spa* font un des meilleurs toniques & un ftomachique des plus efficaces, &c.

Nous avons cru devoir charger avec excès nos Eaux minérales acidules de leur principe aëriforme, quoiqu'elles n'exiftent point telles dans la nature, parce que cet excès les rend fupérieures aux Eaux minérales naturelles dans plufieurs maladies, & que l'on peut facilement, en laiffant évaporer le furplus de ce principe volatil, les adoucir & les rendre par-là propres aux perfonnes les plus irritables.

Les Eaux minérales que nous compofons font les Eaux de *Seltz*, de *Spa*, de *Pyrmont*, de *Buffang*, de *Courmayeur*, de *Vals*, de *Seidfchutz*, de *Sedlitz*, de *Balaruc*, de *Paffy*, & en général toutes les Eaux minérales qui ont de la réputation.

L'Eau de notre Lac, ainfi que celle de la plupart des fources que nous avons à Genève, contient plus ou moins de félénite & de terre calcaire, ce qui peut contribuer à la production des Goëtres, des Obftructions & des Hydropifies affez fréquentes dans ce pays. Nous croyons pouvoir prévenir ces inconvéniens par la vente à bas prix de l'Eau diftillée dont nous avons parlé ci-devant.

Nous invitons Meffieurs les Médecins & les Malades à nous demander les Eaux minérales dont ils pourroient avoir befoin, & que nous ne fpécifions pas ici ; nous les affurons que nous nous occuperons promtement & avec exactitude de leur imitation.

Gosse kept notes of the proceedings at meetings of the partners, providing an illuminating insight into their activities. They also show why Gosse later found Paul difficult to work with. Paul undertook to arrange with the notary for the new agreement with Dr Belcombe covering the English project. A week later he had taken no action but promised to see the notary that day. When at the next meeting Paul still had nothing satisfactory to report, the matter was given to Gosse to deal with. Gosse immediately left the meeting and returned later to say that the notary would prepare the deed.

There was no lack of enthusiastic ideas at that time. Pondicherry and Calcutta were even spoken of at one meeting as likely to be profitable places to establish branches. Dr Belcombe wrote to a doctor friend in London asking him to rent a convenient place where Jacob could live on his arrival and where he could establish a small factory. Jacob was to await the reply before leaving and in the meantime to prepare for the journey. Belcombe's friend was also asked to give all possible help to Jacob, and as soon as the waters had been manufactured, to send samples to the principal doctors in and around London. In addition to his friends in the medical profession Belcombe would bring the firm's mineral waters to the notice of the Secretary for the Navy and various naval officers and would send them samples. An establishment close to Ranelagh was suggested, to popularise the products, with suitable encouragement being given to the director of the gardens. (There is an interesting accent here on the social aspects of the products as distinct from the medical.) It was agreed that to compete with sellers of natural mineral waters in London substantial discounts should be allowed on large orders. At Nicolas Paul's suggestion Seltzer water was to be made in two kinds; one highly charged with 'fixed air' and the other imitating as closely as possible natural Seltzer water. Belcombe suggested that samples of Seltzer water should be sent to the Duke of Gloucester whom Jacob had supplied with his product when the Duke was staying in Geneva. Nicolas Paul would write to 'his friend' Priestley. Belcombe proposed that when they knew that the waters had found favour in London, an effort should be made to interest Genevans with friends or relatives in England, and that a circular in English and French be prepared for distribution to hotels and cafés for the information of foreign visitors. This would give the names and addresses of agents in Geneva, Lausanne, Morges, Rolle and Nyon where their waters were on sale. The London address would be added later. However, Belcombe advised secrecy regarding Jacob's departure and its purpose until the waters were manufactured and ready for distribution.

Encouraged by Belcombe, the partners embarked on an extensive series of experiments to perfect the formulae and manufacture of the extended range of artificial mineral waters they were then offering in Geneva, obtaining fresh supplies of the natural waters for comparison with their own artificial waters. He urged this on them as the best means of enhancing the reputation of the firm's mineral waters with the doctors of London. The purity and flavour of the products received much attention. Various procedures for generating carbon dioxide were tested and a cask made of chestnut was ordered to compare its effect on the waters with those of oak.

A suggestion came from Nicolas Paul at a meeting on 7 November 1790 for a modification of the plant. He indicated a method of moving the piston by a wheel in such a way that the workman would not have sight of the pump handle. This is good confirmation of the mechanical nature of Jacob's means of compression and also revealed Paul's eagerness to preserve the secret which he continued to show in his later undertakings. It also links with Jacob's subsequent statement that Paul's contribution was limited to improving the ease of operation of certain parts of his apparatus.

Ten days later Belcombe was about to leave for England by way of Paris. Some Seltzer water was sent to Paris for him to distribute there. Gosse handed him letters for two friends, one of which was for Mons. De Fourcroy whom he reminded of the proposition he had made two months earlier on the subject of mineral waters, perhaps for a joint venture in Paris. Belcombe remained full of ideas. He proposed installing a pressure gauge in the plant similar to that on the gasometer invented by Lavoisier the previous year. He also suggested that several meaningless parts should be fixed to the apparatus to mislead any strangers who saw it, and said that Jacob was not sufficiently discreet and allowed his apparatus to be too easily seen. The partners' response was to agree that, for security, all apparatus should be enclosed. Finally Belcombe suggested that in preparation for his task Jacob should brush up his English and, oddly, that he should engage a German servant in London, to be better understood. After providing this brief glut of information, Gosse's notes cease. There is no certain answer to the question of why a further whole year passed before Jacob left for England, late in 1791. Was it found that his continued presence was necessary in Geneva? It can easily be imagined that Jacob would have been reluctant to leave the business he had created and nursed during the past ten years in the hands of newcomers, whatever their respective abilities were. There was also perhaps some measure of tension below the surface between the partners. On 13 December 1791 Paul wrote to Gosse. He was not well enough, he said, to brave the bad weather but the first fine day he would call on Gosse to consider with him the conditions applicable to Jacob's proposed stay in London. They should also consider their attitude to Jacob, he continued; it was best that they should be of one mind on this, since he still had certain 'little vanities' which were vexing to one's self-esteem. Considering how Jacob's invention, born of his great dream, had been usurped, schemes of 'aggrandisement' formulated around him, he himself required to depart for London leaving his wife and daughter in Geneva for an unspecified period, in troubled times, it was not surprising if on Jacob's part there might be some 'little vanities' about which he was sensitive.

A week later the partners mutually agreed on the conditions for the overseas operation. The payment of Jacob's expenses was only to continue provided he had not been required by the other partners to discontinue the operation, in which case Jacob would be under an obligation to withdraw the greater part of the partnership property and return promptly at the firm's expense.

Chapter 2

Jacob Schweppe in England

1792–1799

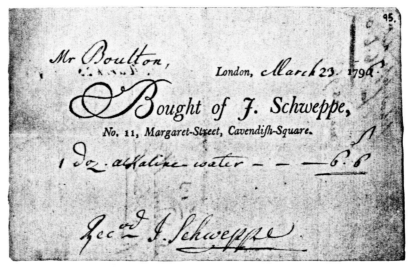

Invoice, in Jacob Schweppe's own hand, to Matthew Boulton of Birmingham

Travelling through the depths of winter, Jacob Schweppe arrived in England on 9 January 1792 bringing with him a letter of recommendation from Professor Pictet of Geneva, which he presented to the Government. Professor Pictet had been thought of as a possible member of the partnership but there is no evidence that he was ever invited to join. He was clearly a friend of all the partners. Gosse's notes record that at one of their meetings, held in Jacob's house, Professor Pictet was present and joined in the discussion on technical problems.

The first factory was set up at 141 Drury Lane, a very poor quarter of London at the end of the eighteenth century. Whether Dr Belcombe had any hand in choosing this address before Jacob's arrival is not known. Production commenced in the spring or early summer. The business met with no immediate, easy success; rather the reverse. There were in London then numerous apothecaries and others dispensing mildly aerated mineral waters prepared on the rudimentary machines that Jacob Schweppe had dismissed in 1780 as inadequate. Horse-drawn wagons carted

mineral water machines through the streets for whoever would buy. Artificial mineral waters, such as they were, were no novelty before Jacob's arrival. His success had to await the recognition, chiefly by the medical profession, of the superior carbonation of his products, which he alone achieved by the use of a compression pump.

In July Jacob reported a decided lack of progress to his partners in Geneva. At the same time he told them that for this reason a firm and resolute decision had to be taken, either to abandon the business there and then, or for them to agree that he should remain in London through the winter, since he saw no hope of progress in a shorter time. Jacob asked that, if they wished him to stay, they should urge his wife to allow his daughter to join him in England, as in his state of health it was not good for him to live for too long alone. A reply came the following month urging Jacob to have courage and patience; he must have lost his reason, his partners said, to think of abandoning the establishment for so small a set-back; he would see that in seven or eight months things would be altogether different.

Colette Schweppe, then only fifteen years old, travelled to London at considerable expense to Jacob, and not without danger in the revolutionary turmoil of 1792, to be by his side.

As he had feared, there was no sign of business improving, even when fashionable society returned from the country for the London season. In November he wrote to his partners that he had hardly done anything since September. Even the doctors, on whom so much reliance had been placed, appeared to be showing no interest. Nevertheless he was committed, at the insistence of his partners, to carry on, at least until the spring, and was therefore astonished to receive in December a peremptory letter requiring him to close down the business and return home. The reasons advanced for requiring Jacob's return were first the lack of success in England; but this they had not long before brushed aside. Next among their reasons were the internal troubles in Geneva, the rumblings of revolution which appeared to be only just beginning and the political changes which they thought imminent in England; last, but not least one imagines, the firm's sales in Geneva were diminishing every day. No one would have known better than Gosse the likely effects in Geneva of revolutionary ideas spreading from France, but neither he nor Paul could speak with the same insight on the situation in England. As to the decline of sales, it seems likely that the conflicting personalities and interests of Paul and Gosse were already proving detrimental to the business and that without Jacob's steadying influence things had begun to fall apart. The letter, with its bombshell, written on the 6th, arrived on 21 December. Jacob was allowed the rest of the month to dispose of property belonging to the partnership and to arrange his return, as the Geneva partners were not willing to incur another month's expenses.

Clearly Jacob felt the situation with his partners was becoming impossible. He replied on 28 December with unrestrained feeling. 'I can only believe,' he said, 'that you wrote without thinking, or in a moment when you didn't have your heads on your shoulders, for such a letter could not possibly have been written in good faith after reflection.' He reminded them how they had urged him to stay on in London and to have patience and courage; how Colette had made the perilous journey to be with him and how he had entered into commitments and incurred expense both on account of the firm and privately. More explosively he expressed his astonishment that they should believe him so imbecile as to want to be their dupe again, to agree to their ridiculous orders. He did not intend to be the plaything of their caprices. He would hold to their

earlier letter and spend the rest of the winter in London at the expense of the partnership, not wishing to suffer the punishing journey in winter for a second time, to the total ruination of his health and that of his daughter, to satisfy their fantasies. If however they preferred that he should personally suffer the expense they had occasioned, he would leave them that choice and all would be broken off between them in London and in Geneva as well if they wished; it being a case of having to deal with people with so few scruples, for one could not find a parallel example among gentlemen. Hard words indeed from Jacob! They were all faithfully recorded by Gosse in his notes.

The situation was thus that Jacob had refused to return to Geneva at the request of Paul and Gosse, his subsequent actions showing that he considered he had been abandoned by his partners. On the other hand Paul and Gosse continued to believe that Jacob would return to Geneva in the spring and wrote to Dr Belcombe to tell him that because of the lack of progress of the business in England and of the political situation they had recalled Jacob to Geneva, indicating the end of the English enterprise.

On 1 February 1793 another crisis struck when France declared war on Great Britain. Jacob heard that Parliament had decreed that all foreigners who had arrived in London during the previous year must leave town and, having been there only a matter of days beyond the prescribed period, was afraid that he might be at risk. On 8 February he wrote to the Government, to whom he had presented his credentials a year earlier, seeking reassurance. 'Since then,' he said, 'I have been busy perfecting my factory and it is only now that I am hoping to begin to reap some benefit from my considerable investment in it.' Prophetically, he affirmed his belief that the business could become of advantage to the country. The impression given by this letter is that he regarded the business as his own with his future at stake in it. A glowing testimonial was added by the optician and mathematical instrument maker, Dudley Adams of Charing Cross, for whom Nicolas Paul had worked some years earlier, and who had been in constant contact with Jacob Schweppe in London. He affirmed that he had been eyewitness to Jacob's activities since his arrival in England; that he had been wholly occupied in perfecting the manufacture of artificial mineral waters, and that he was the first to have brought such waters to their present high state of perfection. He believed Jacob to be as good a friend to the English Government as it was possible for any Englishman to be.

On 7 May 1794 Jacob sent to Geneva an account of

Jacob Schweppe's letter seeking assurance that he would not be required to leave London because of the war with France.

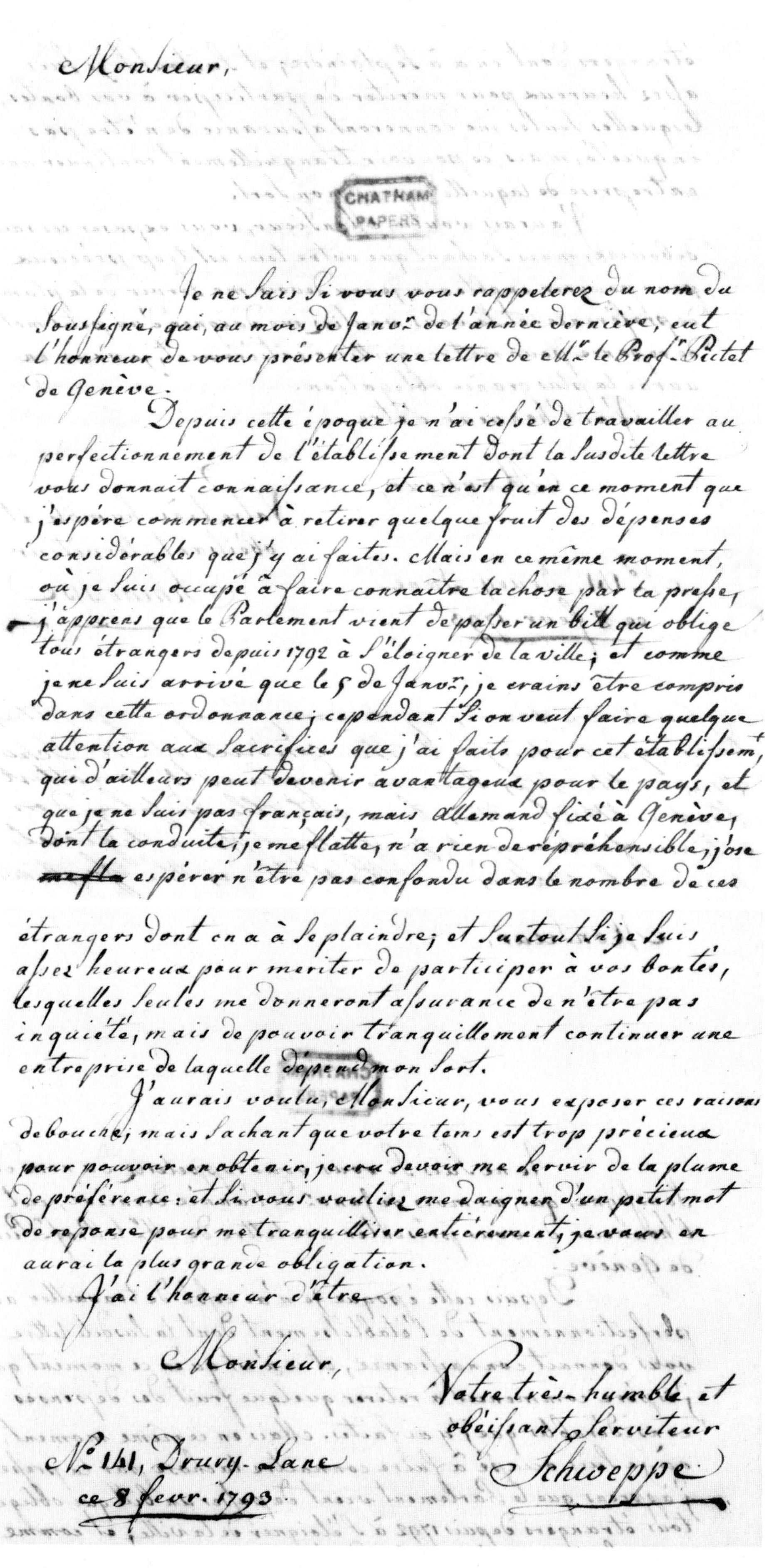

Monsieur,

Je ne sais si vous vous rappelerez du nom du soussigné, qui, au mois de Janvr. de l'année dernière, eut l'honneur de vous présenter une lettre de Mr. le Profr. Pictet de Genève.

Depuis cette époque je n'ai cessé de travailler au perfectionnement de l'établissement dont la susdite lettre vous donnait connaissance, et ce n'est qu'en ce moment que j'espère commencer à retirer quelque fruit des dépenses considérables que j'y ai faites. Mais en ce même moment, où je suis occupé à faire connaître la chose par la presse, j'apprens que le Parlement vient de passer un bill qui oblige tous étrangers depuis 1792 à s'éloigner de la ville; et comme je ne suis arrivé que le 5 de Janvr., je crains être compris dans cette ordonnance; cependant si on veut faire quelque attention aux sacrifices que j'ai faits pour cet établissemt, qui d'ailleurs peut devenir avantageux pour le pays, et que je ne suis pas français, mais Allemand fixé à Genève, dont la conduite, je me flatte, n'a rien de répréhensible, j'ose espérer n'être pas confondu dans le nombre de ces

étrangers dont on a à se plaindre; et surtout si je suis assez heureux pour mériter de participer à vos bontés, lesquelles seules me donneront assurance de n'être pas inquiété, mais de pouvoir tranquillement continuer une entreprise de laquelle dépend mon sort.

J'aurais voulu, Monsieur, vous exposer ces raisons de bouche; mais sachant que votre tems est trop précieux pour pouvoir en obtenir, je crû devoir me servir de la plume de préférence; et si vous vouliez me daigner d'un petit mot de réponse pour me tranquilliser entièrement, je vous en aurai la plus grande obligation.

J'ai l'honneur d'être

Monsieur,

Votre très-humble et obéissant serviteur
Schweppe

No. 141, Drury-Lane
ce 8 fevr. 1793

his expenses attributable to the partnership up to 16 February 1793. In a later letter he made the comment: 'If I have not sent you an account since the time that you abandoned me, that is because I do not have to account for what I do with my own money'. Not unnaturally the Geneva partners looked to the agreement governing Jacob's stay in England to establish the extent of his breaches of its terms.

On 4 November 1794, before a notary public in London, Jacob appointed his friend Jean Antoine de Choudens in Geneva, his attorney, to represent him in settling affairs with his partners. De Choudens found in fact that the agreement for the English venture was invalid. Jaques Paul should have been made a party but had been omitted and had not therefore consented. On 20 February 1795 Jaques and Nicolas Paul and Henry Albert Gosse signed a joint declaration stating that for the purpose of bringing their dispute with Jacob Schweppe to a speedy conclusion, they would regard the partnership agreements, both the original and the supplementary one by which Dr William Belcombe had been included, as terminated with effect from 23 February 1793. The basis of settlement proposed was that Jacob Schweppe would keep the London assets and Nicolas Paul and Gosse would be entitled to those in Geneva in equal shares, Jaques and Nicolas Paul settling their interests between themselves. This arrangement was formally embodied in an agreement dated 18 July 1796 executed in Geneva by Jaques and Nicolas Paul, H. A. Gosse and by Jacob's attorney on his behalf.

In the dissolution of the partnership, Jacob sacrificed his share in the goodwill of the business he had created in Geneva in ten years of dedicated work. In exchange, he kept the London business, still in its extreme infancy, and which in 1792 his partners had shown themselves ready to abandon so hurriedly for lack of success. Perhaps the same vision and faith in artificial mineral waters which originally led Jacob to forsake his craft of bijoutier sustained him in staking his future on the new business he would build in Britain. His confidence in his product was not misplaced, despite the critical wartime situation.

The Geneva business did not last long. Within months of the dissolution of the original partnership, Gosse and Paul agreed to separate and run their own businesses. The relationship between the two had soured to the extent that Gosse produced a lengthy list of Paul's defaults and sought legal arbitration. The accusations included failure to provide free accommodation as promised in the premises of *La Machine Hydraulique*, bad account-keeping (with mistakes 'un-

pardonable in a mathematicican'), inefficient maintenance of the machines, and so on. Gosse then claimed that Paul had tried to steal a march on him by starting separate production earlier than agreed, and that Paul had wrongly pretended to be the inventor of the Geneva System, and tried to discredit Gosse's waters. Eventually however, in November 1796, Paul declared in an affidavit that he had had no intention of harming Gosse, and published an advertisement disclaiming the invention of the system of manufacture. Gosse acknowledged that there had been extenuating reasons for Paul's actions and one can sense that some of their earlier friendship still remained.

Gosse continued to manufacture for a few more years but his trade declined after 1802 with his increasing involvement in his many other interests. Nicolas Paul left Geneva for Paris where by 1799 he had founded a new mineral water business and health centre, and, according to one report, he had excellent partners from whom he soon separated. By 1802 he was manufacturing in London in competition with Jacob's successors, but before long had returned to Geneva where he died prematurely in 1806, aged forty-three. The firm he established in London continued into the twentieth century when its letterheadings erroneously proclaimed 'Established in Geneva as Paul, Schweppe and Gosse in 1789.... The Oldest Firm of Mineral Water Manufacturers in the World'. This was wrong on three counts. The partnership was formed in 1790; Schweppe was always named first among the partners in acknowledgment of his seniority; and the partnership deeds acknowledge Jacob Schweppe's ten years previous experience in the manufacture of artificial mineral waters back to 1780. There are no known challengers to Schweppes as the oldest mineral water manufacturers in the world.

While Jacob remained in England production was confined to London though sales extended far beyond. From 1792 Colette was with him to care for him and assist him in the business. In Geneva, while she was still only fourteen years old, he had given her all the necessary instructions to carry on the business in the event of his death or incapacity through accident or illness and she would have assisted him here in the processes of manufacture. Jacob also worked on the accounts. Invoices in his own handwriting have survived with dates of 1795 to 1797.

Jacob, the self-confessed enthusiastic amateur scientist, would surely have found time to pursue his interests in London. Nicolas Paul had undertaken to write to 'his friend' Dr Joseph Priestley about the new establishment; it is therefore possible that Jacob met great Priestley himself in London. We know for certain that in his first year here Jacob had seen much of Dudley Adams, a person with whom he would have found common ground. Dudley's father, George Adams, had been one of the leading manufacturers of scientific instruments in London in the eighteenth century and had manufactured microscopes for King George III. One of these, together with a compound engine which he also made for the King, is now in the Science Museum, London. On his death in 1778 his business was continued by his sons George and Dudley. A beautiful example of a planetarium or orrery by George Adams had been presented to the Geneva Academy in 1775. This may have been seen by Jacob and discussed with Dudley Adams and been the inspiration for an orrery which Jacob himself made during his retirement.

For further relaxation, at the end of the day when the key was turned on the room where the secret apparatus was kept, there must surely have been music. It is inconceivable that Colette, accomplished musician as she was, should not have continued to make music in London. And in those days, a century before the roar of motor traffic in London streets, did passers-by hear, from upper windows, the magical sounds of Colette's harp?

In London, Jacob Schweppe was free, at least from 1793, to continue to develop the business in his own style, without the distracting influence of his partners. In Geneva, Dr Belcombe had proposed that until the waters had been given a favourable reception in London there should be no general publicity. Therefore no trumpets were sounded on the launch and no elaborate prospectus was published such as had appeared in the *Journal de Genève* announcing the formation of the 1790 partnership. With limited funds and the facilities of Gosse's laboratory not available, the business began in a small way. The range of products offered was much less ambitious than had been the case in Geneva.

The plant, so modest in scale by comparison with later standards, could easily be moved and Jacob did not stay long in Drury Lane. By 1794 he had moved to 8 King's Street, Holborn which has long since disappeared under re-building. Jacob soon moved the factory again to 11 Margaret Street, Cavendish Square, Westminster, at Michaelmas 1795. In this street, though at several different addresses, he remained until he retired, and the firm stayed on until 1831.

In Geneva, Jacob had received the fullest support of the medical profession and the leading physicians recommended daily use of his artificial mineral waters. In England no less a man than Dr Erasmus Darwin, grandfather of Charles Darwin, became their advocate. In his great philosophical work *Zoonomia*, published in 1796, Darwin made reference to both Nooth and Schweppe. For the treatment of 'Stone of the bladder' he prescribed:

A dram of sal soda, or of salt of tartar, dissolved in a pint of water, and well saturated with carbonic acid (fixed air), by means of Dr Nooth's glass apparatus, and drunk every day, or twice a day, is the most efficacious internal medicine yet discovered, which can be easily taken without any general injury to the constitution. An aerated alcaline water of this kind is sold under the name of factitious Seltzer water, by J. Schweppe, at No. 8, King's Street, Holborn, London: which I am told is better prepared than can be easily done in the usual glass vessels, probably by employing a greater pressure in wooden ones.

Erasmus Darwin was the centre of the circle of eminent philosophers and inventors who formed themselves into the Lunar Society of Birmingham. (They met in each other's houses when the moon was full for greater safety when travelling home at night). In this informal circle of friends were such famous men as Josiah Wedgwood, the great potter, James Watt, Matthew Boulton, the Birmingham industrialist who made Watt's first steam engine, and Dr William Withering, the discoverer of digitalis and the designer of Witherings Aerated Water Apparatus. Matthew Boulton was a regular imbiber of Schweppe's waters from at least as early as January 1794. It was he who had told Erasmus Darwin about them. In reply to an enquiry from Darwin he wrote, in October 1794, 'Mr J. Schweppe, preparer of Mineral Waters, is the person whom you have heard me speak of and who impregnates it so highly with fixable air as to exceed in appearance Champaign and all other Bottled Liquors. He prepares it of 3 sorts. No. 1 is for common drinking with your dinner, No. 2 is for Nephritick patients, and No. 3 contains the most alkali and given only in more violent cases, but I know not the quantity of alkali in either. It is contained in Strong Stone Bottles and sold for 6s.6d per doz. including the Bottles'.

It was soon after this that the term 'Soda Water' came into use, although the product had existed under other names for some thirty years, since Richard Bewley first prepared his 'mephitic Julep'. In 1798 Dr Tiberius Cavallo, FRS, a Neapolitan physician who settled in England, stated in *An Essay on the Medicinal Properties of Factitious Airs* that 'The soda water which

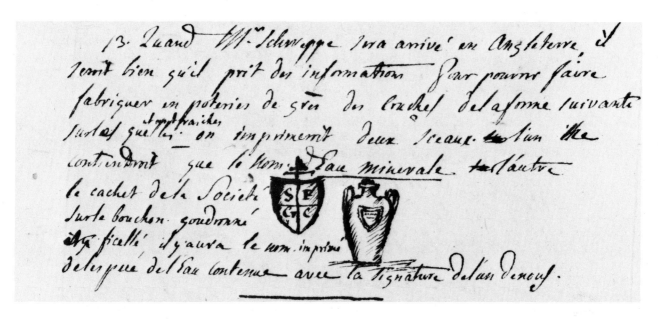

Record of the design of a bottle which it was proposed Jacob Schweppe should have made in England

is now being prepared and sold in London by a Mr Schweppe contains an incomparably greater proportion of carbonic acid gas' (than it was possible to obtain by using Nooth's apparatus). Soda water was named in a Schweppe's advertisement of around 1798 and the use of this description ranks unchallenged as a 'first' for the company.

The advice from Erasmus Darwin and from other leading members of the medical profession did not go unheeded. In the Berkshire County Archives, there is a testimony by a satisfied consumer, Sir Joseph Andrews, Bart., of Shaw House near Newbury, to the faith placed in the prescription of soda water by the medical profession. In his memoranda book Sir Joseph made the following entries:

April 23rd 1796 – Took first advice of Dr Pearson for stone and gravel. Ordered six bottles of Soda Water – double – of Mr Schweppe to be particularly well corked. To take a pint at least per diem.

April 24th 1796 – Passed a small red stone easily after the first taking of the Soda Water D. G. – recommended and prescribed by Dr Pearson.

Sir Joseph continued drinking the water, apparently with further success. Dr Pearson practised as a physician in Doncaster and London, where he became head-physician in St George's Hospital.

The advertisement of 1798 previously referred to was in much greater detail than the usual brief notices inserted in the newspapers by suppliers of mineral waters. It was published in the form of a hand-bill and began: 'From the very great sale of the Acidulous Soda and Artificial Seltzer Waters, Mr Schweppe is emboldened to speak of their virtues; more particularly as the first physicians in this metropolis recommend their daily use.'

The products were listed as *Acidulous Soda Water* ('prepared according to the Proportions prescribed by Dr Pearson') in single, double and triple strengths; *Acidulous Rochelle Salt Water* in single or double strengths; *Seltzer*, *Spa* and *Pyrmont Waters*; and, as an extra, *Tooth Lotion of Soda*. Acidulous soda water was recommended for, among other things, complaints of the kidneys or bladder, the stone, acidity, indigestion and even gout. It could serve, in modern terms, as a 'mixer' if a little rum or brandy or any spicy medicated tincture were added. Seltzer water was recommended for its pleasant taste as well as for its medical virtues. It was ascribed a wide range of uses, for feverish ailments, biliousness, nervous affections ('invigorating the system and exalting the spirits') and the debilitating consequences of hard living. It was described as a safe and cooling drink for 'persons exhausted by much speaking, heated by dancing or when quitting hot rooms or crowded assemblies'. The Acidulous Rochelle Salt water was a purgative 'not ungrateful to the palate'. The manufacture of artificial Pyrmont water by Jacob Schweppe and others no doubt owed much to the fact that it was from experiments upon the waters of the Pyrmont spring that the nature of the gas in mineral waters was discovered. There was an added interest for Jacob, Pyrmont being only about fifty miles from his birthplace, Witzenhausen.

Not surprisingly the authorities regarded artificial mineral waters as being in the nature of patent medicines and imposed an excise duty of three half-pence on every bottle manufactured. Duty stamps were fixed over the corks. When the tax was eventually discontinued about 1840, the traditional appearance of the bottles was preserved by continuing to fix paper straps over the corks, a custom which persisted until the introduction of crown corks.

The medical profession in general recognised Schweppe's soda water and artificial mineral waters as desirable substitutes for natural spa waters, then, as now, frequently sold in bottled form, and specifically recommended them for their superiority over the waters of other manufacturers.

Soda water in this period was a carbonated water in which soda was an ingredient included for medicinal purposes. It was not an exact imitation of any natural water and was distinguished from 'artificial mineral waters' in the firm's notices. Today soda water refers to water charged with carbon dioxide whether or not with a soda content – a transition which took place in America as early as 1830 or so, though not until the twentieth century in Europe.

Speculation on the design of bottles used by Jacob Schweppe in the early 1800s raises the question of the origin and date of introduction of the famous egg-shape bottle. This bottle was evolved or specially designed to contain aerated waters. It became the standard bottle in the trade and remained in use for well over one hundred years. Apart from ensuring that the bottle was kept on its side, so keeping the cork saturated and expanded to retain the precious gas more efficiently, the ovate shape had other advantages. It lent itself to the even distribution of glass during manufacture, reducing the possibility of weak spots so dangerous in a glass vessel under pressure. Because of its inability to stand up on its own, it became known familiarly as the drunken bottle, and sometimes, because of its shape, as the torpedo. In trade literature however, it was more correctly described as the egg bottle or 'egg-soda' although other drinks such as lemonade were often bottled in this shape.

Since the spread of interest in recent years in the hobby of collecting old and interesting bottles, the egg-soda has become widely known as the 'Hamilton'. William Francis Hamilton was granted patents in England in 1809 and 1814 for improved methods of preparing soda water and other mineral waters. In the 1809 patent, he stated 'I generally use a glass or earthen bottle or jar of a long ovate form' and went on to describe the advantages of this shape. No drawing accompanied the specification but in the later patent of 1814 (which makes no reference to bottles in the text) a drawing of his carbonating and filling apparatus showed an ovate bottle in position. Hamilton made no claim in these patent specifications to be the originator of the bottle. Among the earliest Schweppes bottles known are some fully oviform bottles in glass and stoneware with the address of 79 Margaret Street; they may therefore be dated between 1809, the year Hamilton patented his improved machine, and 1831.

When, in Geneva in 1790, plans were first made for Jacob to come to England, a year before he actually came, he was provided with a sketch of a bottle or jar to be manufactured in stoneware potteries. The shape of the bottle was distinctly ovoid but with a small flattened base, which would enable it to stand upright when required. Over the cork, which would be tarred and secured with string, would be placed a label bearing the name of the product and the signature of one of the partners. Two lugs or handles were shown attached to the shoulders which continued the ovoid line upwards and would not have prevented the container from being laid fully on its side. It was to have two seals impressed upon it, one bearing the initials of the firm, S.P.G.C. for Schweppe, Paul, Gosse & Co., and the other the name of the product. The container embodied the principles of the later egg bottle. The advertisement of J. Schweppe & Co. issued from 75 Margaret Street in about 1798 contained the following words – 'To keep these waters good, the Bottles must be laid on their Sides, in a cool Place, Or if convenient, it is still better to keep them covered with Water'. No such bottle has ever been found. Had Jacob by that time modified the Geneva design to the familiar form of the egg bottle? The mystery seems likely to remain unless some further clues are found, perhaps from bottles of the early 1800s which may yet come to light.

Chapter 3

Jacob Schweppe in Retirement

A corner of Jacob Schweppe's country home at Bouchet, near Geneva

After six years devoted to the development of his business in England, publicising and extending it throughout the country, Jacob Schweppe, at the age of fifty-eight, prepared for retirement. He sold three-quarters of his interest to three Jerseymen, retaining a one-eighth share for himself and one-eighth in the name of Colette. His business had achieved a solid basis of success. His clear profit in the year to 14 May 1798 had been £1200, a handsome sum in those days. His artificial mineral waters had met with even more acclamation and commercial success in England than they had enjoyed in Geneva. It is true that the supreme quality of the waters was a major factor in their success but it is also certain that Jacob's own exceptional qualities, through which he had first succeeded in the art of aeration, played their part.

His wife Eléonore had died two years earlier at their home in the Rue de Cornavin on 27 April 1796. So far as is known, Jacob and Colette were unable to go to her, cut off as they were in England by the war. The political and military situation had not improved since and 1797 had been a dark year for England in its struggle against the greatest military alliance yet seen. And, still more depressing for Jacob and Colette, in March 1798 the French invaded Switzerland and annexed Geneva.

For whatever reason Jacob was ready to unloose the shackles of his business and regain some freedom of action for himself and Colette. A faded parchment copy of Articles of Agreement of 14 May 1798 in the company's archives sets out the details of his new partnership. The parties were Jacob and Colette and the three Channel Islanders; Henry William Lauzun, Francis Charles Lauzun and Robert Charles George Brohier. The new partners acquired three-quarters of the business in the proportions of a half share to H. W. Lauzun and an eighth share each to F. C. Lauzun and R. C. G. Brohier. The partnership was to be carried on under the name of Schweppe and Company in the Margaret Street premises, and was established for a term of fifty years. Jacob and Colette could continue to reside at Margaret Street while they desired to do so, paying half the costs, but otherwise another partner would take up occupation, and whoever resided in the premises would be charged with receiving all monies and settling all accounts. Jacob and Colette would reveal to the partners 'the whole art, mistery and process of making and composing artificial mineral waters'. The partners covenanted not to disclose any part of the 'said art, mistery or process' and to be true, just and faithful to one another.

The consideration for the shares acquired by the incoming partners was £2250, equal to less than two years' profits, payable over five years – a price perhaps affected by the war situation and the threat of invasion. This valued the business at £3000 in the money values of the day, assuming the price was a fair one. There were carefully constructed provisions to secure future payments, and collateral charges were deposited with Dr Christopher Stanger of Lambs Conduit Street, Middlesex, as trustee nominated by Jacob Schweppe for their due performance. Dr Stanger was probably one of Jacob's circle of friends in London.

During the following months Jacob and Colette initiated the Lauzuns and Brohier into the arts and mysteries of their trade or craft. Although the three new partners were from the island of Jersey, H. W. Lauzun occupied the property called Walfield near Whetstone, Middlesex, which he held on copyhold from the Manor of Friern Barnet. R. C. G. Brohier was also residing at the same address. Jacob provided for the replacement of his and Colette's labours in the business by the introduction of Stephen DeMole, described as a working jeweller, which indicates an affinity of interest with Jacob. Previously of Poland Street, Stephen took lodgings at the Margaret Street factory.

Jacob was then ready to complete his retirement. By an agreement dated 14 February 1799, he and Colette relinquished to Stephen DeMole one half of the combined quarter share which they had retained, in return for Stephen's undertaking to employ the whole of his labour and skill in the business and giving a bond as security for not disclosing its secrets, and for his good conduct, in the penalty of £20,000. Stephen was to be entitled to his equivalent share in the future profits of the business and the same privileges and obligations as the other partners, but to have no right of disposal of his share, which, in the event of his death or inability to meet the service conditions, would revert to Jacob and Colette, who were released by the other parties from any obligation to act in the business in any way in respect of their remaining shares and interests.

So, as the eighteenth century ended, Jacob Schweppe and Colette withdrew from the scene. By his ingenuity and determination twenty years before, Jacob had transformed both the quality and the scale of production of artificial mineral waters. In so doing he had found himself at the hub of a commercial enterprise in Geneva. Transplanted in England that commerce had, from small and precarious beginnings, flourished exceedingly, inspired by his genius. He now left his incomparable name and reputation in the hands of his successors.

By the annexation of Geneva by France under Napoleon, and its union with the Republic of France, Jacob and Colette had acquired French citizenship. In September 1798, while his retirement arrangements were in progress, Jacob applied for a passport through an intermediary in Geneva. The new municipal administration in Geneva granted an authority to Citizen Jacob Schweppe and Citizeness Colette Schweppe, his daughter, (who were then said to be in Hamburg) to return to their country. It seems doubtful if any use was made of this passport immediately as it is believed that Jacob and Colette were in London to sign the agreement of 14 February 1799 completing their retirement. The same authority granted them, in May 1802, again on the application of an intermediary, a certificate of 'non-emigration' which in effect attested that their names were not included in a famous list of émigrés established in the first years of the French Revolution. It would have provided additional security on a journey through French territory.

Some details of Jacob's life in retirement can be gathered from the records in Geneva. His name appears in a list of the inhabitants of Petit-Saconnex in 1804, and he was there in 1806 when Colette was married to Henri-Louis Maunoir, a merchant of Lyon; she was then twenty-nine, Maunoir a year older. It seems that after their marriage they lived in Geneva, so no doubt she saw Jacob frequently.

In February 1814 Jacob, then almost seventy-four years old, and Colette, were granted a new passport to travel to Rotterdam through Switzerland and Germany; it appears that Jacob, though not perhaps Colette, was away from Geneva for nearly two years. One can guess that they visited London to see old friends and check on the progress of the firm, and that Jacob at least made a sentimental journey to Witzenhausen, his birthplace.

That Jacob was home again in June 1816 we know from an entry in the diary of Charles de Constant, one of the leading figures of the district where he lived. Charles de Constant, cousin of the more famous Benjamin, had a house beautifully situated by the Rhône where on his terrace he entertained many famous and important visitors. One of these, a Mr

Wickham, who had been the British Minister in Switzerland during the Revolution, he took to Jacob's home to see his fine peach trees. But de Constant said, 'I find M. Schweppe more interesting to see than his peach trees; his great age, his white hair, contrast strongly with his vivacity and his energy; he has an originality of expression and a fire which belong only to genius'. He added that Jacob had brought back a 'pretty fortune' from England, where he was the first to make artificial mineral waters, which were now so widely used.

At this time Jacob was living quietly but remaining active, with a wide range of interests. A close friend and near neighbour was François Huber, a blind naturalist who, with the help of his wife and devoted servant, studied the lives of bees and became famous for his discoveries. It was Huber who described the career of Jacob Schweppe to the second Earl of Minto, who was living in Geneva in 1820. The Earl had a strong amateur interest in meteorology and physics and had many contacts with leading men of science and letters.

Jacob was then nearing the end of his life. It is our great good fortune that Lord Minto recorded Huber's words in his diary. These for nearly two centuries have lain unconsidered by those who pondered on what manner of man Jacob Schweppe was. Huber, who commented on Colette's accomplishments as a musician, described Jacob as a man of very great genius and originality, though only known in England as the inventor of the best means of impregnating factitious waters with fixed air. He also described Jacob's last years at his home at Bouchet, and there could be no more fitting tribute to him than to repeat the words of his old blind friend.

Here Schweppe has occupied and amused himself by agriculture, gardening and mechanics in which he has shown the same originality and talent for which he was distinguished in his early youth – and such was his energy in his eightieth year that because one or two parts of a very detailed and intricate orrery which he made did not work so smoothly and silently as he wished, he threw it aside and in twelve months completed another which did not offend him by the ticking of its wheels. He is now in a very alarming state of health having just experienced an attack which it is feared is apoplectic. He is a man of learning but so modest and of such retired habits and so much simplicity of character that none but those whom mere neighbourhood or some accident may bring into contact with him are aware of his merit or even of his existence.

A month later Jacob was dead.

After Jacob's death in November 1821, Colette inherited his estate, including the Petit Crêt, his house at Bouchet. Her husband at once put in hand the enlargement of the house and about the same time Colette extended the property by the purchase of an adjoining vineyard. In 1824 she and her husband sold the interest that Colette had inherited, under Jacob's will, in the English partnership, which was then dissolved.

Colette made her own will in 1833. In it she said, 'I nominate as my sole and universal heir my dear husband Henri-Louis Maunoir in recompense for the care and affection he has lavished upon me. I leave it entirely to him to give whatever he thinks is fitting to the poor and to persons that he considers deserve some recompense or souvenir'. Colette died three years later on 21 February 1836, aged fifty-nine. We must hope that the gentle phrases of her will truly reflect the serenity of thirty years of marriage to Henri-Louis Maunoir, in contrast to the turbulent story of her early youth.

Two olive green glass bottles of J. Schweppe & Co. The one on the right, embossed 79 Margaret Street, dates from 1809–1831 and the other, from Berners Street, from the 1830's

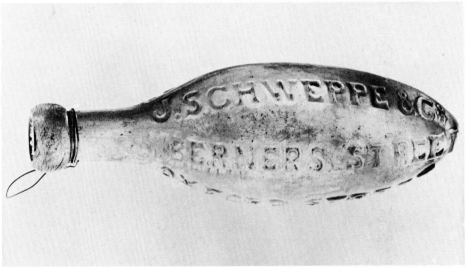

A typical specimen of the millions of egg shape bottles issued from Berners Street for most of the 19th Century. They were embossed J. SCHWEPPE & CO./51 BERNERS STREET OXFORD STREET/GENUINE SUPERIOR/ AERATED WATERS

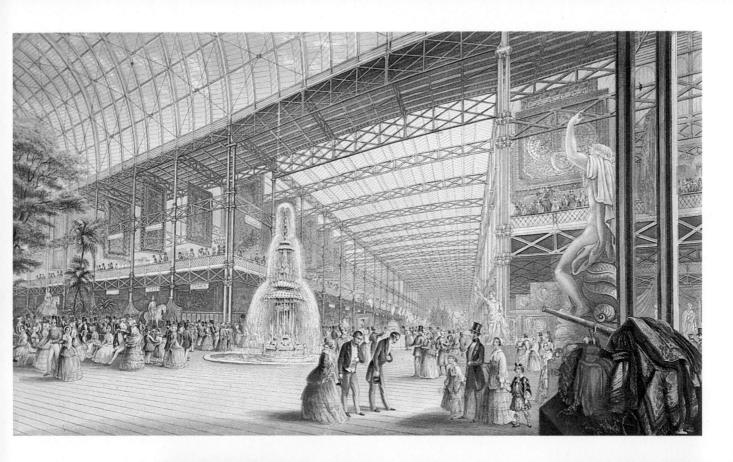

The Great Exhibition of 1851. The fountain, which faced the dais erected for the opening of the Exhibition by Queen Victoria, was echoed in the design adopted by Schweppes for their Fountain trade mark.

A selection of attractive bottles from Schweppes memorabilia.

Examples of sales aids from Schweppes' collection, dating from 1897 to the present day.

Chapter 4

Schweppes under the three Jerseymen

1799–1834

Matthew Boulton
F.R.S.
(1728–1809)

Dr Erasmus Darwin
M.D., F.R.S., F.L.S.
(1731–1802)

*Leading members of the Lunar Society of Birmingham
and advocates of Schweppe's mineral waters*

In the early 1800s the firm continued steadily to establish itself on a national scale. Tantalizingly little is known about the three Jerseymen who had taken over from Jacob and Colette the major interest in the business, Robert Brohier and Henry and Francis Lauzun. The records show, however, that Robert Brohier was a great-grandson of Mathieu Brohier, a merchant, and refugee from Provence after the Revocation of the Edict of Nantes in 1685. Both of Mathieu Brohier's sons married into prominent Jersey families and the Brohiers had trading links with Southampton throughout the eighteenth century. One of Robert Brohier's activities in the island had been the manufacture of soap. His nephew, Henry Brohier, an MRCS, wrote a thesis for his medical degree at Paris University in 1821 on the subject of natural and artificial mineral waters, clearly inspired by his uncle's association with Schweppe's. This Brohier married the sister of a Bailiff of Jersey. When he died he was much praised for his concern for the poor and exiled and for his support of public works as well as arts and science. The Lauzuns appear not to have been born in Jersey and may have

been descendants of an aristocratic family of France. Henry Lauzun was a Captain in the Royal Staff Corps and as a surveying draughtsman for the Duke of Richmond, Master General of the Ordnance, is listed with others on a map of Jersey in 1795, known as the 'Richmond Map'. Francis Lauzun, probably the brother of Henry, had married Robert Brohier's sister.

An adjustment of the new partners' shares took place in November 1801. Henry Lauzun, who before had had the largest interest with a half share, became a sleeping partner with one-sixteenth only. Possibly he was unable to fulfil the requirement that partners should employ themselves in the business in proportion to their interests. Apparently his military duties still continued since in 1809 he was one of the officers concerned in the building of military roads in the island and for this work the States of Jersey, in commending the officers on completion of their task, singled him out as 'Captain Lauzun of the Royal Staff Corps who . . . has acquitted himself in a manner which reflects honour on his zeal and abilities'.

In the re-arrangement of shares Francis Lauzun,

One of a series of three paintings by Maynard Brown, c. 1900, for Schweppes advertising

Stephen DeMole and Robert Brohier all took a proportion of Henry Lauzun's share, and thereafter Brohier was the chief shareholder with five-sixteenths, which he increased further at a later date. From the money passing in these transactions, it is evident that the business was increasing rapidly in value.

Schweppe's waters were consigned carriage paid to any part of England, Scotland or Wales so there was no disadvantage to those residing at a distance from London. A network of agents was established covering most of the country well within the first decade of the nineteenth century which helped to curtail distribution costs, as may be seen from an advertisement of 1809 in the *Lincoln, Rutland and Stamford Mercury*:

Schweppe and Co.'s Soda, Rochelle and
Artificial Mineral Waters
J. Schweppe & Co. beg leave to acquaint the medical gentlemen and the public in general that they have established a respectable agent in each principal town in the Kingdom where the above waters may be had genuine, and in as great perfection as at their warehouse, 79 Margaret Street, Cavendish Square. They have also, from this new arrangement, been able to fix the prices considerably lower than formerly, and have taken such steps that a constant supply may always be depended upon. Their sole agent in Lincoln is Francis Sympson, druggist . . . etc.

Each agent was supported by advertisements in the local press and in this way Schweppe's took its place among the very first major advertisers on a national scale. Advertisements in the leading newspapers were, typically, directed to the Nobility, the Gentry, Members of the Faculty and others. The 'Members of the Faculty' continued to spread the news that Schweppe's waters were better than could otherwise be obtained and recommended their consumption in appropriate cases.

Matthew Boulton of Birmingham, who in his later years drank Schweppe's soda water for his own complaint, received a letter from Heneage Legge of Aston Hall in 1803 saying: 'Our friend, Dr Carmichael, having advised the use of a little Soda Water for the correction of a weak stomach, will you have the goodness to send me two or three small bottles which will be ample for my purposes till I can procure a supply from Mr Schweppe.'

It is significant that Matthew Boulton purchased Schweppe's waters from London since Birmingham was a stronghold of Thomas Henry who, assisted by his son William, had launched out as a mineral water manufacturer probably using the original apparatus he had designed, perhaps as improved by Dr Haygarth. In Henry's apparatus the gas was forced into the water

by squeezing a pig's bladder in which it had been collected, but Dr Haygarth substituted a bellows for this operation. Early in 1804 William Henry wrote to James Watt junior seeking his assistance in setting up a factory in Birmingham. This may be an indication of further technical advances in Henry's plant. The Henrys had observed that J. Schweppe & Co. were spreading across the country and feared that they might establish themselves in Birmingham, 'and thus deprive us of a very good market'. He cautioned Watt to keep the matter secret 'lest the enemy should steal a march on us'. In another letter to Watt, written shortly after, William Henry considered the prospect for a factory at Bath but clearly thought that the competition from Schweppe at Bristol would be too great and that the trade at Bristol itself was already monopolised by Schweppe. There was obviously keen rivalry. Notwithstanding the Henrys' presence in Birmingham, Matthew Boulton continued to purchase Schweppe's waters from London – a sufficient testimony that their quality remained unmatched.

After supplying him regularly from at least as early as 1794, J. Schweppe & Co. ventured to write to Matthew Boulton asking him to recommend a suitable agent in Birmingham. The letter is a delightful example of the business style of the day. It reads as follows:

London August 4 1802
Sir,
 We beg pardon for the liberty we take in troubling you with a commission which nothing could warrant us in doing, but the uniform support you have given to our establishment of preparing mineral waters; and from our being constantly favoured with your commands we are emboldened to flatter ourselves that our exertions meet your approbation. We have, Sir, for long time been in want of a proper person to retail our waters in Birmingham, but not knowing to whom to apply (we having no correspondents there), we have been deprived of that advantage. We have however, Sir, at last ventured to solicit your aid in appointing us as agent there, being well convinced that if you will oblige us so far, the person you may nominate will, in every respect, answer our purpose.
 We cannot conclude, Sir, without again begging your excuse for this liberty we have taken which we have been tempted to do from having been hitherto honoured with your support and patronage.
 We have the honour to be,
  Sir,
   Your obedient humble servants
   J. Schweppe & Co.
P.S. Your Hamper of 12 dozen ½ pints Soda Water was sent off on Monday by Deykins waggon.
 The reference to Deykin's wagon is a timely re-

minder that the railway age had not yet arrived; the London and Birmingham Railway would not be opened for another thirty-five years. Goods moving about the country went by canal boat or coasting vessel, or by the well-developed system of horse transport operated by firms of wagoners. Deykin & Co. ran 'The Birmingham and Coventry Flying Wagons' from The Bell, Wood Street, Cheapside. The schedules of the many wagoners were published collectively in the contemporary equivalent of our modern railway time-tables. Not all wagoners gave equal satisfaction. On one occasion a consignment to Matthew Boulton had been entrusted to Phillips' wagon. When after more than a fortnight it had still not arrived considerable heat was generated in Birmingham. Matthew Boulton's agent, William Cheshire, instructed Schweppe's to bill Phillips for the goods not delivered through their 'shameful remissness' and to threaten them with an action; also to send a fresh consignment without a moment's delay to the Bell Inn for Deykin's wagon, to avoid any further disappointment. Moreover, they were requested to 'send all future parcels of water by this conveyance, the regularity of which we have daily proof of'.

Another insight into the transport used by the firm in those days, and an indication of the spread of trade, is provided in a letter dated 24 January 1811 from J. Schweppe & Co. to 'the Rt Hon. Lord Elgin of Broom Hall, Fifeshire': 'We beg to advise our having forwarded by the Old Shipping Company's smack Queen Charlotte, William Nesbitt, Master, a hamper containing 5 dozen half pints Soda Water which (we) hope will arrive safe. We have the honour to be . . . etc.'

The level of carbonation of mineral waters in those days was an important and sometimes a sensitive issue. It had been realised from the beginning that artificial mineral waters could be made more efficacious than the natural waters they imitated by introducing an increased and unvarying content of salts and a higher volume of gas. Drs Darwin and Cavallo and many others had borne testimony to early Schweppervescence. Jacob Schweppe's erstwhile partner Nicolas Paul, however, carbonated his products well beyond the natural levels, when in Paris, and afterwards on coming to London in about 1802. It was reported by the French Faculty of Physicians, who inspected his works, that his waters 'opened with the noise of a pistol shot'. That the issue was a continuing one can be gathered from a Schweppe's advertisement which appeared in the *Manchester Courier* in June 1838, which read as follows:

Real judges of Soda Water need not be told that its main excellence consists in the *length of time* during which it retains its life and pungency *after it is poured out* and not (as many erroneously suppose) on the force with which it expels the cork. This latter is rather the characteristic of the commonest Soda Water, for the obvious reason that the air is disengaged, whereas, by the *peculiar* principle of Schweppe's process, the carbonic acid gas does not escape with the cork, but, being thoroughly amalgamated with the water, *remains* as a valuable medicinal feature in their manufacture. The same observations will apply to their Aerated Lemonade, Potass and Magnesia Waters.

It is said that contemporary cartoonists depicted Nicolas Paul's customers appearing like inflated balloons. Probably Schweppe's products more closely resembled the natural waters in carbonation, and the steady growth of their trade witnessed the public's general satisfaction. An interesting first-hand comment on carbonation was made in a letter written in 1808 by Anthony Clapham Jnr of Newcastle-upon-Tyne, to Luke Howard, the proprietor of a manufacturing laboratory at Stratford, Essex. Written in the Quaker style, the letter commences, 'Respected Friend, I shall take the liberty of giving thee my opinion on thy Soda Water which thou hast sent me; on comparing it with what Schweppe & Co. make here, it appears to me to be very far short in point of briskness'. The letter goes on to confirm however that the products of Paul & Co. were even brisker than Schweppe's. In the *Morning Chronicle* of 20 May 1823, and in other advertisements, the theme was the quality of Schweppe's waters:

SODA-WATER – J. SCHWEPPE and CO., 79 Margaret Street, Cavendish Square, the Original Manufacturers of SODA-WATER, having, for a series of years, experienced the decided preference and continued support of the Nobility, Gentry, the Faculty, and the Public in general, beg to observe they continue the careful preparation of their Soda-Water, Magnesia Water, Artificial Seltzer, Seidlitz, and other aerated Waters, and from their long confirmed practice and experience, they can confidently recommend their Soda Water, Magnesia Water, and other artificial Mineral Waters, as prepared in the highest possible state of perfection – J. S. and Co. have Agents in every Town, and any supply can be had at a short notice for exportation.

In this, as in other advertisements, J. Schweppe and Co. asserted their claim to be the original manufacturers of soda water which was supported by the earliest known reference to soda water (prepared and sold in London by a Mr Schweppe) made by Dr Cavallo in 1798.

Another feature of the *Morning Chronicle* advertisement of 1823 is the interest shown in export trade. The ovate recumbent bottles of heavy glass or stoneware were ideally suited to transport mineral waters over long distances. Supplies for ships' stores also provided substantial additional business judging from finds of the egg-shaped bottles on the sea bed and in old wrecks of sunken ships. Robert Brohier's nephew, Henry Brohier, when writing his thesis for his medical degree, had said 'the English have a large business in their artificial waters in the Cape of Good Hope, the East Indies, the Antilles, etc.' In this he was speaking with knowledge available not only from his uncle in London, but also from his own father, Jean Henry Brohier (a Captain in the Royal Jersey Militia) who, at his warehouse in Southampton, was agent for the waters and in an advertisement as early as 1803 said 'these waters have been found by gentlemen travelling to the East or West Indies to be the most cool and grateful beverage possible'. Schweppe's, as the well-established leader of the mineral water trade, must have enjoyed the major share of the export trade referred to.

Press advertisements repeatedly stressed quality. Owing its very existence to the leap ahead in quality which Jacob's apparatus permitted, the firm's preoccupation with the maintenance of the highest standards of quality was natural. Throughout the vast expansion of the business and through successive generations of management, this ideal has always remained at the forefront. Other advertisements reveal, by the frequency with which the theme recurs, that the mineral water trade had, over the years, a fair share of unscrupulous members. 'Pray observe,' said one typical advertisement, 'the red label over the cork, representing their signature, as many of the other manufacturers impose upon the public by filling Schweppe's bottles with their own spurious composition'.

The early years of the nineteenth century saw the opening of three branch factories. The first was in Bristol. Many times it has been written that Jacob Schweppe landed at Bristol from Geneva and set up his first factory there, but that was not so. It was in February 1803 that the following advertisement appeared in the *Bristol Journal*:

J. Schweppe and Co. beg leave to acquaint the Nobility, Gentlemen of the Faculty, and others that on account of the increased demand for their ARTIFICIAL MINERAL WATERS at Bath, Bristol and the Western parts of England, they have been induced to commence the manufacture of them at No. 18, corner of Philadelphia Street, Bristol.

N.B. J. Schweppe and Co. also intend to impregnate the Bristol Hotwell and Spa Waters with fixed air.

Only a quarter of a mile away, in Union Street, was a chocolate factory where the newly-invented steam engine of James Watt had been installed for grinding cocoa beans by Joseph Storrs Fry, son of the founder of the firm which, with Cadbury Brothers, became part of the Cadbury Schweppes Group in 1969.

What precisely happened in Bristol at that juncture is not clear, but advertisements in the *Bristol Journal* in 1814 and 1820 show that the firm was at those dates manufacturing soda water at Upper Hotwell Spring and Sion Spring respectively; at this time the firm's address was at Clifton, the attractive district of Bristol by the River Avon where these springs were situated.

The factory at Newcastle-upon-Tyne was the next to be opened. The exact year is not known but it was certainly operating in 1808 when Anthony Clapham of Newcastle wrote to Luke Howard about 'the soda water now being made *here* by Schweppe & Co.' By 1824 this factory no longer existed. Elizabeth DeMole, widow of Stephen DeMole who had been engaged to work in the business when Jacob retired, was then recorded as living in Newcastle, which suggests that Stephen DeMole was sent north to manage this factory, which on his death was closed down.

The third branch factory was at Derby where manufacture was commenced at premises in Friar Gate in 1812. This factory continued until 1893 when production was halted after an analysis of the local water pronounced it unsuitable. The choice of Derby as the location for a factory in the East Midlands, rather than, say, Nottingham, was almost certainly influenced by the local sources of bottles from the salt-glaze stoneware potteries of Derbyshire. The East Derbyshire coalfields, local clays, and salt from across the border in Cheshire provided the materials on which this industry flourished. J. Schweppe & Co.'s advertisement announcing the Derby factory especially mentioned that 'the bottles being manufactured on the spot will admit a reduction of the present prices'. Derbyshire potteries known to have supplied bottles to J. Schweppe & Co. at that period were Burton's of Codnor Park, Edward M. Mundy and Joseph Bourne.

Therefore within fourteen years after Jacob's retirement there were four factories at strategic points across England. Jacob's successors were doing well. There were numerous competitors and a rash of imitators: but with a headstart springing from superior technical knowledge, 'the secret of Schweppes', Jacob's initiative had been maintained. Much of the credit for the continuing progress must be due to Robert Brohier, who had demonstrated his commitment by increasing his investment when opportunity offered. Brohier,

A selection of billheads

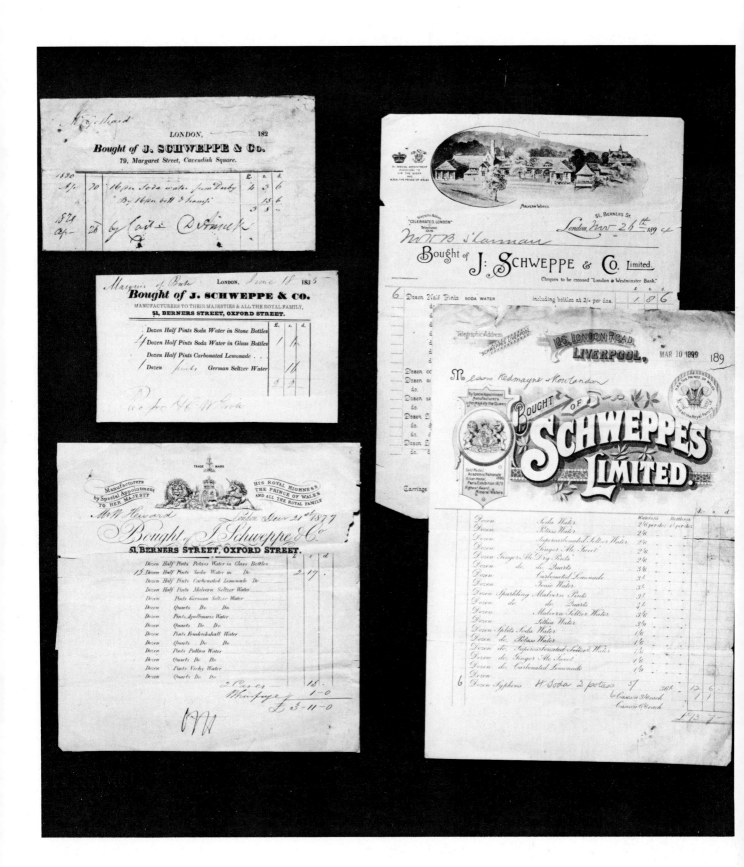

though, was growing old. The partnership of 1798 with the three Jerseymen was dissolved by a deed dated 3 May 1824. Colette's name appeared in the deed as Jacob's heiress, coupled with the name of her husband, Henri Maunoir of Geneva. The two Lauzuns departed from the business. Henri Maunoir and Colette, the two Lauzuns and Elizabeth DeMole assigned their interests to Robert Brohier, R. J. Brohier and Richard Annesley Sparkes of Oaking in Surrey.

Robert Brohier was, of course, one of the original partners from 1798. Since 1801 he had had the largest share in the business. He had taken up residence at the Margaret Street premises and assumed reponsibility for the commercial management of the business. For twenty-five years therefore, following Jacob's retirement, he had borne the heaviest burden. Surely he must be numbered among the stalwarts of Schweppe's. His signature, laboriously appended to the deed of Dissolution of Partnership and Assignment, indicated his failing strength. His knowledge of the 'art, mistery and process' had been imparted to him directly by Jacob Schweppe himself and he was the last member of the firm to have known the founder personally.

We do not know in what proportions Robert Brohier and R. J. Brohier held the business with the other purchaser, R. A. Sparkes, nor how long they continued in partnership together. By 1834, when R. A. Sparkes himself sold the business, he had acquired the interests of the Brohiers and become the sole owner.

A new note was struck in an advertisement which appeared in *The New Times* published in London on 12 July 1824 after the dissolution of the 1798 partnership, which read:

SODA, AERATED MAGNESIA and other MINERAL WATERS J. Schweppe and Co. deem it necessary to state that they are the Original Inventors and Manufacturers of the above-mentioned MINERAL WATERS and that their method of preparing the same is entirely confined to themselves, the knowledge never having been imparted to any other person.

This advertisement sounds like a challenge against all detractors and a declaration by the firm of its birthright which it felt necessary to make to reaffirm its position. It must therefore have been gratifying to the owners when later they became suppliers of soda water to the Household of King William IV. The date of commencement of this honour is uncertain. The Post Office Directory for 1831 recorded J. Schweppe & Co.

as 'Soda and Mineral Water Manufacturers to Their Majesties and the Royal Family' and in the British Imperial Calendar for 1833 J. Schweppe is listed as purveyor of soda water to His Majesty's Household.

During this period, at the close of the year 1831, the firm left its old home in Margaret Street and moved to new premises close by at 51 Berners Street, off Oxford Street. Several different addresses had been occupied in Margaret Street since 1795; it was relatively easy to transfer the modest plant and machinery of those days. Margaret Street must retain special significance for Schweppe devotees, as the situation of the London home of Jacob and Colette for four years before their retirement. No. 51 Berners Street was to be Schweppe's London factory for sixty-four years from 1832 to 1895. Until 1900 it remained the head office and nerve centre of the business, a period which embraced, all but a few months, the whole of the reign of Queen Victoria.

The address was also destined to achieve celebrity for another curious reason. Millions of the famous egg-shaped bottles of the mineral water trade, embossed with the legend 'J. Schweppe & Co., 51 Berners Street, Oxford Street, Genuine Superior Aerated Waters', were distributed in Great Britain and despatched overseas – bottles which today are sought after with considerable interest by collectors of memorabilia. Many are dug up or found in old cellars or lofts, under floorboards, on river banks or the beds of oceans. Others come to light in circumstances linked with memorable events of the past, as did those found by divers in 1972 in the wreck of the *Royal Charter* which foundered in a hurricane off Anglesey in 1859, with the loss of 450 lives. In 1903 Schweppes advertised that they had in their possession a bottle, bearing their Margaret Street address, that had been dug up on a Crimean battlefield. This bottle is probably one of the Margaret Street bottles still in the company's collection. It can no longer, unfortunately, be identified. Abroad they have been found buried in Arabian sands and among overgrown piles of empty gin bottles left by hard-drinking prospectors in the rain forests of South America. Although the greater part of a century has elapsed since Schweppes left Berners Street, the address is still linked with the firm in the minds of collectors through the fame of the egg-shaped bottle.

Chapter 5

John Kemp-Welch and William Evill

1834–1885

Royal Warrant of Appointment granted to
J. Schweppe & Company in 1836 by Their Royal Highnesses
The Duchess of Kent and the Princess Victoria

The 1st of June 1834 was a significant day in the history of Schweppe's. It marked the commencement of a new ownership of the business, under two partners of outstanding character. The impetus thus given to the development of the business world-wide continued throughout the Victorian era. The new owners were John Kemp-Welch, a wine merchant of Bath, and William Evill, also of Bath. Together they purchased the business from R. A. Sparkes.

William Evill had been a prosperous silversmith in Bath but in the depression of trade and industry which came with the peace after the Battle of Waterloo his business declined. After a while he decided to give it up and retire until an opportunity arose to invest his capital again with a prospect of success. Somewhat later he advanced a part of his money to a relative who wished to expand his business of a wine merchant. However the relative neglected the business for other matters, albeit worthy ones, and when difficulties arose

agreed with William Evill that it should be sold. The purchaser was John Kemp-Welch.

Like William Evill, John Kemp-Welch came from an influential nonconformist family and was a man of religious character. Coming to Bath, where the business was, he soon began to improve it. He liquidated part of the stock, reduced the capital employed, and by hard work succeeded in obtaining a good return on the remainder invested. Then he heard that the business of Schweppe's mineral waters was for sale. He had been greatly impressed by the character of William Evill, and of his wife and family, and he invited him to become his partner in purchasing Schweppe's. William Evill agreed. John Kemp-Welch was then not quite twenty-four years old and William Evill was forty-four. So began the association of the Kemp-Welch family with the firm of Schweppe's which continued through four generations.

John Kemp-Welch and William Evill showed com-

John Kemp-Welch

William Evill

plete trust and confidence in each other's judgement and integrity. It was said that throughout the long course of their partnership, which ended with William Evill's death in 1877, no disagreement ever took place between them. It was agreed that John Kemp-Welch would take a two-thirds share in the business and William-Evill one-third, for the first five years, after which William Evill would purchase an additional one-sixth share, and the business would then be held equally. The firm then held the leasehold premises in Berners Street, Riding House Lane close by, Bridge Street, Bristol and Friar Gate, Derby. William Evill took up residence at the Berners Street factory in succession to R. A. Sparkes, good evidence that it was he who would be fulfilling the key role in the commercial management of the business.

Although before long John Kemp-Welch wound up his wine business and also came to live in London, it was first agreed that he should remain in the West of England and apply himself more particularly to the management of Schweppe's business at Bristol. This, however, was not to prejudice the conduct of his own business in Bath. It was even contemplated at first that

Schweppe's at Bristol might be moved to Bath

The introduction of Schweppe's Aerated Lemonade, in 1835, was clearly an innovation of John-Kemp Welch and William Evill, soon after they took control. For more than fifty years J. Schweppe & Co. had concentrated on their soda water and artificial mineral waters. For a simple pleasing drink they had offered artificial Seltzer water, to be drunk straight or with milk or wine or syrup. It was a departure from that tradition when aerated lemonade was added to the range. Still lemonade had for long been drunk as a thirst-quencher. On the Continent in the seventeenth and eighteenth centuries it had been sold by *limonadiers*, sometimes being dispensed from tanks carried on the backs of itinerant vendors. In 1676 the French Government recognised the trade by granting a patent or monopoly to the 'Compagnie de Limonadiers'. Carbonated lemonades began to be produced in the 1830s. Some rare records which have survived of suppliers to the firm from 1835 onwards show that lemons were being bought, no doubt to be processed for this product. By the introduction of their aerated lemonade Schweppe's took the first step in adding to their range of artificial mineral waters and other alkaline beverages the sweetened flavoured drinks and 'mixers' of later years. Another century was to pass, all but a few years, before another fruit drink, an aerated orange drink, was introduced in 1931.

There is evidence however that before lemonade, J. Schweppe & Co. had supplied ginger beer from time to time. Two invoices of 1821 confirm sales of ginger beer at that date but the supply seems to have been intermittent and not established on a permanent basis until 1898.

John Kemp-Welch and William Evill were soon to be honoured, on 31 March 1836, by the grant of a formal Warrant of Appointment as manufacturers of soda water to Their Royal Highnesses, the Duchess of Kent and The Princess Victoria. From a technical viewpoint, this Warrant is unusual as only the firm's name is mentioned and not the personal name of the proprietor as Grantee as is usual. In August 1837, two months after coming to the throne, Queen Victoria granted a new Royal Warrant of Appointment to the firm as purveyors of soda water. This Appointment was to William Evill of J. Schweppe & Co., as Grantee, further evidence that although John Kemp-Welch was at the time the major shareholder, William Evill was the chief executive at the heart in London. It is a matter of intense pride in the company that it has been honoured by Royal Warrants of Appointment by all successive monarchs (with the exception of King Edward VIII, in whose short reign no Warrants were

Extract from William Evill's annual record of trade debts

granted) and by Her Majesty Queen Elizabeth The Queen Mother.

Another product innovation was the importation of 'German Seltzer Water', in quarts and pints, direct from the Springs; Schweppe's claimed to be its largest importer. In this the firm was no doubt responding to a vogue which had arisen for this water, at least among persons of fashion, and to competition from the 'German Spa' opened in Brighton by Dr Struve in 1825. Dr F. A. Struve M.D. of Dresden had the idea of setting up centres for dispensing artificial mineral waters in popular resorts not endowed by nature with natural spas. Brighton was just such a resort. After starting artificial spas at Dresden, Berlin, Leipzig and eventually in several other cities in Europe Dr Struve set up his German Spa within easy reach of the Steine at Brighton where there was a ready-made fashionable clientele. The Doctor obtained the patronage of King George IV, and called his establishment the Royal German Spa. In addition to importing Seltzer water from Germany, Schweppe's also became 'Special Agents for Struve's Brighton Seltzer Water' which had its adherents in London and several provincial towns. The Spa reached its peak of popularity in the 1830s but during Queen Victoria's reign it declined and by the 1880s its days of glory were over.

John Kemp-Welch and William Evill took another step forward in 1838 when a new branch factory was opened at 148 London Road, Liverpool. This seems to have been a well judged move as sales records show

that from the second year of production Liverpool results regularly exceeded those of the other branches at Bristol and Derby.

Perhaps a not wholly surprising result of the entry into Schweppe's of John Kemp-Welch, a wine merchant, was the diversification into wines. A carefully selected and comprehensive range of wines usually in demand was offered. The reputation of the firm for upwards of half a century was invoked as a guarantee of quality and an assurance given that quality would not be sacrificed to price. Cellars were at 27 Marshall Street, Regent Street, London. Advertisements for the wines were placed in such periodicals as *Ainsworth's Magazine* and *The Spectator*. The adventure into wine seems to have lasted for only a short time before being abandoned for over a century until, in the 1970s, Schweppes once again became involved in the wine trade.

Unquestionably the Great Exhibition of 1851 was an event of major importance in the progress of Schweppes. Sales, which in the year of Queen Victoria's accession had been 88,800 dozen, had leapt up by 47% to 130,900 dozen in the next two years but after that further growth came slowly. In 1850, sales were 157,366 dozen. The Exhibition was to provide a further welcome impetus. The daringly conceived structure of glass and iron known as the Crystal Palace, built to house the Exhibition, was erected in Hyde Park; nearly two thousand feet long, it covered more

*The Great Exhibition of 1851. Right: a handbill
announcing Schweppe's appointment as caterers.
Below: 1851 sales from the Berners Street factory,
from William Evill's notebook, showing 84,914
dozen sold at the Exhibition.*

Stock char'd 1851

January	4700 Doz
February	5043 "
March	5271
April (CR 700)	7581
May (5520)	20600
June (19917)	32850
July (22198)	34695
August (16766)	28672
September (11295)	18828
October (6018)	11608
November	3927
December	3962
	177737

177737
84914 &"
92823

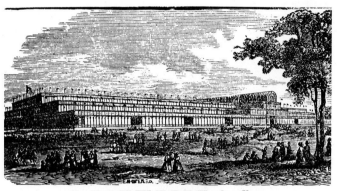

J. SCHWEPPE & Co.,
LONDON,
BY ROYAL APPOINTMENT,
MANUFACTURERS OF SODA AND OTHER MINERAL WATERS.

Having been entrusted by the EXECUTIVE COMMITTEE with the CONTRACT for the supply of
REFRESHMENTS AT THE GREAT EXHIBITION,
very respectfully inform the Public that the THREE DEPARTMENTS IN THE BUILDING, allotted to
that purpose, consisting of the CENTRE AND OF THE EASTERN AND WESTERN ROOMS, have been
transferred to the able management of parties long familiar with the discharge of similar duties.
Messrs. YOUNGHUSBAND & SON, Gerrard's Hall, the centre,
AND
Messrs. MASTERS & Co., Oxford Street,
Purveyors to the Zoological and Botanical Gardens, Regent's Park, the other Areas.
at either and all of which, VISITORS may be supplied with EVERY DESCRIPTION OF REFRESHMENT
permitted by the Committee.

As some apprehension may be entertained that Refreshments provided at so large an outlay and on
so extraordinary an occasion, would be charged *proportionably high*, S. & Co. beg particularly to
inform the Public, that in accordance with the wishes of the Committee, they have arranged with the
Sub-Contractors to provide every thing of the BEST QUALITY and at
VERY MODERATE CHARGES,
Printed lists of which will be exhibited in each department, and will be found, in no case, higher than
the usual shop prices.
The BEVERAGES will be supplied direct from the Manufactory of
SCHWEPPE & Co.
Consisting of—SODA and other Mineral Waters and ÆRATED LEMONADE, GERMAN SELTZER
WATER, in quarts and pints, imported direct from the Springs; and as a novelty, they beg to intro-
duce their
MALVERN SODA WATER,

Comparative annual Sales	A.D. 1834	1835	1836	1837	1838	1839	1840	1841	1842	1843	1844
	£5900 2ms	89200	87000	88.800	100.900	130.900	139470	137360	146520	138220	142000
	A.D. 1845	1846	1847	1848	1849	1850	1851	1852	1853	1854	1855
	146900	183,760	162,216	145.552	145,715	157366	175.136 & 84914 260.060	192076	172566	188.934	207.430
	A.D. 1856	1857	1858	1859	1860	1861	1862	1863	1864	1865	1866
	241,017	271.897	270059	320,361	270.412	322,199	346,174 & 24,804 270.978	392,208	447,918	551,436	535,851
	1867	1868	1869	1870	1871	1872	1873	1874	1875	1876	1877
	566.469	723,540	653,810	674.178	694,739	776.282 Con. 22,664 798,946	757,168 20,480 777,648	797372 15780 813,152	784067 11540 795587	846347 12.106 .85.844	779832 14270 794102

Summary of annual sales from 1834 to 1877, from William and Henry Evill's notebook

than eighteen acres, arching over several large elm trees. Exhibits of manufactures or of produce came from all parts of the globe and there were many foreign visitors. In all, six million visitors passed through the entrance gates. The Commissioners for the Exhibition advertised for tenders for the supply of refreshments and the contract was granted to J. Schweppe & Co. upon payment of the sum of £5,500 for the privilege. This was a considerable speculation when there was little precedent by which to gauge the likely demand. A handbill issued by J. Schweppe & Co. announced that they had sub-contracted the catering in the central refreshment rooms to Messrs Younghusband & Son and in the eastern and western rooms to Messrs Masters & Co., 'parties long familiar with the discharge of similar duties'. They also assured the public that a recent enlargement of their works would enable them to meet any anticipated demand and that in accordance with the wishes of the Executive Committee, they had arranged with the sub-contractors to provide everything of the best quality and at very moderate charges. The refreshments to be supplied would be of every description permitted by the Committee. The Commissioners for the Exhibition had felt that it would be inconsistent with the nature of the Exhibition to permit the sale of wines and spirits, beer or intoxicating drinks; but tea, coffee, chocolate, cocoa, lemonade, ices, ginger beer, seltzer and soda water were in ample supply, as were more solid requirements such as cold meats with steamed potatoes and pickles, sandwiches, buns, bread and cheese, fruits and jellies, milk and cream. J. Schweppe & Co. supplied their Soda and other Mineral Waters, Aerated Lemonade and German Seltzer Water. On this great occasion also they introduced their new Malvern Soda Water 'made at the beautiful Springs in that well known locality, where they have recently established a manufactory'. The company's association with the Malvern district which began in 1850 has continued to the present day, and the special quality of Malvern Water, first recognized over three hundred years ago, is as highly prized as ever.

A report in the *Morning Post* for Monday 9 June 1851 recorded that on the previous Saturday, during the Queen's visit to the Exhibition, Her Majesty inspected the refreshment rooms where the royal party met 'Messrs Schweppe, Welch and Masters, the contractors for supplying the refreshments'. After that the royal party took some refreshments including cream ices produced by the ingenious machinery of Mr Masters for freezing by artificial means which was put into action by *steam power*. There was, of course, no Mr Schweppe in the firm then but it seems likely that John Kemp-Welch and William Evill were among those received. The company holds the medal awarded for services to the Great Exhibition, which remained open for less than six months during which time Schweppe's sales amounted to well over one million bottles. Furthermore their sales in the country generally rose by 18,000 dozen to 175,000 dozen in 1851. In 1852, after a tremendous boost in July, they climbed again to 192,000 dozen. In 1853 and 1854 the figures dropped back but resumed climbing in 1855, the sales for that year being doubled by 1864.

In May 1865 production of Schweppe's was taken north of the border for the first time. The original small factory was in Marlow Street, Kinning Park, which at that time was on the outskirts of Glasgow, almost in the country. There was also a city office at 85 Union Street. As so often in the past, it was the general recommendation by the medical profession of the firm's products which was mentioned, in the announcement of the event, as the reason for expansion. The opening of the factory was an act of faith, since Glasgow was then in the middle of a depression and there was heavy unemployment due to the cotton famine resulting from the American Civil War. The offices moved to 50 York Street in about 1873–4 and to Bothwell Street in 1916, but the factory, although considerably enlarged, remained at Marlow Street until 1924 when both factory and offices moved to Killearn Street in Possilpark. The branch had a notable success in 1901 in securing the exclusive supply of mineral waters to all bars and restaurants at the Glasgow Exhibition. Many hundreds of people tasted Schweppe's waters for the first time and signified their approval by doubling Scottish returns in the next four years.

By contrast with the early days, in the 1960s the increasing prosperity in and around Glasgow was reflected in the rising sales of the Scottish branch. A building site was secured at East Kilbride where the new factory was opened in 1966, Schweppes' centenary year in Scotland. The present team there worthily maintains and enhances the great Schweppes tradition north of the border.

1877 saw the opening of a further manufacturing branch in far away Sydney, Australia. In 1884 and 1885 the firm again reached out overseas, to set up factories, first across the Atlantic in Brooklyn, New York and then in Australia again to open a second factory, this time in Melbourne.

During the 1870s further new products, Tonic Water and Ginger Ale, had been added to the range though there could have been little realisation how important they were destined to become, particularly in the case of Tonic. Ginger Ale was supplied either dry or sweet.

The origin of an aerated flavoured quinine drink is generally believed to date from the days of the British Raj in India. The British took quinine as an antidote for fevers and ameliorated the bitter taste with lemon or lime and gin. On returning home they continued to gratify the taste for the resulting beverage which they had acquired overseas. Although there were recipes of a much earlier date for bitter tonic drinks, sometimes using an infusion of cinchona bark, the development of Quinine Tonic Water as we know it

today began in 1858 when Erasmus Bond, who had acquired the old-established mineral water business of W. Pitt & Co. around 1850, was granted a patent for an improved 'aerated tonic liquid'. Support for this view lies in the fact that for almost a hundred years thereafter Quinine Tonic Water, or Indian Tonic Water, had been a peculiarly British drink, and only became popular in America after Schweppes commenced bottling it there under franchise in 1953. In more recent years the consumption of Tonic Water as a straight drink has grown enormously, particularly in France and Spain.

The excellence of Schweppes Tonic Water today stems not only from the care taken in the preparation of the essence but also from the skill acquired within the company, over many years, in the extraction of flavours from citrus fruits. Since the second world war Schweppes Tonic, for long the leader of its kind in the U.K., has unquestionably become the leading Tonic beverage on a world-wide scale.

The first evidence of Schweppe's manufacturing a cola beverage appears in a minute of 1885 'that Booker Bros of Demarara be sent a sample of Kola as made by

Henry Evill

the Glasgow House', at which branch it was probably being made to meet a local demand. Kola did not make its appearance in the main price lists until 1916.

The nineteenth century was certainly notable for the enthusiasm shown in Britain and France for the promotion of exhibitions featuring agriculture, the works of industry and the arts. After the high point of the Great Exhibition of 1851 another International Exhibition was staged in London in 1862. This was housed in a massive building, constructed mainly of brick, altogether different from its predecessor in Hyde Park. It had magnificent glass domes at either end exceeding in diameter those of St Paul's and St Peter's in Rome! However, the lapse of only eleven years since the Exhibition of 1851 was insufficient to allow a revival of the excitement of the previous occasion, with its great influx of visitors from overseas. Moreover Queen Victoria was in mourning for the Prince Consort. Schweppe's beverages were supplied but sales were less than a third of the million bottles sold at the Great Exhibition. At the Paris

Exhibition of 1878 Schweppe's won the silver medal, the highest award for mineral waters; two years later they were awarded the gold medal of the Académie Nationale of Paris. An International Health Exhibition followed in London in 1884 (a half-page illustration of Schweppe's pavilion was published in the special supplement of the *Illustrated London News*) and in 1886 the Liverpool Exhibition was held, grandly entitled the International Exhibition of Navigation, Travelling, Commerce and Manufacture, where the gold medal for table waters was awarded to J. Schweppe & Co. Limited. Also in 1886 Schweppe's received a medal for their exhibit at the Colonial and Indian Exhibition in London. The new century opened with another international exhibition in Paris in 1900; Schweppe's was awarded the gold, silver and bronze medals.

The last word which by then had appeared in the company's name showed that the days of partnerships were over for Schweppe's; in 1886 the partners had formed themselves into a limited company.

Some historic commemorative medallions. Top left: Bronze medal – For Services to the Great Exhibition, 1851. Top centre: Gold medal of the Académie Nationale of Paris awarded in 1880 for the purity and excellence of Schweppe's mineral waters. Top right: Bronze medal – The International Health Exhibition, London 1884. Bottom left: Silver medal – Highest award for Mineral Waters Paris Exhibition, 1878. Bottom right: Silver medal – Paris Exhibition, 1900.

Chapter 6

Schweppes Limited – Private and Public

1886–1897

The event which precipitated the formation of Schweppes as a limited company was the death of John Kemp-Welch on 24 January 1885 at the age of seventy-four, after fifty years with the firm. (William Evill had died eight years earlier.) A brief history of the company published in 1924 referred to the purchase of the business by John Kemp-Welch in 1834 and described him as the one 'to whose business acumen was largely due the exceptional development of the House of Schweppes'. John Kemp-Welch certainly had the boldness and foresight to take the initiative in acquiring Schweppe's. He also had the wise judgement to invite William Evill to join him in purchasing the undertaking. Unfortunately there are few records of the period from 1834 until his death from which the part played by John Kemp-Welch can be assessed. The 1924 history, while not mentioning William Evill's equal financial stake, also overlooked his long years of service at the heart of the steadily expanding business. Nor indeed did it do justice to his son Henry Evill who succeeded his father, became chairman of the company when it was first incorporated and eventu-

ally, when he retired from active management, handed over to John Kemp-Welch's son Charles Durant. John Kemp-Welch's role is therefore uncertain. His considerable wealth enabled him to act as a banker to the firm. All his instincts would have been to maintain the closest possible interest in the welfare of the business which, no doubt, he did, but nothing has survived to indicate the sphere of his executive activities.

John Kemp-Welch's share of J. Schweppe & Co. was divided on his death among his sons Charles Durant, Stanley, William, Henry and John and his nephew James Kemp-Welch. Charles Durant Kemp-Welch was already a partner, having received an eighth share of the business in 1880 following an adjustment of capital between John Kemp-Welch and Henry Evill, who thereafter held five-eighths and one quarter respectively; on receiving the further share on his father's death, C. D. Kemp-Welch's interest then nearly equalled that of Henry Evill.

In February 1886, Henry Evill and the Kemp-Welch family partners agreed to transfer their interests to a limited liability company registered under the

Companies Act 1862. The authorised capital was fixed at £350,000 in shares of £10 each. The net book value of the business was around £112,000. A purchase price for the goodwill was established at £180,000 and the partners were allotted shares with a total nominal value of £288,000.

The company continued on these lines for seven years until 1892 when there was a capital reconstruction. The capital of the new company was £450,000 in 30,000 preference and 60,000 ordinary shares all of £5 each. The shareholders received one preference and two ordinary shares for each £10 share held in the old company. The nominal value of the issued capital was thereby increased by 50% to £432,000. Goodwill was written up by £136,000 to £316,000.

The new J. Schweppe & Co. Ltd was incorporated on 2 January 1893 and from there onwards complete minutes of board meetings exist to the present day. The share allotment records show that in addition to the directors, there were some 145 shareholders. The shares were traded freely and the number of shareholders increased steadily. The board comprised Henry Evill, chairman, and C. D. Kemp-Welch, John Kemp-Welch, James Kemp-Welch, C. H. Evill and E. Ross Fairfax, directors.

The balance sheet for 1892 had recorded, unfortunately, the write-off of loss on plant, machinery and stocks, including stock of Aesculap (a spring water imported from Budapest) in New York, resulting from the decision to abandon production in America.

In 1888 patents were granted on the continent and in London for syphon heads lined with porcelain to avoid the risk of metallic contamination by heads even of pure tin. Schweppe's adopted the use of syphons during the 1880s and the Christmas number of *Punch* for 1890 announced that their Soda, Potass, Seltzer and Lithia waters would shortly be available in the new patent syphons, the heads of which were lined with porcelain to prevent metallic contamination. In the 1920s Dry Ginger Ale, Lemonade and Tonic Water were also sold in syphons and this continued until the second world war.

In the last decade of the nineteenth century, Schweppe's undertook the construction of two completely new factories, one at Colwall, in the quiet beauty of the Malvern Hills, and the other at Hendon, Middlesex, then still a rural parish, with a picturesque ivy-clad church, six miles north of London.

The building of the Colwall factory was a testimony to Schweppe's faith in the value of Malvern Water, already demonstrated over forty years, and of their desire to establish bottling on a sounder, more permanent footing. For centuries the exceptional quality of the water from certain springs in the Malvern Hills had been recognised. Malvern Water was used for its health restoring powers over two hundred years ago by Dr John Wall, and the beautiful town of Great Malvern developed as a spa during the nineteenth century. Apart from the specialised treatments available at hydropathic establishments, the water could be drunk freely at public fountains at the springs. As Malvern developed into a fashionable health resort, large numbers came to drink the waters and to enjoy the bracing air and invigorating walks along the chain of hills, with exquisite views across the valleys of the Severn and the Wye.

Schweppe's first Malvern Water was introduced in 1850 as Malvern Soda, bottled at the Holy Well. In 1856 this was changed to Malvern Seltzer, which Schweppes continued to bottle for many years. In 1890, however, interesting developments were taking place at Colwall. Mr Stephen Ballard had purchased The Winnings Farm, in 1849, being influenced in his decision by the existence of numerous springs running from the Malvern Hills across the land. He realised the potential of this gravity supply not only for his land but also as a water supply for the village of Colwall. In 1890 J. Schweppe & Co. Ltd entered into a contract with him for a piped supply of spring water of a pure and soft character 'suitable for the manufacture of Seltzer Water and other similar mineral waters' and with this assurance they proceeded to acquire a site and build a factory at Colwall. Drilling was undertaken to establish a water supply within the factory but at a depth of 978 feet an adequate source had still not been found. When water was at last located it was found to be mineralised, and this was marketed for some years under the name of 'Britannis'. Today Schweppes Malvern Water is drawn from the Primeswell Spring, on the western slopes of the Malverns near the British Camp, at an altitude of 700 feet. It owes its fine reputation to its remarkable purity, and the care with which it is bottled. In its well-known red-capped bottles it finds its way to many far-distant parts of the world.

In a firm as long-established as Schweppes, with several branches over one hundred years old – Bristol one hundred and eighty years – it is perhaps not surprising that among its employees there should be instances of families having served for several generations. There have been many such families with a tradition of loyal and devoted service, but it would be difficult to go into details of them and impossible to do justice to them all. With Malvern and the Colwall factory in mind, however, it might be permissible to

Schweppes

'Fairy Queen', painted by W. H. Barribal, c. 1920, for Schweppes advertising

Overleaf left: One of a set of paintings by W. H. Barribal in 1919, for Schweppes advertising
Overleaf right: One of a series of UK press advertisements linking Schweppes with
famous traditions, circa 1947. The claim to fame from 1790 was made when Jacob Schweppe's earlier history was still not fully known

Schweppes

"Naval Occasions"

A privilege of the Royal Navy is to remain seated when drinking the Royal Toast. So far from implying any disrespect, this privilege is a reminder of the days of the old wooden walls where quarters were frequently so cramped that officers and men could not stand up without bumping their heads! The quarters are vastly improved today but the jealously guarded privilege remains.

Schweppes*

Table Waters
famous since 1790

ON THE STEPPES ONE DRINKS KISSLYSCHTSCHY...★

...WHEN ONE CAN'T GET

Schweppes

★ Kisslyschtschy is described by intrepid drinkers as "a beer like sweet wort or treacle beer"... which is probably helpful to anyone who knows his treacle beer. But lately there has been a marked swing-over, on the Steppes, to Schweppes, which not only tastes better but is easier to pronounce.

WHEREVER YOU ARE... THE BEST CLASS BAR SERVES Schweppes

At the International Health Exhibition, London, 1884

A Schweppe's advertisement of 1885

Facing: One of a substantial series of press advertisements reminding consumers of the late 1930's of the international appeal of Schweppes

mention just one such family, the Hill family, which had its first connection with Schweppes there and has been associated with the firm through three generations for nearly a century.

Albert William Hill had a small engineering shop at Colwall and contracted with Schweppe's to install the plant in their factory there when this was first set up. He was taken onto the permanent staff on 21 March 1892. Later he was manager of Schweppes' factories at Hammersmith and Vauxhall where he was succeeded by his sons Albert and Harry. Of his eight children, four sons and one daughter worked for Schweppes. The sons all had a rigorous training in engineering. All achieved senior management responsibility in production, Albert and Harry serving the company at Vauxhall and other branches, Francis in Johannesburg and Jack in Paris. Francis Hill also held the position of company production controller and was elected to the board of directors. A. W. Hill's daughter, Rhoda, served in the office. A brother of A. W. Hill also joined the company and was in charge of Plymouth factory where his son B. H. Hill joined him, later becoming production manager at Colwall. H. F. Hill, son of Harry Hill, retired from his appointment of manager of the company's factories at Birmingham and Colwall in 1979, the last of the family to be in the company's service. Altogether a record difficult to equal!

By 1893 the London factory and head office had been at 51 Berners Street for over sixty years, during which time sales had multiplied twenty-fold. In April the board resolved that it was desirable to remove the factory to more spacious premises and empowered the then managing directors to look for a suitable site in the neighbourhood of London, not too far out. A site of six acres at Hendon was found to be suitable and a lease for 99 years was secured. An adjoining leasehold plot was secured shortly after, bringing the site to nine or ten acres. Isler & Co. were engaged to sink a well and the architect Mr John Slater was asked to prepare plans. A tender by Holloway Brothers for erecting the factory buildings at a cost of £18,919 was accepted but the board cautiously ordered confirmation to be withheld until 'the well sinkers have got the water in the boring'. The freehold of another ten-acre plot was secured on which to erect cottages for employees. Enquiry was made among the men as to how many cottages would be required at 8s. per week and how many at 6s. so that building could proceed accordingly. This work was also done by Holloway Brothers.

Many of the first workers at Hendon were experienced men drawn from the London factory at Berners Street and the Warehouse at Bankside Wharf, Southwark (which was closed and sold in 1897). Those were the days of hand bottling, corks being malleted in and secured by boy 'wirers'. In a very few years, however, rotary fillers were introduced, with crown corking machinery, the forerunners of the all-in-one machines of today which wash, rinse, syrup, fill, crown, label and crate ready for delivery at thousands of dozens an hour.

Mr John Slater was then authorised to prepare plans for the erection of stables for the housing of fifty horses, the building to admit of extension to accommodate seventy horses in case of need. The machinery was moved to Hendon from Berners Street late in 1895. The company's head office remained at Berners Street until 1900, the Post Office providing a private wire to Hendon for better communication. The capacious stabling was completed in 1898. In that year also a special ginger beer factory was constructed on the site which provided brewed ginger beer of superlative quality. The product was in great demand, especially in hot weather. A serious misfortune occurred during one hot summer towards the close of the century, when fire broke out in the roof of the over-taxed brewery boiler, causing havoc for several weeks in the firm's ginger beer trade. The brewery ceased operation during the second world war and was afterwards dismantled.

The pleasant rural surroundings were enhanced by the nearby Welsh Harp, the large artificial lake formed as a reservoir for the Regent Canal, containing an abundance of fish, and a favourite resort of skaters in the winter. The provision of cottages to house employees was desirable in view of the relative isolation of the site, and the fifty families living in the enclave of 'Deerfield' formed a close-knit community. A Deerfield Social Club was in existence in 1896, promoting concerts in the mess-room and arranging cricket matches with teams from Berners Street and Bankside. This club extended beyond the confines of Deerfield and eventually outgrew its sole allegiance to the company. In 1925 therefore the Hendon Social and Athletic Club was formed. The sports field was laid out in 1927. It became the scene of some memorable athletics meetings with keen competition between contenders from the Hendon and Vauxhall branches and head office. Cricket and football teams engaged in local fixtures; there were tennis courts and a bowling green. The Hendon bowls team enjoyed a consistently

Above: Horse-drawn transport at Hendon in 1910
Below: Hendon factory – the Edgware Road frontage

high reputation, one of the highlights of their history being a visit to Schweppes in Genval, Belgium, to play in a match at the inauguration of the Genval Country Club in 1955.

Major changes in the patterns and demands of production and distribution eventually brought the Hendon factory to the end of its useful life. In 1980, the eighty-five year old building was vacated and crumbled under the onslaught of demolition squads. Many people who served the company there will look back with pride on Hendon's great contribution during the major part of the company's second century. Some will remember the impact on the scene made by the fine teams of horses drawing the company's vans, and the pride which they engendered. And many a motorist speeding into London by way of the Edgware Road will spare a thought for the landmark he knew of old – the illuminated ornamental garden fronting the gabled buildings, and the large sign proclaiming Schweppes Table Waters.

The flotation of Schweppes Limited as a public company was accomplished through the offices of that extravagant and ill-starred financier, Ernest Terah Hooley. Hooley's system for company flotation was simple and direct. In the uncertain world of late Victorian company promotion he concentrated on large companies of sound reputation such as the Raleigh and Humber cycle companies, Dunlop, Bovril and Schweppes. For these he was willing to pay a high price, confident that he could obtain an even higher one from the public. For some of his companies this was a recipe for disaster resulting from the effects of the inevitable over-capitalisation. For Schweppes it resulted in years of struggle to service its inflated capital while at the same time providing for the needs of an expanding business.

Hooley agreed to take over the old company for £1,011,000. A new company was formed for sale to the public with a capital of £950,000 in preference, ordinary and deferred shares, all with cumulative dividend rights, and £300,000 of 4% debenture stock. Thus Hooley sold the company for £1,250,000, his apparent profit being £239,000. However, when he was in bankruptcy, in the following year, it was reported that he actually made a loss of about £40,000 on the transaction. He paid all the expenses up to completion and there were many stories of blocks of shares being issued at a discount and sums of money being laid out in other ways to ensure the success of the issue. What was described as one of Hooley's mammoth promotions was a complete success viewed solely as a promotion. Two-thirds of the new share capital

had been reserved for existing shareholders desiring to re-invest, on terms likely to secure their approval. All the shares as well as the debenture stock were fully subscribed, though only about 50,000 of the deferred shares were applied for, the rest being placed privately at well below par.

However, the new company was over-capitalised to the extent of the £350,000 in deferred shares at the very least. Press comment was caustic on the weakness of the balance sheet. One of the more restrained articles lamented: 'Before Mr Hooley purchased and re-sold the company, it was doing a very steady high class business, and if it had only been left alone, it might still have been regarded as a model of enviable prosperity'. Fortunately 'the very steady high class business' continued to increase and enabled the company eventually to surmount its difficulties. The chief controversy arose over the deferred shares. The board maintained that the prospectus showed that the average net profits were sufficient to provide for debenture interest in the new company together with the preference and ordinary dividends, directors' fees and reserve, and it should therefore have been evident that the deferred shares would be a speculative investment.

By scraping the barrel in the first year a dividend of 2% had been paid to the deferred shareholders, but in the next year they received nothing. Sales had increased by two million bottles in the year but a reduction in bottle deposits from 2s. to 1s. per dozen, made in 1897, had not had time to generate sufficient additional business to compensate for the effect on profits of the reduction in the deposit charges.

The question might be asked why the directors entrusted the promotion to Hooley. The answer almost certainly lies in the fact that in 1897 Hooley had reached the culminating point of his success and even of glory, and his confidence was infectious. Bluff and straightforward, he had the disarming characteristic of open dealing. He did not attempt to hide his gains by subterfuge, but frankly disclosed what he would make from a promotion. Equally the public were persuaded that by participating they would also benefit.

Born in 1859, Hooley had started work in his father's lace factory in Derbyshire but when still in his twenties he boldly established himself as a stockbroker and company promotor first in Nottingham and later in London. Encouraged by early success with the Humber and Raleigh cycle firms, in seventeen years he floated twenty-six companies, netting millions of pounds. In the grandest style he acquired Risley Hall near Derby and Papworth Hall in Cambridgeshire, where he entertained lavishly. He was appointed High Sheriff of Cambridgeshire, Deputy Lieutenant of the City of London and was made a magistrate. He gave vast sums to charity. In 1896 he bought and sold Dunlop and Bovril. It is not surprising that, in this euphoric situation, the Schweppes prospectus of 1897 contained a statement by the directors that as a result of the extra publicity from the promotion they anticipated a considerable addition to profits both at home and abroad.

In the year of the Schweppes promotion came Hooley's final grand gesture. He presented to St Paul's Cathedral a gift of communion plate in solid gold. This caused much comment and after his bankruptcy the price of the service was returned. Hooley was to have been knighted but before he could be summoned before the Queen to receive the accolade he crashed, with liabilities of £1.5m. His bankruptcy brought Schweppes' affairs under closer scrutiny than they

otherwise might have had, and every financial paper analysed the situation according to its own point of view. It was clearly realised that companies such as Dunlop, Bovril and Schweppes had been placed by Hooley's methods at a disadvantage in relation to competitors in similar businesses. The lessons were plain for all to see.

Of the directors of the old company, only C. D. Kemp-Welch joined the board of the new company, as managing director. So Schweppes said goodbye here, sadly and with gratitude surely, to its old chairman Henry Evill, and director C. H. Evill, after a great contribution by the Evill family extending over sixty-three years.

The company entered the twentieth century overburdened with its capital structure and with a board on which C. D. Kemp-Welch alone was rooted in its traditions. Gradually it grew stronger but it was to be nearly twenty years before it placed its feet firmly again on the road to financial strength.

HOOLEY UP   AND HOOLEY DOWN.

1897, Millionaire.   1898, Bankrupt.

Chapter 7

Expansion and Constraint

1897–1918

Major-General Baden-Powell and Schweppes at Mafeking in 1900. He is seen reading Lord Roberts' telegram asking him to hold out until 18 May.

In the aftermath of the Hooley flotation there were rapid changes on the board. The two leading names appointed in May 1897 had departed within two years. One of these, the Earl of March, the original chairman, resigned after five months for personal reasons, and never faced the shareholders at a general meeting. The Earl De La Warr, who succeeded him as chairman, resigned before the second annual meeting in March 1899, finding that he had insufficient time to devote to the company's affairs. Another original director departed before either of the two earls; this was A. Drucker, M P, who resigned after two months and never attended a board meeting. F. W. Towle resigned in September 1898, having accepted another important appointment. The board was thereby much reduced from its original numbers. C. D. Kemp-Welch, the managing director, became also chairman, at no extra fee, upon the departure of the Earl De La Warr. The other remaining directors were H. J. Gurdon-Rebow, Walter H. Harris, C M G, a Sheriff of London in 1889–90, and Lieut-Col. Hugh H. Ley.

Thus the board remained, except for the addition for a short while in 1898–9 of J. E. Dudley Ryder, until the election of Sir Ernest Clarke in June 1901. J. E. Dudley Ryder was chairman of the company controlling Kronthal, a German mineral water, and sat on the board while Schweppes held the agency for it. Col. Hugh H. Ley died in December 1906, H. J. Gurdon-Rebow resigned in April 1908, leaving only C. D. Kemp-Welch and Walter H. Harris from the original board of 1897; Sir William P. Treloar, Bart., Lord Mayor of London in 1906, was elected to fill the vacancy caused by the resignation of Gurdon-Rebow. No further changes occurred until 1914.

The head office of the company had continued at Berners Street after production had transferred to Hendon in 1895 but in the summer of 1900 was moved to 49 Pall Mall, where it remained until transferred to 64 Hammersmith Road in 1906. The company continued to use the Pall Mall offices, however, and board meetings were held there until October 1910; thereafter the board met at offices rented at 49 St James's Street.

An episode which had repercussions for years to

come had its beginning in 1900. There was some concern over the state of the Bristol branch, so the managing director, C. D. Kemp-Welch, appointed an able employee, J. A. York Harris, to manage the branch jointly with his son Brian, then in his twenties and in training in the company. This disgruntled one of the Bristol clerks who, after unsuccessfully presenting before the board his application for the post to which he considered he was entitled, commenced a virulent campaign against the management and against C. D. Kemp-Welch in particular. He circulated shareholders, got his case taken up by some sections of the Press, had himself proposed for election to the board and disrupted several annual meetings, from one of which he had to be forcibly ejected. The extremities of vituperation in which he indulged eventually lost him most of the sympathy he had ever gained.

Although 1900 saw continued growth of sales, profits were slightly down and the directors thought it wise to pass payment of the dividend on the deferred shares. Addressing the shareholders at the annual meeting in 1901, the chairman said, 'The question of a dividend to the deferred shareholders must necessarily be deferred to the necessities of the stability and the proper finances of the company'. It is interesting to find this view expressed personally by C. D. Kemp-Welch, since the precept was not adopted by the board as a whole, as subsequent events showed. Only the next year an increase of under £7000 in the profits was immediately sacrificed by the directors in paying 2% on the deferred shares. This was to be the way of things at that time, while arrangements were constantly being made at the bank, especially when the dividends were due. Moreover, for additional finance, further debenture stock was issued in amounts of £100,000 in 1903, £60,000 in 1909 and even a further £100,000 cumulative ordinary shares were issued in 1914, thus further worsening the already serious capital burden.

Britain was fighting the Boers and the claims of the soldiers and sailors serving their country had not been forgotten; the company had sent out supplies of Schweppes waters to the Cape for the solace of those in hospital. At the annual meeting in 1901, C. D. Kemp-Welch spoke of the 'irreparable disaster' of the death of the country's beloved Queen and of the effect on trade of the war in South Africa which 'has taken from the country thousands of officers who have been brought up on Schweppes, and when at home and at their clubs, always see that they get it'. One newspaper took exception to these remarks since, in spite

of such lamentable events, sales were well up for the year. Entertainments were then certainly the exception rather than the rule, and sales were no doubt a good deal less than they might overwise have been. 'We as a company,' the chairman said, 'cater for the upper and middle classes', a comment which aptly summed up the policy in that era and which in some degree remained true until after the second world war. The company was looking for its business in the principal clubs, hotels, restaurants, theatres, railways and shipping companies, and similar high class outlets. Schweppes' pre-eminence in London theatre bars, for example, was evident from a comment in the *Licensed Victuallers Gazette* in 1900 where the correspondent referred to the 'wise policy' of the management of the Empire and the Alhambra in stocking only Schweppes. 'I am constrained to remark,' he added, 'that the theatres are ahead of the variety houses, for with two solitary exceptions, at all the West End temples of drama Schweppes articles are the only waters kept.' There were other more modest sections of the market where Schweppes did not seek business in the belief that to do so would detract from its prestige. It was not until 1948 that Schweppes resolutely set out with a clear determination to seek sales wherever they could be found.

Fortunately, having regard to the financial constraints which were the legacy of the public flotation, the board could take heart from the continuing buoyancy of sales in spite of keen competition from other manufacturers and the general commercial depression of the times. In part this owed something to the reduction in bottle deposits made by the directors of the old company in June 1897. An increase of upwards of one and a half million bottles in 1897 was followed by increases of two million bottles in 1898 and two and a half million bottles (a record) in 1899.

Haulage from the fine new factory in the Hendon countryside (a complaint was received in the summer of 1898 from a neighbouring landowner that the company's employees were trespassing in his hayfield) to the London warehouse, some eight miles distant, became an increasing problem as the sales grew. In 1900 a Thornycroft steam wagon was purchased to ease this task and a satisfactory saving was effected, the rate of carriage coming out at 3d per ton per mile, or about half the cost of horses and vans. This original 'Puffing Billy' brought forth a complaint from a Kilburn crockery merchant that the vibration of its passage wrought havoc among the display of his wares. It was the first mechanical vehicle ever operated by

THE

THORNYCROFT

STEAM WAGON Co., Ltd.

LONDON DEPOT:
HOMEFIELD,
CHISWICK, W.

WORKS:
BASINGSTOKE,
HANTS.

SCHWEPPES
MINERAL WATERS

ALL HIGHEST AWARDS
FOR STEAM VEHICLES ON TRIAL
DURING 1899.

Above: Schweppes' first mechanical vehicle, purchased in 1900
Below left: A well matched pair of greys, prize winners at the Dublin Spring Show in 1931
Above right: Steam wagons, photographed in 1920, were used for heavy work during the transition from horse-drawn to petrol driven vehicles
Below right: A fleet of three Swiss 'Berna' 4-tonners, in 1915

the company and was kept in service for thirteen years. Acquired by way of an experiment, it proved that mechanical power would be indispensable to the company's transport arrangements. Motor wagons were in use in growing numbers at that time. A journalist of the day recorded that in travelling between Chiswick and the Mansion House via Hammersmith, Chelsea and the Embankment, he had seen no less than ten such heavy motors in forty-five minutes engaged in active work which made him rub his eyes. The last of these was Schweppes' Thornycroft moving along Cheapside. As an example of performance, one vehicle was quoted as having carried a cargo of five tons for a journey of thirty-four miles at an average speed of seven miles an hour.

The pressure on production necessitated extensions to premises where these could be made. At the London Road factory in Liverpool, the restricted space had for some years hampered development, notwith-

standing the addition in 1903 of a four-storied building at the rear, extending to Marquis Street, and considerable warehousing accommodation and stabling some distance off in Farnworth Street. The Corporation offered a property in Gill Street which was adequate in size and otherwise suitable except that it adjoined a raw hide and skin store! There was no way of overcoming that drawback. About a year later in 1905, new premises were found at 34–38 Chatham Street which, with the addition of adjoining premises in 1911, served the company until after the second world war. In London, to keep pace with development and in view of the expense caused by the transit of goods from Hendon, the board decided that a new factory, with stables adjoining, was necessary. In 1901 they were able to acquire premises in Hammersmith Road in West London, formerly the Kensington Stores, then in liquidation. Isler & Co. certified that they could sink a well on the premises to supply at least 10,000 gallons of water a day, similar in quality to that obtained from the well at Hendon. But Schweppes only stayed at Hammersmith Road for ten years. During that period a 50% increase in sales brought the factory to the limit of its output, there being no space for expansion. Moreover, the quality of the water from the well deteriorated and became unsuitable for bottling so that water had to be carted from the well at Hendon in a 400-gallon tank drawn by a team of four horses. In 1911 therefore a piece of land was found near the Albert Embankment at Vauxhall where a factory twice as large as that at Hammersmith could be built, with stabling for fifty horses. The situation was also more convenient for deliveries to the City and the West End. The board proceeded with the construction of the new factory when it was confirmed that a supply of satisfactory water was obtainable from a well sunk on the site. Completed in 1914, it was one of the first structures in which the technique of reinforced concrete construction was used.

The occasion of the move provided a worthy example of the versatility and output of the craftsmen of the day. Frank Sheen, the factory carpenter, made the wooden patterns for the castings required in iron and phosphor bronze which were machined and finished, with interior tinning where necessary, by the Hill brothers on lathes and on drilling, shaping, milling and welding machines installed for the purpose at Hammersmith Road. Frank Sheen also made all the tables and chairs required at Vauxhall. Hammersmith Road closed at 5 p.m. on 30 September, and at 8 a.m. the following day production started at Vauxhall with most of the staff from the old factory. In that fateful year of the Great War some of those who had worked to achieve that well organised move were not at the opening ceremony, having already joined Kitchener's Army or transferred to war work.

The Vauxhall factory remained the principal south London factory for forty years. Close to London's famous Lambeth Walk and drawing many of its workpeople from the neighbourhood, it had its own distinctive character. Many strong family links were forged and the names of many stalwarts were indelibly linked with its history; and until the thirties and the advent of motor transport there was the pride in the horse-drawn vans and the clattering hooves of the horses.

Although restricted in their actions by shortage of funds the board took steps, in 1903, towards the formation of a company for the better exploitation of Schweppes' products in the United States, where negotiations were carried on by Walter Harris and Brian Kemp-Welch. However, these were abandoned by the board on grounds of the depression in the mineral water industry in the States at that time. Serious consideration was also given, in 1905, to the purchase of the American White Rock business; the money was to be raised, so far as possible, by a public issue of shares, but terms could not be agreed.

In 1902 an interest was taken in a company known as the Air-Tight Sealing Development Syndicate which controlled the rights to a patent cap and cork known as the 'Phoenix', widely used in America and France by preserving companies, but also adapted to mineral waters. The cap consisted of a cork-lined disc held in position by a pull-away metal binding strip. No form of opener was therefore required. Sealing with full corks, wired on, had been for Schweppes part of the original process of bottling for well over a hundred years and they had not been tempted to adopt any of the numerous forms of patent closures which had been tried and often soon abandoned. Schweppes in England, for example, never adopted the internal glass marble and rubber ring closure invented by Hiram Codd in 1870, although this enjoyed a very long life extending well into the twentieth century. Hiram Codd's bottle was, however, used for a time by Schweppes in Australia. Corking and wiring was a cumbersome, costly, time-consuming process and was also wasteful of cork. The weight of these disadvantages grew as the volume of production increased. Each new type of closure presented a technical problem for bottle manufacturers in forming a new neck shape. The difficulty of obtaining satisfactory supplies of bottles suitable for the Phoenix Cap delayed its introduction until 1904. Unfortunately the company had backed the wrong horse. The British patent for the Crown Cork had been granted in 1892 and although at first received by the bottling industry with some scepticism, its overwhelming advantages met all requirements; its simplicity of design, which in essential principle remains unchanged to the present day, understandably resulted in its ultimate triumph. Schweppes' use of the Phoenix Cap was short lived.

In 1905 the directors had good reason to be upset by the outcome of a legal action taken for the protection of Schweppes' soda water label. Action had originally been taken against two other firms to prevent their using labels which the company considered to be colourable imitations of its own and therefore confusing to the public. These cases were lost in the High Court and in the Court of Appeal, and on the advice of Counsel the company took one case, that of *Schweppes Ltd* v. *Gibbons*, to the House of Lords. They trusted that finally their well-known and distinctive soda water label would be given the protection of the law, but the highest tribunal in the land affirmed the decisions of the inferior courts. Such was the attitude of the courts at that time that whilst manufacturers could obtain protection for a single distinctive word or symbol, protection of a combination of features was much more difficult to obtain. The decision, which of course had been costly, caused consternation. Even fifty years later when an infringement of the company's ginger ale label was being considered, where the facts closely corresponded to those in *Schweppes Ltd* v. *Gibbons*, Counsel's comment was that it would be a brave judge that reversed the House of Lords' decision.

Schweppes' involvement in fruit juices began when it became sole selling agents within the Empire for juices, especially of lemons, oranges and grapes, pressed from fruit ripe from the trees and sterilised by a new process invented by Professor Kuhn, a disciple of Pasteur, which permitted them to be kept in bottles without the use of preservatives. The company promoting the Kuhn process was expected to commence supplies in June 1907, but production in the factory in Sicily failed to start in time to catch the lemon crop, although a large quantity of pure grape juice was processed and delivered to Schweppes in London. This was marketed as a pure non-alcoholic wine under the name of *Vin de Vie*. Alas, the lemon juice factory, fully equipped with expensive plant, situated at Tremesteri, a few miles from Messina, was destroyed by an earthquake on the morning of 28

December 1908. As a result of the problems which ensued, the arrangement ended. The sale of *Vin de Vie* was abandoned in 1911.

Another major and memorable exhibition was staged in London in 1908 – The Franco-British Exhibition. To accommodate the vast collection of exhibits from all parts of Great Britain and France and their colonies, a magnificent 'White City' was created comprising twenty white palaces and many other interesting pavilions and courts. On the same site was the great stadium, specially erected for the Olympic Games of that year. Schweppes responded by commissioning their architect to design an English house and shop of the eighteenth century which they christened the Fountain House. Unfortunately they also associated with it a legend which had gained credence in the company, and represented it as the shop where Jacob Schweppe first made soda water in Bristol, giving the date of this as 1787, when Jacob was, in fact, still making mineral waters in Geneva. The architect worked into the building a delightful collection of old timber, genuine old tiles and glass panes from ancient cottages, and ironwork forged in the days of Queen Anne. It was a relief to the eyes of visitors, dazzled by the white palaces, to step inside and see the way their forefathers lived and be reminded of the antiquity of the firm of Schweppes – who received the Exhibition's highest award for the excellence of its products.

In December 1909 Schweppes commenced bottling their own lime juice and other cordials and a considerable trade in these quickly resulted. Lime juice, lemon squash and peppermint cordial were on sale at 'Schweppes Cottage' at the Ideal Home Exhibition at Olympia in April 1910. At the same time, manufacture commenced of a range of British wines such as green ginger, orange, raisin and blackcurrant, raspberry, cowslip, elderberry, clove cordial and other old-time beverages. Schweppes were justly proud of the quality of their lime juice cordial and lemon and orange squash and of their range of wines which were real brewed wines. Another product, manufactured under licence, which should be mentioned was 'Proset', a name signifying 'Good Health', introduced by Schweppes in July 1908; a non-alcoholic fruit beverage in which the flavours of raspberries, strawberries, oranges, lemons, bananas and pineapples were blended but of which none predominated. Proset was then selling at the rate of a hundred million bottles a year on the Continent, where it was known as Bilz Sinalco. It met with initial success here but production was halted by the 1914–18 War.

The Fountain House. Built by Schweppes to contain their display at the Franco–British Exhibition, 1908

At the annual meeting in April 1911 the chairman, C. D. Kemp-Welch, deplored the death of King Edward VII in May of the previous year and, as he had done on the death of Queen Victoria, referred to the effect of that event on trade through the curtailment of the usual season's festivities, the Court being in mourning and many large town houses staying closed. In addition there had been a poor summer in 1910. Notwithstanding, and again as happened following the Queen's death, he had to report a considerable increase of sales. However this did not show through in increased profits, which were less than the year before, due mainly to some exceptional charges. An additional £3000 however had been spent on general advertising. Of this the chairman said, 'We have to regard the future as well as the present, so that the rising generation may not lose sight of the name of "Schweppes", which has stood first for over one hundred and thirty years in the mineral water trade, and continues to hold that position, and its products are the "standard of comparison"'. He regretted that in spite of a recent All-British Week there were still many who patronised imported mineral waters, which was another reason for the company

to increase its advertisements. In stirring words he continued, 'In naval matters wise men say Great Britain shall continue to hold the premier position on the waters, and that two keels shall be laid down to every one laid down by her possible enemies. So we will fight our competitors in like manner, so that Schweppes shall continue to hold the premier position in the mineral water trade'. This challenging proclamation was greeted with applause by the shareholders present.

An advertisement far removed from traditional style was adopted a few months later, in the form of support for the first official United Kingdom Aerial Post, when, as part of the celebration of the coronation of King George V, mail was carried by air between Hendon and Windsor. Balloons had been used to carry letters in and out of Paris during the siege of 1870 but when the Wright brothers flew their heavier-than-air machine in 1903, regular point-to-point flights became a possibility. Some six years later the practice developed of sending postmarked mail by air unofficially, but the first 'official' mail-carrying flight took place at Allahabad, India, during an exhibition there in February 1911. The twenty mail-carrying flights of the

Coronation Aerial Post between London and Windsor from 9 to 26 September 1911 were on the same basis. Only special pictorial postcards and envelopes issued with the authority of the Postmaster-General were conveyed, and many thousands of these were purchased by the public for despatch. Schweppes were one of about twenty commercial concerns who despatched cards for trade advertisement purposes. The cards depicted a Farman biplane in flight over Windsor Castle. On the other side, Schweppes sent a suitable message to their customers, prophetically adding as a P.S., 'This stamp will some day be of great interest to collectors'. In connection with the coronation celebrations there must also be recorded an extremely effective presentation by Schweppes at the Festival of Empire display at the Crystal Palace.

The 1914–1918 War brought all the difficulties that can well be imagined. Within a month the War Office had requisitioned seventy-five of Schweppes' best horses, with some of their harness, seven vans and two motors. Ninety-four employees had enlisted or rejoined the colours. Further requisitions continued and, of course, enlistments, and by 1915 there were acute staffing problems at the Vauxhall and Hendon factories. Soon Schweppes' men in France writing home to their branches reported it a common sight to see convoys of fifty 'General' buses transporting troops with Schweppes and Dewars advertisements still showing. One sighted a Halley Lorry from Liverpool at Ypres and another two of Schweppes' three-ton Fodens doing good work. In all, 439 employees joined the forces, of whom forty-one lost their lives. Among these was Anthony Kemp-Welch, brother of Brian Kemp-Welch, who was long remembered affectionately in the company by those who knew him. He was a great judge of horses and did much towards

Charles Durant Kemp-Welch, drawn by Lucy Kemp-Welch

establishing the high reputation for its horses which Schweppes enjoyed.

Inevitably rumours began to circulate on the outbreak of war that Schweppes was a German company and, indeed one public statement to this effect in Liverpool was made the subject of a prosecution by the company to enforce a retraction. The company decided in September 1914 to insert advertisements in newspapers giving a short account of its origins to allay false rumours and stating that all the directors were English and of its many shareholders there was only one, holding twenty-five £1 shares, who lived in Germany or Austria. The new factory at Vauxhall, with contents, was insured against 'aerial craft' until a Government scheme of insurance was introduced

One of the cards carried by the Coronation Aerial Post from Hendon to Windsor in 1911

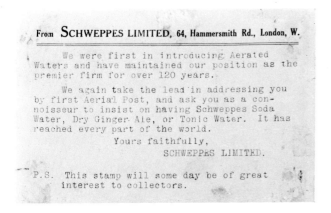

in 1915. Efforts were made to husband stocks of sugar. In December 1916, when the company's sugar supplies were 75% of 1915 requirements, a further cut of 15% was imposed. By January 1917, supplies were down to 50% and by May to 25% of 1915 requirements. Sales declined slowly at first but a bolt from the blue in the form of a tax on mineral waters, introduced in April 1916, contributed to a drop of one million dozen bottles in the following year. In 1918 sales were about 60% of those of 1914. Costs of labour, bottles, cases, fodder and other materials seriously increased but due to the circumstances of the mineral water trade generally, the directors did not feel it possible to raise the price of the products to the full extent that would otherwise have been justified. Although there were off-setting economies, profits suffered and the deferred shareholders had no dividend for the years 1916 to 1918.

The first twenty years in the history of Schweppes as a public company, culminating with the Great War, proved to be exceedingly perplexing ones for members of the board. The company could ill afford to pay the full dividend on its 7% ordinary shares and much less so the dividend on the deferred shares, but nevertheless the directors paid full dividends on the preference and ordinary shares and an average of $2\frac{3}{4}\%$ on the deferred shares over the years 1897 to 1917; consequently there had been a chronic shortage of resources within the company for development. The last few years of the period particularly were positively unhappy ones in the boardroom because of the deteriorating personal relationships between some of the directors.

Fortunately, it was all to come right for the company in the end. Underneath there was considerable momentum in the business, as of old, which continued to sustain it, and many loyal and competent employees maintained the reputation of the company's products and promoted its best interests. A new board was on the way, with the right leadership in the person of Sir Ivor Philipps. As sometimes happens in history, the hour of need produced for the company a leader with the right qualities for the task. Sir Ivor, then Colonel Ivor Philipps D S O M P, was first elected a director in February 1914 on the proposition of C. D. Kemp-Welch. At the same meeting Sir W. H. Dunn, a future Lord Mayor, was elected a director on the proposition of Sir William Treloar, a past Lord Mayor.

The following month, when the annual accounts came before the board for consideration, Sir Ivor unhesitatingly set about his business. In line with a

Sir Ivor Philipps

memorandum circulated to the directors before the meeting, he moved that additional depreciation of £25,000 be written off assets, including £10,000 off goodwill, and that the dividend on the deferred shares be reduced from 6% to 3%. He found a seconder in Sir William Dunn. W. H. Harris however moved an amendment to delete the writing off of £10,000 on goodwill. On this the board were equally divided and the chairman exercised his casting vote against Sir Ivor. W. H. Harris thereupon moved a further amendment to pay the 6% on the deferred shares originally projected. On this the board also divided equally and the chairman again exercised his casting vote against Sir Ivor, whose initial efforts were thus frustrated. War came in August and Sir Ivor rejoined the Army. General Sir Ivor Philipps raised the 115th Brigade of the Welsh Army Corps in 1914 and in 1915 took over command of all the troops being raised by the

Welsh Army Corps Committee. Standing six feet four inches, he was one of the tallest men in the Army. The board gave him three months' leave of absence, which they prolonged for a year while he was a soldier. Then Lloyd George, the Minister of Munitions, recalled Sir Ivor and appointed him his Under-Secretary. In July 1915 his leave from the board was up and the last day came on which he could attend a meeting to avoid jeopardising his seat. 'As I was a reformer,' he said, 'I was very doubtful if they would prolong my leave any further.' As he left the door of his office in Whitehall Gardens to go to the meeting at the company's office in St James's Street, a messenger put a note into his hand from Lloyd George: 'Come and see me at once'. Sir Ivor went to see Lloyd George and did not go to the board meeting. The board invoked the Articles of Association and declared his seat vacant. Although in 1918 circumstances conspired to bring him again on to the board, his reforming work had been delayed for four years.

In January 1913 the board brought Brian Kemp-Welch, who since 1900 had received a broad training in the business, one step nearer succeeding his father by appointing him general manager and requiring him to attend board meetings. In March of the same year

C. D. Kemp-Welch underwent an illness involving an operation, but missed only two board meetings – the first for fifteen years. The following September he was again struck by a serious illness resulting in a prolonged absence from the board until December. The board then confirmed that Brian Kemp-Welch would be managing director from 3 April 1914, the day following the annual meeting when his father would retire.

C. D. Kemp-Welch remained as chairman until February 1916, when Sir William Treloar was elected his successor. He remained a director until he died on 17 December 1916. His record was certainly a remarkable one. He was actively associated with the business during the whole of his working life of forty-three years, twenty of which he spent as managing director of the public company. In his address to the shareholders after his illness in 1913, he said: 'I hope so long as there is any strength in me to continue as long as I possibly can to carry on the business'. In those words came through a glimpse of his commitment and complete identification with Schweppes. Since 1834 the names of Kemp-Welch and Schweppes had become synonymous, and the family association was now left to be carried on by his son Brian.

An advertisement of the Edwardian era

'Schweppes Table Waters are supplied exclusively to the Savoy, Claridge's & Berkeley Hotels and can be obtained at all first-class clubs, hotels & restaurants throughout the world'

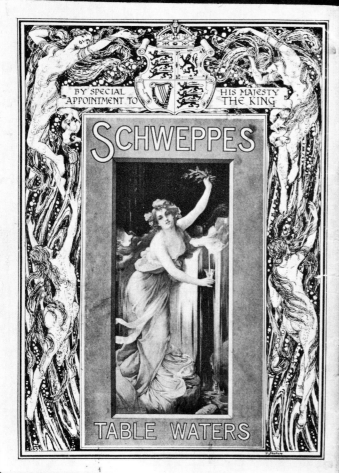

BY SPECIAL
APPOINTMENT TO HIS MAJESTY
THE KING

SCHWEPPES

TABLE WATERS

London
Coliseum

Mme Sarah Bernhardt
Season

Commencing Sept, 8th, 1913.

Price 3ᵈ nett.

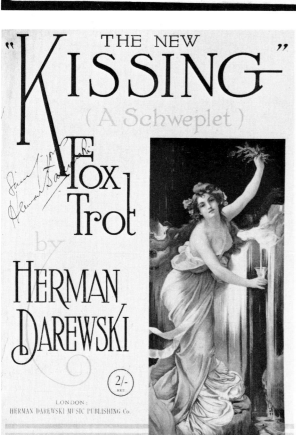

THE NEW
"KISSING"

(A Schweplet)

Fox
Trot

by

HERMAN
DAREWSKI

2/-
NET

LONDON:
HERMAN DAREWSKI MUSIC PUBLISHING Co.

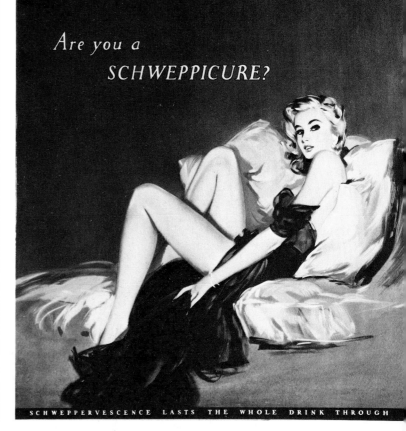

Are you a
SCHWEPPICURE?

SCHWEPPERVESCENCE LASTS THE WHOLE DRINK THROUGH

*Far left: Music
cover of the 1920s*

*Left: One of a
series of UK full
colour showcards,
c. 1950*

Schweppes TONIC WATER
(GIN & TONIC)

In 1917 Walter Harris was appointed joint managing director with Brian Kemp-Welch. In 1918, when it appeared that the latter might be called up, the board proposed the appointment of a third managing director, J. A. York Harris, subject to confirmation at the next annual meeting, in a move which reflected lack of trust in Walter Harris (who was no relation of York Harris). No particular functions were assigned to any of the three managing directors which led to confusion on questions of management and authority. Eventually the tensions within the board could be contained no longer and the storm broke at the annual meeting in June 1918.

Two events, the affair of the Hendon factory and the proposed appointment of a third managing director, brought the situation to a head. The state of trade was such that it would have been possible to close all or part of the Hendon factory and make up the lost production, with the possible exception of brewed ginger beer, at Vauxhall. Brian Kemp-Welch and Walter Harris, the two managing directors, hoped for a requisition of the premises by a government department. In a typical state of dichotomy, the other directors had authorised the company's agents to look for a commercial tenant. Notice of the government's intention to requisition was presented to the board at the same meeting as the agent's recommendation to accept an offer received to take the premises on lease. The two managing directors opposed the latter proposal with great determination in the face of which the other members of the board felt unable to proceed. When, after that, the board appointed J. A. York Harris as an additional managing director, opposed by the two existing managing directors, a deeply incensed Walter Harris gave notice to the chairman that he would oppose him on the issue at the annual meeting. Accordingly, at that meeting he spoke out frankly to the shareholders of his dissatisfaction with the control of the company. After this Walter Harris's contract as joint managing director was not renewed at 30 September and in November, having had enough, he resigned his directorship.

The upshot of Walter Harris's revelations was that the shareholders decided to appoint a committee of investigation. Sir Ivor Philipps, then Major General Sir Ivor Philipps, was present at the meeting and was asked to be one of those forming the committee. This he declined; he was a very busy man, he said, and having been a director in the past, thought it better that he did not serve on the committee. He suggested however that to solve what was a difficult problem for the meeting to handle, a selection committee of three persons, including the Public Trustee, should be formed to appoint the committee of investigation. This was agreed and Sir Ivor was proposed by the meeting and consented to be one of the three. The selection of the committee still proved difficult; some of the larger shareholders were written to but there were no volunteers forthcoming among them. Sir Ivor adhered to his view that he should not sit on the committee but was eventually persuaded by the Public Trustee to take up the task. 'As I had put my hand to the plough in the first place, I was prepared in the interests of the shareholders to see the matter through', was his comment. The committee included Lewis Haslam MP, John McLaren, a city accountant, C. W. Sloper, a stockbroker and A. Williamson Milne, deputy chairman of Liptons, with Sir Ivor as chairman. All the members were public men who had already done good work and the consequent strength of the committee was generally acknowledged.

After the most careful investigation, the committee circulated its report to shareholders in January 1919. The directors made their reply a few days later but did not make much impression. The Press supported the committee and its recommendations. The report of the committee was in restrained terms and as little acrimonious as possible. It was critical of the board's failure, since 1897, to make adequate provision for depreciation whereby the stability of the company had been so seriously imperilled that it was necessary from time to time to increase the capital indebtedness by issue of shares and debentures to an extent which should not have been necessary if a sound system of management and finance had been followed. 'Hooley made the capital big enough, and the board have out-Hooleyed Hooley' said Sir Ivor when the report was debated by the shareholders. There was stern censure for the board's practice of showing the chief assets in the balance sheet, unspecified as to the value, lumped together with 'purchase of business' in a total figure of (for 1917) £1,364,130, of which no less than £1,039,903 was represented by goodwill alone. The committee found that there was not only disharmony among the directors, but a continuous lack of grip and capacity on their part. They considered that Walter Harris was fully justified in calling attention to the unbusinesslike methods of the board, although he was himself apt to embark on important negotiations vitally affecting shareholders' interests without previous consultation with the board. Walter Harris having already voluntarily resigned his directorship, the committee recommended that the shareholders should dismiss the remaining directors with the exception of Brian Kemp-Welch, whose continued presence on the board they considered desirable on account of his long experience with the details of the business. Realising that the shareholders would look to the committee to make arrangements for the continuity of the business, they declared themselves willing, if the shareholders so wished, to accept office as directors on the understanding that they should all retire and come up for re-election at the next annual meeting. Mr Sloper however considered that his position as a principal dealer in the company's shares on the Stock Exchange made it undesirable that he should serve.

An extraordinary general meeting was called to consider the report and recommendations. It was the last time Sir William Treloar presided over a meeting of the shareholders. A director since 1908 and chairman since February 1916, he had won by personal achievement many city and civil distinctions, no cause being dearer to his heart than his foundation for handicapped children which continues today as the Lord Mayor Treloar College, at Holybourne, near Alton. It was his misfortune to have become involved in the uphill struggle for stability in the post-Hooley era in the company. Sir William presided over the meeting with equanimity and it passed off in an orderly manner. A resolution to adopt the committee's report was carried. Resolutions to dismiss the directors, other than Brian Kemp-Welch, and appoint the new board were carried on a show of hands but on a poll, demanded by the chairman, the requisite majority of three to one was not obtained. The committee had foreseen this contingency and a further resolution increasing the number of directors to eight and appointing the four committee members offering to serve, which required only a simple majority, was duly passed.

At the following board meeting Sir William Treloar and Sir William Dunn, the two ex-Lord Mayors, resigned with good grace in the light of the shareholders' action in appointing the members of the committee directors. They expressed their appreciation of the courtesy with which the enquiry had been conducted – and took their leave. Sir Ernest Clarke, who through serious illness was absent during the proceedings and for some months after, did not seek re-election at the next annual meeting.

Thus early in 1919 the company found itself with a new board, under the chairmanship of Sir Ivor Philipps, with Brian Kemp-Welch the only continuing link with the past, as C. D. Kemp-Welch had been at the incorporation in 1897.

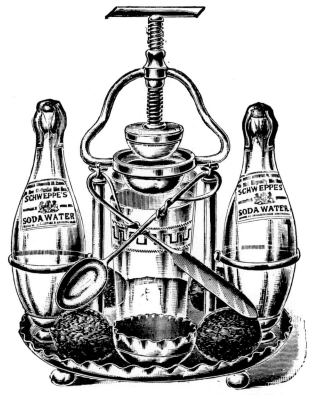

'Lemon Squash Frame', advertised by Mappin and Webb in 1890

Chapter 8

Sir Ivor Philipps

1919–1940

Connaught Place, c. 1830

The new board went into action in a calmer atmosphere than had hitherto prevailed, delving deeper into the state of the company. It was not an easy matter to take over such a large concern and to re-establish it on sound lines. The representative in the United States attended an early board meeting and again the prospects of re-establishing production there were debated. It was clear that such a venture would be very costly indeed with a minimum of three factories being necessary, say in New York, San Francisco and Chicago – a scale of operations for which the company was not then prepared. E. S. W. Paul, the manager in Australia, came to London to report, and the formation of an Australian subsidiary company was discussed but not proceeded with: instead Paul was appointed to the main board as managing director in Australia.

When the accounts for 1918 came before the board, Sir Ivor Philipps' reforming influence was at last unfettered. For the first time since the flotation by Hooley in 1897, the values of freehold and leasehold properties were separated from the old 'Purchase of Business' account revealing that goodwill stood in the

books at over a million pounds. Had this been done before, the late board would probably have found it impossible to have issued 100,000 ordinary shares, thus placing a heavy charge permanently in front of the deferred shares. £14,000 was transferred to Reserve Account and the total amount in that account, £139,000, was applied in writing down goodwill. This was the first of regular annual reductions in goodwill until in 1930 it stood at £400,000. The full preference and ordinary dividends were paid for 1918. For the third year in succession the deferred shareholders received no dividend. This could be attributed to the results of the financial methods of the previous years but the new policy of economising resources, combined with businesslike development of trade, held hope for the future.

Early in 1919 the Hendon factory had been recovered from the Government's war-time requisition for munition works and great efforts were made to restore it to full production. This was sorely needed as the post-war revival in trade, which was being met only by long spells of overtime at other factories, demonstrated that the public appreciation of the company's products was as great as ever. By the annual meeting in June 1919, Sir Ivor was able to report that normal conditions were gradually returning. Sugar was no longer a problem but the supply of bottles was causing great anxiety. The stock of horses, in the turnout of which the company had always taken pride, had been seriously depleted through commandeering and efforts were being made to return to the pre-war standard. Motor transport also required considerable renewals and overhaul. Sir Ivor did not fail to remind shareholders that he and his colleagues on the investigation committee had agreed to accept office as directors on the understanding that they would retire at the next annual meeting. The board had taken some trouble beforehand to ascertain if they had the support of the shareholders and they were re-elected unanimously and congratulated on the company's improved position.

No doubt encouraged, the directors pressed on and the following year again reported good progress in the post-war recovery and in the financial position. The balance sheet showed no loan from the bank which had seldom been the position for the past twenty years, while on the other side, there was nearly £100,000 in investments and cash. The deferred shareholders were rewarded for their patience with a payment of 5%, the highest for six years. Hendon factory had been partially refitted and was producing again but was still restricted by shortage of bottles. Motor transport had been strengthened and the recovery of horse transport, almost to its pre-war standard of excellence, was evidenced by the remarkable achievement at the first post-war van horse parade in Regents Park on Easter Monday of April 1920 when an old rivalry in the pairs classes between the horses of the great distilling firm of James Buchanan and those of Schweppes was revived. Schweppes exhibited thirteen teams and obtained twelve first prizes and one second, the awards being presented by Princess Louise, Duchess of Argyll. The standing of the company was in all respects as high as ever, its reputation for quality bringing increasing demands for its products not only at home but in all parts of the world.

The termination by the landlords of the lease of the company's cordial factory in Belvedere Road led to the further development of the Vauxhall site for manufacturing purposes and the consequent need to remove the head offices to new quarters. After a year of searching, it was decided in July 1920 to acquire the lease of 1 Connaught Place, then known as Marble Arch House. Notwithstanding the immediate reasons which motivated the change, it was in a measure symbolic of the new regime. The old boardroom in St James's was given up and board and staff were re-united under one roof. For many years it was also possible to invite shareholders to general meetings at Connaught Place until their numbers grew altogether too great. The directors had borne in mind the desirability of obtaining a building with ample accommodation for the clerical staff in a prominent position which would be a credit to the company. Marble Arch was known to everyone, not only in London, but in the provinces and abroad. It also had the advantages of a fine prospect over Hyde Park and lay on the direct route between the two London factories at Hendon and Vauxhall. As opportunity offered, the leases of adjoining houses were acquired.

Much historic interest attaches to the property. The construction of Connaught Place began in 1807 in an area formerly associated with the ominous name of Tyburn, for centuries the place of public execution. By 1807 it was seen as a desirable area for development on the edge of London, which ended abruptly at the junction of Oxford Street and the Edgware Road; Paddington was then a rural parish. Connaught Place soon attracted fashionable inhabitants, No. 1 being the town house of Princess Caroline of Brunswick, the unhappy wife of the Prince Regent. It was here that, one night in July 1814, their daughter, the Princess Charlotte, took refuge from the Prince Regent's anger, after breaking off her engagement to the Prince of Orange.

It was a moment of drama, since Charlotte was as popular with the people as her father was unpopular, and a bye-election was about to take place in Westminster amid much excitement. Her mother's close adviser Henry Brougham persuaded Charlotte to return to her father to avert a riot – 'I have only to take you to that window, and show you to the multitude, and tell them your grievances, and they will rise on your behalf'.

Princess Caroline went abroad that same year, and a sale of her effects at Connaught House (as No. 1 was then known) took place in October 1814. Later the mansion was known as Arklow House; Augustus D'Este, a son of the Duke of Sussex, who was also Baron Arklow, lived there for a time.

A wholly Victorian resident of 2 Connaught Place was Lord Randolph Churchill, from 1883 to 1892 at the height of his political career. As a child, young Winston Churchill manoeuvred his toy soldiers in an upper floor nursery.

Schweppes took pleasure in their new offices and wrote of them, 'The beauties of the interior decoration have been preserved with the greatest of care, and the atmosphere of the spacious Victorian age still lingers midst the hustle of present day business'. (The buildings were of course of the late Georgian period). The effects of a road widening scheme have since forced some sacrifices of the old elegance, but fortunately much still remains. The closure of the entrance to 1 Connaught Place from the Edgware Road frontage was followed by the removal of the grand staircase in the entrance hall, so the ghost of a lady in white that used to walk upon this stair is seen no more.

The old general offices, the Town and Country ledger departments, were originally set up in the ballroom which ran through the depth of the house from the north light of Connaught Place to the brightness of the south-facing casement windows and the balcony overlooking Hyde Park. Two white marble fireplaces, at each end of the room, were surmounted by ample mirrors, and the walls were decorated with carved festoons of musical instruments, fruits, cupids, bows and arrows and ribbons. In such an atmosphere, until World War II, the clerks stood, or sat on their high stools, at mahogany desks writing up the massive ledgers. Here when a spell of hot weather stretched out to a second or even a third week, excitement mounted as messages came over the telephone from Hendon or Vauxhall of record orders received. The exhilarating news would soon spread through the whole building. Today this historic terrace, a familiar part of the London scene, is being reconstructed, skilfully and sensitively, to preserve much of its old Georgian grandeur while providing office accommodation appropriate to the twentieth century.

1920 proved a good trading year and the opportunity was not missed of writing another £30,000 off goodwill. This was of course a book transaction requiring no hard cash. By contrast important developments within the business required real money and the reduction of the deferred dividend from 5% to 4%, which showed only a small saving, demonstrated the board's determination to conserve resources. A climate of monetary stringency had also developed and the industrial outlook was less bright than it had been. Some of the cash retained in the business by the board's refusal to divide profits up to the hilt was used for the purchase, in January 1921, of large freehold premises in the old cattle market in Leeds, for conversion to a mineral water factory. This was to supply the densely populated area including the North-East coast which had hitherto been supplied from Liverpool and Glasgow and to eliminate escalating rail charges.

Mr Lewis Haslam, MP, a member of the 1918 Committee of Investigation, who had since served loyally on the board, was compelled to resign in September 1920 owing to the state of his health and in his place William J. Barnett was elected, who was later to play a leading role in the company's expansion in South Africa and France.

1921 was blessed with a phenomenal summer, the benefit of the long spell of warm weather being somewhat offset by the adverse effects of a coal strike, with consequent curtailment of power in the factories, as well as by depressed export trade due largely to unfavourable exchange rates; but the results were still good and the pattern was becoming predictable. Once again £30,000 was written off the goodwill; twelve of the horse vans, which were such a well known sight in the London streets, were exhibited at the Easter Monday van horse parade and each was awarded a first prize. The products of the new cordial factory at Vauxhall were of the highest quality and sales were gaining ground rapidly. The Hendon ginger beer plant was again being extended to meet the great demand for Schweppes' supreme brewed ginger beer. Another small factory had been opened in Southampton Docks, on the principle of further reducing the cost of carriage, to handle the ships' stores traffic with ocean-going liners.

1924–5 were the years of the British Empire Exhibition at Wembley. As the setting for their own exhibit in 1925, Schweppes acquired from the government of Burma, the Burmese pavilion, of graceful design and exquisite carving, described as the most beautiful building at the Exhibition. In association with it they created a reconstruction of an English Tudor village. The Burma Pavilion was constructed of teak, carved by the best craftsmen of Mandalay and Rangoon, the entrance guarded by a monster pair of fabulous beasts. Its eastern dignity was set off by surrounding gardens with Indo-Malayan shrubs and splendid Burmese peacocks. The pavilion and grounds were an outstandingly picturesque feature of the Exhibition providing a cooling rendezvous for refreshment, visited by tens of thousands. The highlight of the occasion for Schweppes was the visit to the pavilion on 9 June 1925 of Their Royal Highnesses the Duke and Duchess of York. The pavilion was later shipped to Australia and erected on a site in the permanent fair ground at Sydney and so continued to be an attractive and popular advertisement.

As year followed year, the story continued the same – of profits larger than ever before in the history of the company, further strengthening of the financial position, development and modernisation of the business

The British Empire Exhibition, Wembley, 1925; Their Royal Highnesses, The Duke and Duchess of York passing through the gateway approaching Schweppes' Burmese Pavilion. The Duke and Duchess are accompanied by Sir Ivor Philipps (Right). Mr Brian Kemp-Welch is behind Sir Ivor.

at home and expansion abroad. The company's improving fortunes permitted payment to the deferred shareholders of their full cumulative dividend of 7% in 1924, for the first time since Hooley twenty-seven years before.

In 1928 Sir Ivor put forward his carefully thought-out scheme to deal with the long outstanding problem of the arrears of the deferred dividend which then amounted to 95%. The company could not hope to pay up the arrears except over a long period of years. The plan was therefore to capitalise £175,000 from the reserve fund and issue one new deferred share free for every two of the 350,000 held. A deferred shareholder who sold the new shares at the then market value would recover in cash at once the whole of his arrears. The shareholder who retained his increased holding and received the increased dividend at the rate of 10%, which it was expected could be paid, would receive the equivalent of his arrears over about twelve years. A compensatory gesture was proposed for the ordinary shareholders, increasing their cumulative dividend from 7% to 8% to equalise their rights and secure their consent. The scheme, which was widely described in the financial Press as a good and fair one, was agreed by the shareholders, so eliminating at last the old thorn in the flesh of so many years.

At the next annual general meeting Sir Ivor reviewed for shareholders the board's ten years of management of their 'great business'. A few shareholders, and occasionally the Press, had shown impatience at the conservative policies adopted, of which Sir Ivor was often at pains to point out the basic principles. The building up of reserves, the writing down of goodwill and the refusal to pay out in dividends cash needed for vital development had provided the additional capital to carry on the expansion of the business and to maintain the plant in the most modern and efficient form. During ten years the pursuit of these policies had resulted in the paying off of £111,000 of charges on properties and the reduction of goodwill from £1,039,000 to £450,000; new factories had been added at Glasgow, Brighton, Cardiff, Leeds and Dublin; large additions had been made to factories at Vauxhall and Hendon; the Sydney factory had been extended and that at Melbourne almost entirely rebuilt. New depots had been formed for improved distribution. New machinery had been introduced and motor transport extended. Cider had been added to the other products, cider mills and orchards acquired. Large interests were held in Schweppes factories in Belgium, South Africa, the Transvaal and in Paris. There had been no issue of new shares for cash, no calling upon

shareholders to put up more capital, no issue of debentures. Net profits had risen from £55,000 in 1918 to £173,000 in 1928, dividends improved and the long outstanding question of the arrears of deferred dividend settled to the satisfaction of the ordinary and deferred shareholders. The remarkable transformation in the strength of the company, prior to the onset of the trade depression of the 1930s, was reflected in the stock market valuation which had risen from £479,000 in 1918 to £1,855,000 in 1928.

Not all new activities during this period prospered, as indeed they rarely do at any time however enthusiastically undertaken. One such activity was Schweppes' entry into the cider trade. Schweppes' Cyder (the alternative spelling was used for the first few years) was launched on 1 June 1923, the product being bought at the outset in bulk from other manufacturers. The progress of sales was encouraging and the company embarked on the purchase of its own cider orchards and mills at Weare in Somerset, Hele in Devonshire and Bledisloe in Gloucestershire. By 1927 the business was well in its stride. The company was firmly settled in its policy which was to market a pure English-made cider neither blended with imported cider nor manufactured from concentrates, thus maintaining the highest standard of quality always exercised with regard to its table waters. The west country orchards were a protection against periodical shortages of English cider-apples and these were extended by the purchase of additional land which was planted with the best types of cider-producing apple trees. Schweppes' cider clearly had a following among the public who appreciated its fine quality, and sales continued to grow. At the Brewers' Exhibition held in London in 1928, Schweppes' cider was awarded in open competition the championship gold medal, the highest possible award which could be obtained for cider in the country. Having succeeded thus far, however, the business began to give rise to some anxiety. The policy of providing an unadulterated English cider was having its effect on profitability. The annual meeting in 1930 found the chairman speaking of the tendency on the part of brewers to tie their houses for cider and in some instances to buy up cider manufactories. Every effort was made to boost sales but further progress became increasingly difficult. The range of ciders offered was reduced by discontinuing dry and very dry cider and also draught cider. The Hele cider factory was sold in 1934 and production concentrated at Bledisloe. Hope still survived and further plantings of trees were made at Bledisloe in 1936. However, early in 1939 the decision was taken to cease production and stocks were running out as the war with Germany began.

A vastly more significant event was the formation in 1923 of a wholly owned subsidiary company then known as Schweppes (Colonial and Foreign) Ltd specifically for the purpose of investing abroad in countries where it was considered advisable to manufacture locally. This was to lead progressively away from the traditional reliance on exports, with the attendant drawbacks of costly freight and foreign exchange problems, first to local manufacture through overseas subsidiary companies and later, after the second world war, to local manufacture by franchised bottlers. The new company was assigned the goodwill of the Schweppes business, and the use of its name and trade marks in all quarters of the world except the British Isles, Northern and Southern Ireland, the Channel Islands and the Isle of Man, Australia and its dependencies and New Zealand, which were the territory of the Sydney branch. The new company's first subsidiary overseas was in Belgium.

For many years Schweppes' minerals had been imported into Ireland and distributed through an agent in Dublin. Schweppes decided to establish a small factory there and in 1928 acquired and equipped premises in Upper Gardiner Street. All branches of the company have, in the course of time, acquired a particular character of their own, deriving in the main from the personalities of the staff who build up their traditions. Dublin was no exception and a team was created there which, in the office and on the road among customers, won many friends for the name of Schweppes. The Irish branch continued until 1956, when it was sold and bottling continued under a franchise appointment.

Schweppes' relationship with W. & J. Burrow Ltd of Great Malvern dates back to the 1850s; for many years the two firms were friendly rivals in the sale of spring water from the Malvern Hills. In the 1850s Walter Beeken Burrow and John Severn Burrow were partners in the firm of Lea, Perrins and Burrows, 'chymists and druggists' of Malvern who held leasehold rights over the water from Holy Well, which they sub-leased to Schweppes. Later Walter and John Burrow set up a separate business in Malvern. They acquired the right to bottle water from St Ann's Well, situated on the Worcester Beacon, and were mineral water manufacturers and wine merchants at Belle Vue Terrace, Malvern. Later they also secured rights over the water from the Primeswell Spring, which rises on the Herefordshire Beacon. Walter and John Burrow were granted a Royal Warrant of Appointment by Princess Mary Adelaide, Duchess of Teck, the mother of Queen Mary, in 1895; by King George V in 1911; and subsequently by King George VI. In 1927 Schweppes acquired Burrows from the company to which the founders had sold in 1917, and considerably consolidated its position in regard to Malvern Water. The board had faith in the future of natural spring waters, particularly those of Malvern, and believed that their value was not sufficiently realised. The same may still be equally true today.

An opportunity was taken in 1930 of purchasing a 51% interest in Kia-Ora Ltd. Kia-Ora Lemon Squash was widely known and enjoyed a high reputation. It was considered that the purchase would provide a valuable addition to Schweppes' interests in fruit beverages as well as permitting considerable economies by the closer working of the two businesses. Kia-Ora's history goes back to 1896 in Australia, when John Dixon left his father's farm in search of a wider life and fortune and set up in Sydney making and selling ice. Soon he added lemonade and ginger beer to his products but his real success came with a new drink, a chilli punch, hot and spicy, with the effective designation of 'O.T.' By 1909 the Australian business was so flourishing that it was decided to enter the British market, where O.T. was also successful, being sold chiefly to the licensed trade for use as a flavouring added to beer, spirits and the like, and described as 'The Sauce of Drinks'. A few years after Schweppes had embarked on the large-scale production of fruit squashes, cordials and British wines, the O.T. company commenced the manufacture of a lemon squash in which the actual pulp of the fruit was included, a distinct departure from the clear varieties of similar drinks previously on the market. This was launched under the name of 'Kia-Ora', a Maori word meaning 'Good Health'. During the first world war the shortage of beers and spirits had a disastrous effect on the sales of O.T. but on the other hand very large orders were received for Kia-Ora Lemon Squash for supplies to the Services. The factory at Rushworth Street was kept busy working two shifts on supplies for the Services for every one for the home market. A natural result of this was that on demobilisation, servicemen carried a taste for Kia-Ora beverages with them into civilian life. Other fruit flavours were added, each in turn meeting with a favourable reception from the public, until by 1924 the Kia-Ora brand had a dominant position in the market. John Dixon, in Australia, then decided in 1929 to dispose of the London undertaking, including extensive trading rights overseas, and a public company was formed with the title of Kia-Ora Ltd, in which Schweppes purchased a controlling interest.

Winners of the Sagamore Cup – International Horse Show, Olympia 1912

Schweppes completed the acquisition of the whole of the outstanding share capital of Kia-Ora Ltd in 1943.

The range of Schweppes' products was expanded about this time by the addition in 1932 of two new fruit juice products, Sparkling Grape Fruit and Sparkling Lemon, joining Sparkling Orange which had been in the list for a few years, though previously known as Orangeade and later 'Palato'. Sales of these products forged rapidly ahead as all-the-year-round beverages. Sparkling Lime and Sparkling Lemon Barley were added in 1935.

The trade depression in Great Britain and Australia, coupled with a bad summer here in 1930, had resulted in a decrease in gross profits for that year of 19%. The outlook remained uncertain and so, despite the reserves in the balance sheet, the directors, still pursuing conservative policies, cut back dividends to the basic cumulative rates and increased the carry-forward. The staff bonus, tuned to the year's results, fell from 20% to 12½% and no salary increases were made to senior staff in 1931. Having trimmed its sails, the company rode out the storm and in a few years was moving forward again. The *Joint Stock Company's Journal*'s report on the 1937 results bore the caption 'Schweppes – Ever Onward!'

It was a portent of things to come when the board resolved, early in 1932, that there should be no further purchases of horses and that consideration be given to the extension of motor deliveries and the pensioning of old horse drivers. This decision inevitably led to the closure of the stables and final dispersal of the horses in 1937. Traffic conditions were no longer suited for horse transport, restrictions were being imposed on their use in certain thoroughfares, and the continued stopping and starting was imposing too great a strain on the animals. It is doubtful if a finer collection of van horses than Schweppes' existed anywhere in the world, as the trophies won in the ring at the International Horse Shows at Olympia bear witness. Their magnificent appearance and the perfection of their turn-out were one of the sights of the London streets. The striking pairs of greys, the wagons in dark green, red

Her Majesty Queen Elizabeth The Queen Mother receiving the Schweppes Gold Trophy won by her horse Tammuz at Newbury, 1975. In the picture are Donald Methven, deputy chairman of Schweppes, and Mrs Methven who made the presentation.

and gold livery, the gleaming brasses and well turned out drivers, were a fine advertisement for the company. These horses sometimes assisted on great State occasions such as the Jubilee procession of King George V and King George VI's Coronation procession. Some of them were real characters, endearing themselves to the men who worked with them and the customers at whose premises they called. But they were all sadly missed. Schweppes' interest in horses continued in other ways. Their Sporting Calendar, picturing each year twelve outstanding horses of the past season, already well established in the 1930s, remains ever popular; and in 1963 the company promoted the Schweppes Gold Trophy handicap hurdle race which has become one of the most prestigious events in the National Hunt Calendar.

Naturally, pride in its transport of whatever kind was instinctive in the organisation, and Schweppes lavished the same care on their subsequent fleet of motor vehicles as they had on their horse-drawn vans. The splendid appearance of the bodywork in the same dignified colours was the work of the company's own highly-skilled coach painters, who also did the lettering in gold leaf. The care given to the exterior appearance was also applied under the bonnets. Again this was largely done in the company's own workshops. With considerable stability of employment, drivers were trained from boyhood, starting as mates. So far as possible they always drove the same vehicle and a competitive spirit developed among them in keeping their own vehicles spick and span.

After a detailed study carried out by Hanning Philipps at the request of the board, a formal pension and life assurance scheme for all employees – production, transport and clerical – was introduced on 1 January 1933. Hanning Philipps, later the Hon. Hanning Philipps, nephew of the chairman and destined to succeed him, had joined the board in March 1930. The new scheme, which included benefits in respect of past service, was to replace the discretionary allowances traditionally made by the directors and by the owners of the business when in

Brian Kemp-Welch, from a newspaper cutting

private hands from time immemorial. Some of these allowances had continued to be paid for many years. On the other hand, the company had often allowed men who wished to do so to remain at work well beyond pensionable age. As an example of the former, in 1928 a retired foreman died aged ninety, who had been pensioned at £60 a year in 1898 after forty-five years' service; and as an example of the latter, in the same year, an under-foreman was pensioned having expressed the wish to retire after sixty years spent in the service of the company.

Another director, George D. Kemp-Welch, was elected to the board in January 1936. The fourth generation of the family since John Kemp-Welch and William Evill purchased Schweppes in 1834, he had been in training in the business for seven years after leaving university. The underlying confidence generated by the strengthening of the company's finances under Sir Ivor was reflected in the decision, early in 1938, to build a new factory at Liverpool, equipped with the most modern machinery, to replace the old

and inconvenient premises in Chatham Street. This was to be the first purpose-built factory constructed since Colwall and Hendon were built in the 1890s. A suitable ten-acre site was found at Aintree. While the negotiations progressed, however, the international situation worsened and in September came the Munich agreement with Hitler. The lease of the site from the Liverpool Corporation was completed the following April as minds were turning to questions of civil defence and the possible consequences of war with Germany. The building of Aintree factory had to wait until 1951. When war came, but not the immediate aerial onslaught that some had predicted, there was breathing space to make preparations. Air raid precautions officers had been appointed throughout the company and much good and essential preparation had already been made, but no one knew quite what to expect. The board agreed a scheme of allowances to be paid to employees joining the services, some of whom were quickly mobilised. The two younger members of the board, the Hon. Hanning Philipps and G. D. Kemp-Welch, were given leave of absence whilst on military service.

At Marble Arch, strategically situated at the junction of two great thoroughfares, some people fell to calculating the number of the enemy's bomber aircraft, the number of bombs each could carry and the devastation each bomb could wreak, and concluded that the head office would cease to exist within an hour or two of the outbreak of hostilities. The company was prepared with alternative accommodation at Woodlands, a large house near Tibbet's Corner by Putney Heath, away from central London, and some departments were sent there as soon as war was declared. Apart from numerous air-raid alerts and the sight of vapour trails in the sky over the city where dog-fights were in progress and some very ugly incidents at fairly close quarters, the Marble Arch offices remained relatively unscathed until a night raid early in the 1940–41 blitz on London, when Schweppes' offices, then confined to Nos 1 and 2 Connaught Place, were severely shaken and many of the heavy plaster ceilings descended on the desks beneath like tablecloths and on the surrounding floors like white carpets. In the morning there was much shovelling-up and carting away being done and several passers-by indulged their humour in an old wisecrack, by enquiring if we were being 'Schwepped away'. The company's architect expressed fears for the safety of the building and the remaining staff moved out to Woodlands, perhaps needlessly. Fairly soon afterwards the offices were requisitioned and occupied by a Government Department, which was slow to be dislodged when hostilities were over. In 1942 the garages and flats of Connaught Mews suffered a direct hit from a powerful bomb, fortunately without loss of life. The blast totally demolished 5 Connaught Place and wrecked No. 6.

Whilst at first the attack from the air was delayed and its possible future consequences uncertain, there was no doubt that the vulnerability of sea routes to Britain would quickly bring shortages of all imported supplies. Every effort was made to maximise stocks of manufacturing ingredients not under government control. For the soft drinks industry the chief concern was for sugar and fruit juices, particularly sugar. The Government declared a standstill on the usage of sugar in October 1939, limiting manufacturers to quantities equal to their usage during October to December of the previous year. Cuts in this allocation were soon imposed and by March 1940 the rate was reduced to 40% of pre-war usage. The manufacture of Tonic Water soon had to be discontinued as the company's stocks of quinine were urgently required for medical use in the national interest. The demand for Schweppes drinks remained at a very high level. Movements of troops and of the civilian population, with additional earnings from increased employment in the war effort, stimulated sales. Indeed in the industry as a whole, production actually expanded,

though with a loss of quality where some manufacturers 'stretched' the use of raw materials in short supply. But the evacuation of the British army from Dunkirk and the cessation of hostilities in France brought the threat of enemy invasion. The dramatic change in prospect demanded the mobilisation of the resources of all sections of industry for defence. So there began between the soft drinks industry and the Government and within the trade itself the months of anxious planning and debate which finally led to the concentration scheme which operated from 1943–1948.

About this time the company suffered a great loss from the death in August 1940 of Sir Ivor Philipps, its chairman for the past twenty-one years. In paying tribute to his memory and to his wide experience and sterling qualities, the board recalled the extent of his achievement in bringing the company through the difficulties which had prevailed when he took over the chairmanship. *The Times* obituary notice of Major-General Sir Ivor Philipps, K C B, D S O, Governor of Pembroke Castle, spoke of his distinguished career in the Army and subsequent career in politics (he was for many years Liberal MP for Southampton) and in the City. His influence in Schweppes' affairs at a most critical period in its history was of immense value. Those that appreciated this the most felt that on his death they had seen the end of an era.

Scenes from production units in 1924

Chapter 9

J. W. Joyce and
the War Time Association

1940–1948

*If we had some Gin
we'd have a Gin & Tonic
if we had some*

Schweppes

Bereft of Sir Ivor and with Hanning Philipps and George Kemp-Welch away in the armed forces, Hanning with the Welsh Guards and George with the Grenadiers, the board acted promptly to co-opt Lord Milford, brother of Sir Ivor, as a director. The Hon. Hanning Philipps succeeded Sir Ivor as chairman and Sir Henry E. ap Rhys Pryce, KCB, CMG, DSO, who had joined the board in 1938, was elected deputy chairman.

The family gift for finance, latent in Sir Ivor Philipps until he returned to the City after the first world war, was brought to bear by Lord Milford on Schweppes' affairs. A large proportion of the company's liquid resources at that time were invested in government stocks. A substantial part of this was redeployed under his direction in first-class industrial securities and his management of the portfolio, at a time when there was no other outlet for the funds, substantially benefited the company.

Towards the end of 1940, Brian Kemp-Welch expressed the desire to retire from the managing directorship due to his state of health and the board

agreed that he should relinquish that responsibility from the end of the year. After twenty-six years as managing director, it was with great sadness that he felt it necessary to hand on to another the task of dealing with the considerable problems then arising, and which would arise when the war was over. During his years of office he had been a constant guardian of the company's reputation for quality and service, which remained second to none, and had maintained the closest personal contact with the trade. A rather reserved man in contact with the staff, he was nevertheless always approachable by them and he won their complete loyalty and affection. Brian Kemp-Welch remained on the board as an ordinary director until the end of 1949, when he retired after fifty-one years of service to the company, having reached the age of seventy. Unfortunately he did not long survive his retirement and died on 1 August 1950.

The gap was filled by the appointment in January 1941 of James W. Joyce as general manager. J. W. Joyce was the managing director of Kia-Ora Ltd in which Schweppes held the controlling interest, and his abilities were therefore well known to the board. He was not however appointed to the board and made managing director until April 1942. His dynamic personality was to make a long-remembered impact throughout the company.

For head office staff at Woodlands the new situation added considerably to travelling problems. It was always the objective to get home before the blackout and the routine of air raids. 'Dig for Victory' was a watchword of the day to which Woodlands staff rallied with enthusiasm. The perfect lawn was dug up for growing vegetables. Pampered for years with fertiliser, the ground produced phenomenal crops.

In March and April 1941, Plymouth suffered two intensive bombing attacks, the second of five nights' duration. The civic buildings and the shopping centres of Plymouth and Devonport were wiped out. The company's Plymouth factory was completely destroyed, fortunately with no loss of life, though hundreds of civilians in the city were killed. Premises were quickly found at Newton Abbott from which to carry on distribution.

The board, concerned over the question of conserving raw materials, agreed in August to the modification of formulae but only such as would still permit the quality of the drinks concerned to maintain their usual superiority over the best competitors. Contact was made with Schweppes in Cape Town with a view to encouraging shipments of fruit juice. If production fell short of demand, pre-war customers' orders were supplied in full and others received as high a proportion as possible.

Having strategically deployed the investment of the company's reserves, Lord Milford succeeded in bringing about a simplification of the capital structure. As a legacy of the Hooley flotation, the company had been left with a complicated and cumbrous share capital in which the three classes of shares all had cumulative rights. Profit available for distribution, after the fixed rates had been paid, was shared as to one quarter to the ordinary shares and three-quarters to the deferred. The disadvantages of this had been felt in the past when, because of the unusual dividend rights, further issues of shares had only been possible under schemes of arrangement and sanctions of the Court. The board had in mind the acquisition of the outstanding capital of Kia-Ora Ltd still in public ownership, by an exchange of shares, but freedom from the shackles of the old structure, already overdue, would clear the way for other future developments. Lord Milford brought before the shareholders a skilfully designed scheme of capital reorganisation which

eliminated the problems and was equitable in the matter of earnings. It was approved by the Court and the resolutions adopting it were passed by the shareholders unanimously.

While these somewhat dry formalities had been taking place, events of a momentous and controversial nature were moving the industry relentlessly under Government pressure towards concentration. Lord Woolton, Minister of Food, recognised the valuable part the beverage industry would play in maintaining the morale of the nation, and the importance of supplies of citrus drinks for the nation's health, but rightly demanded a maximum economy in production and distribution. Preliminary surveys were made of total output, factory space, manpower and sales, based on which the Ministry of Food decided upon a target for the whole industry in gallons of drinkable liquid, whether of ready-to-drink beverages or of squashes and cordials after dilution. In the division between the two types, the emphasis was placed heavily on concentrated beverages, to save the transport of millions of gallons of water from factory to customer. Eventually the proposed production of mineral waters was cut from a total level of 116 million gallons in 1940–1941 to 85 million gallons, the loss of drinkable liquid to be made up by doubling the concentrated beverage gallonage from 6.2 million to 12.4 million gallons. It was left to the trade to adapt itself to this change.

After several months of debate, the regional and sectional trade associations were still not of one mind on the best approach to a scheme of concentration. The Ministry insisted that the carbonated and concentrated sections of the trade should be regarded as one. Having set a deadline for a scheme to be worked out by the industry itself, it called a meeting, as widely representative of the trade as possible, with a view to establishing a War Time Association. On 12 May 1942, 160 members of the industry met and approved the formation of the Association. The Ministry also proposed the names of twelve trade representatives to serve as the first executive committee to draft the constitution and rules. A compliment was paid to the company by the appointment of J. W. Joyce as chairman of the committee. Despite some misgivings the meeting supported these arrangements, as a result of which the Soft Drinks Industry (War Time) Association, afterwards known familiarly as the S.D.I. or the W.T.A., came into being.

The atmosphere prevailing at the time can be sensed from the following extract from the official history of the S.D.I.:

The Association was not, however, launched and equipped

*A Schweppes bottle with a standard
S.D.I. label of the period 1943–1948*

Concentration of the Soft Drinks Industry

Schweppes LTD

REGRET TO ANNOUNCE THAT THEIR

TABLE WATERS
SQUASHES AND CORDIALS

ARE, OWING TO THE INTRODUCTION
OF THE CONCENTRATION SCHEME
SPONSORED BY THE MINISTRY OF
FOOD, NOW UNOBTAINABLE UNTIL
AFTER THE WAR.

*UK press advertisement early in the
second world war*

without considerable labour and confusion. Since the sole reason for its coming into being was to draw up and operate a Concentration Scheme, controversy over the make-up of the Association and discussions as to the best scheme were inextricably mingled. At times the judgment of the committee was criticised. At others, its very powers were called into question. And as these committee men journeyed each week to London, with the enemy's air offensive providing an incessant reminder that speed was essential and with the Ministry already closing factories, they wondered whether, in the time at its disposal, the trade could cope with its two gigantic tasks; that is to say, the reorganisation of the trade from top to bottom to meet the production targets and the introduction of a fair and workable system of concentration. Subsequent tribute has rightly been paid to the work of this Committee of Twelve during this time and particularly to the chairman in keeping a clear head and (to keep to the simile) in holding the vessel on an even keel.

The devising of the scheme of concentration reconciling the many and varied interests was a matter of great intricacy and took over six months to complete. When announced it was naturally subject to some criticism and some adjustments were made. Nevertheless it was generally approved by the trade and was accepted by the Government. It came into operation on 1 February 1943.

The principles of the scheme were simply efficiency and equity. Government licensing powers ensured that all manufacturers were members of the Association.

The abandonment of individual labels, as a means of economy and of protecting the interests of a closed firm, was also the subject of Government decree. The new national label, which merely specified the name of the drink and the initials S.D.I. with a code number identifying a production point, was a focal point for opposition groups who felt that it threatened to erase from the public mind the well-known brand names, so that all the years of goodwill built up by old established firms would vanish away. Schweppes, who had most to lose, made it clear that they were prepared to make this sacrifice in the national interest. The public came readily to accept 'S.D.I.' beverages, though some cynics, unable to obtain their favourite brand of soda water or lime juice, suggested that 'S.D.I.' stood for 'some die instantly'. The committee had power to close any business and to direct how and by whom raw materials and facilities and, subject to Government requirement, even labour should be used and distributed. They also controlled the zoning of distribution

Facing: A 1949 example from the UK press advertisements which were then establishing the relatively new word 'Schweppervescence' (drawing by Felix Topolski)

*Overleaf left: The first recorded use of the word 'Schwepping' was in 1951; e.g. in this pre-Christmas advertisement
Overleaf right: One of the many memorable Schweppes press advertisements designed by the French cartoonist Siné*

NEW WORDS for NEW TIMES

" Escalator "   —   " Schweppervescence "

The Grand Staircase has gone the way of the Grand Manner.

Schweppes, quietly lending its name to the language, changes only to get, if possible, better.

How many Schwepping Days to Christmas?

SCHWEPPERVESCENCE LASTS THE WHOLE DRINK THROUGH

HOW MANY SCHWEPPING DAYS
TO CHRISTMAS ?

SCHWEPPERVESCENCE LASTS THE WHOLE DRINK THROUGH

Schweppervescence lasts the whole drink through

More Troopers

Trooper in Sparkling ★ *Bottledress*

The Duke of Schweppshire's Own
Lemonade Hussars

Dolman—

Tail
of Charger

Shadow—

Schwepp**
LEMONA**
SCHWE**

THIRSTY?—TAKE THE NECESSARY

SCHWEPPES

B SQUADRON, SCHWEPPES THIRSTKILLING DRAGOONS

and the type and quality and the standard formulae of all drinks manufactured as well as the type of packs and the prices at which they would be sold. The rights of individual members were safeguarded, including a provision for the eventual replacement of, or alternatively compensation for, production or distribution facilities loaned under the scheme. The receipts by members from all sales, less a pre-determined allowance for the cost of production, distribution and certain other operating costs, were paid to the Association's Pool Fund. Each member, whether operating or closed, received a share of the Pool Fund in proportion to his share in the profits of the industry before the war.

The provisions for the democratic control of the Association were naturally a thorny problem. Fears had to be allayed that it would be dominated by the larger firms and that the squash section would be inadequately represented. The original Committee of Twelve had been a temporary body to set up the Association. They had been under constant fire for being men picked by the Government, meeting in secret and dictatorial. Eventually, five months after the commencement of concentration, an election scheme giving representation on a sectional and regional basis, and including Ministerial and Trade Association representatives, was agreed at a general meeting. A reconstituted committee of twenty-four, including the original twelve, was appointed to serve from September 1943. The meeting provided a last opportunity for criticism after which the Association moved into calmer waters. One final formality was necessary, namely the election of the chairman of the reconstituted committee. A proposal was advanced for an 'independent' chairman but was rejected. The rejection of this proposal, taken in conjunction with the conditions of the meeting, was tantamount to a popular mandate for J. W. Joyce himself to lead the Association.

So for five years until de-concentration on 1 February 1948, Schweppes, like all other mineral water manufacturers in the country, operated under these conditions. By reason of its national character, Schweppes was drastically affected, four of its factories and fourteen depots being closed. The War Time Association took control of distribution and Schweppes' fleet of vans came under its control. The sales force was seriously dislocated and undoubtedly the greatest setback suffered by the company was the absence of its labelled products from the market. Nevertheless the board was fully satisfied that the scheme operated in the interests of the nation and the soft drinks industry as a whole. The company's name

was kept before the public by advertisements and the board remained confident that the goodwill between the company, its numerous customers and the public would enable trading to be resumed under the Schweppes brand with good results when the Scheme of Concentration ceased to operate.

From the outset the Association had been required to give priority in distribution to ships' stores and establishments such as Service canteens and those conducted by Naafi, Y.M.C.A., and other organisations, and also hospitals and the very many industrial canteens that had been established during war-time. A special demand arose in the latter part of 1942 and during 1943, when large numbers of U.S. and Canadian troops were arriving in this country. It was made clear to the War Time Association that British standard soft drinks would not be acceptable to these troops. Cola drinks of full sugar quality were required. Protests that the British Tommy was receiving the standard S.D.I. drinks were of no avail. In high-level talks between the British and U.S. Governments it was agreed that purchases of cola by the U.S. Army in Britain would be paid for under the reciprocal aid arrangements devised as part payment of lease-lend goods. Supplies of sugar, additional to the industry's block allocation, were made available for the cola drinks so required. By the peak period of demand just prior to D-Day in 1944, members of the Association were supplying these troops with cola drinks at the rate of two million bottles per week.

As soon as the company's scheme of capital reconstruction had been carried through in 1942, the board went ahead with its intention to make an offer to acquire the shares in Kia-Ora Ltd not already owned by the company. The offer was successful and Kia-Ora became a wholly owned subsidiary in July 1943 which assisted the concentration of both companies and resulted in considerable economies.

The company suffered a loss of particular poignancy by the death on 18 June 1944 of Captain George Durant Kemp-Welch, Grenadier Guards, who was present at the morning service in the Guards Chapel, Wellington Barracks, when the building was struck and destroyed by a flying bomb. He had served the company faithfully and well on the staff and as a director. He was an exceptionally talented sportsman (a double blue at Cambridge, he had captained Warwickshire and taken part in an M.C.C. tour of the West Indies) but took his business career most seriously. Had he survived the war he would undoubtedly have played a significant role in the future of the company. The sad consequence of this tragedy

Facing: A typical lighthearted press advertisement used in the popular UK weekly publication 'Picture Post' during summer 1953

J. W. Joyce

was that when Brian Kemp-Welch finally retired from the board in 1949, his son was not there to succeed him and the association of the Kemp-Welch family with Schweppes, which had lasted for 115 years, came to an end.

The flying bombs (the V-1s or doodlebugs) caused considerable disruption to production in southern England. The first of these fell in June 1944. At Woodlands during the period of the flying bombs, a watcher was mounted at a vantage point on the roof to sound a bell for those below to take cover when one came close. The roar of the bombs' jet engines was distinctive and in clear weather they could be seen approaching at 300/400 m.p.h. Sooner or later the engine stopped. There followed several seconds of waiting while the bomb plunged unpredictably to earth, then a violent explosion. A potentially more sinister event

was the arrival the following September of the first V-2 rocket which fell in Chiswick about three miles from Woodlands. Preparations were then made for the complete evacuation of soft drinks production and staff from the danger areas.

Woodlands came through unscathed. Its closest call had come the previous February when in a night raid a high explosive bomb had fallen outside the gates but had failed to explode. The offices were cordoned off when the staff arrived in the morning and remained closed for a few days while the bomb was dealt with. However someone slipped into the house and extricated the 1943 end-of-year accounts and a few other items.

The Concentration Scheme, when introduced, had laid emphasis on an early return to normal trading when hostilities ceased and J. W. Joyce had pledged himself and the committee of the War Time Association to secure the most equitable arrangements possible for the return of competitive conditions. Consequently in the autumn of 1944, when it appeared that the war in Europe might be nearing its end, the committee turned its attention to the preparation of a deconcentration scheme. Nevertheless, it did not prove possible to commence the deconcentration period until 12 October 1947. The practical problems of reversion to normal trading were dealt with with the utmost care. But the delay was largely due to the fact that in the economic state of the country at the end of the war, the shortage of materials in some cases grew worse; and there were difficulties in getting factories which had been closed repaired and re-equipped. In such circumstances, a return to fair competition could hardly be achieved.

The deconcentration period ended on 1 February 1948, the great day on which there was a joyful return to individual labels and brand names, though there were still restrictions on the supply of sugar. The resumption of normal trading went with remarkable smoothness and the following summer the trade manufactured a record gallonage of all types of drinks.

The Association dealt with its final claims from members and all other outstanding matters and in October 1948 the members resolved that it should be wound up. Amid emotional scenes, a great tribute was paid to the committee and in particular to 'Jimmy' Joyce, as he was known to his colleagues, for the outstanding service rendered to the industry. The Government, through the Minister of Food, had also congratulated the industry on the great success of the scheme which had proved a model of its kind in plan and operation. They gave great credit to the generosity of the committee members and others who had given so freely of their time and knowledge and finally paid tribute to J. W. Joyce as chairman of the Association for his energy, idealism and thorough knowledge born of long experience, without which the scheme could not possibly have been the success that it was. Jimmy Joyce was offered a knighthood but declined saying that the whole industry had earned recognition. In the concluding words of his foreword to the official

PERSONAL — BY AIR

Dear Mr. Gerald :

    I take up my pen in good time in order to send you Best Wishes on the occasion of your Birthday which should reach you five weeks from today. All at the Hall are well except old Mr. Macgregor who sustained a slight flesh wound near his asparagus beds by a bow and arrow discharged by a young evacuee. This evacuee is one of the ones stopping at the Lodge, and Mr. Macgregor had made him the bow and arrow himself, so he cannot complain. The silver is put away for the duration, but I take it out periodically and give it a careful clean. Last year we lifted a fine lot of potatoes from what used to be the Clock Golf Lawn. I am also looking after the cellar to the best of my ability. In particular, I have made a point of laying in a case of Rose's Lime Juice against your return. Like many good things, Rose's is hard to obtain in England these days. Still, there will be ample Rose's Lime Juice after the war, when all headaches and hangovers will be where they belong — on the other side of the Rhine.

    In anticipation of that day, I sign myself, in haste.

        Yours respectfully,

        Albert Hawkins

        (Sergt., Home Guard).

There is no substitute for ROSE'S Lime Juice

The remembrance of these things will prove a source of future pleasure

Schweppes

Typical Schweppes and Roses press advertisements during the second world war years of shortages and discontinuation of branded soft drinks

history of the S.D.I. he wrote, 'The rich store of memories which that experience has left with me is my abundant reward'.

    The enormous amount of personal effort which he gave to the affairs of the S.D.I. was, of course, in parallel with his normal duties as managing director of the company. After the end of the war, he began intensive preparations within the company for the return to competitive trading and for the post-war future of Schweppes. Several groups of staff were sent to the U.S.A. over the following months to study developments in the beverage industry there, American methods of salesmanship and the latest production methods. Additional representatives and trainee salesmen were engaged and appointments made to strengthen management. Every possible step was taken to boost production facilities; as many of the latest machines as could be obtained were installed and old plant re-conditioned.

    It was vital for the company to be able to meet the

Press advertisements heralding and celebrating the return of Schweppes branded products in the UK after the second world war. From a series of ideas by the cartoonist David Langdon

demand for Schweppes wherever it arose and to recover contact with those customers from whom it had been severed under zoning arrangements. With freedom of trading scheduled for 1 February 1948, stocks of S.D.I. quality were run down and on 29 January J. W. Joyce reported to the board that after several weeks of canvassing by representatives, there were orders in hand equivalent to about four weeks' production. Schweppes received a great welcome back. But for the restricted supplies of sugar and of bottles, the results would have been even better. As it was, the volume of sales in 1948 was in excess of the pre-war figure and the expansion continued. Exports had also received their due share of attention and sales to the U.S.A. were also substantially in excess of 1938.

The successful transition to normal trading took place under the guidance of J. W. Joyce but this, unfortunately, was his last major service to the company during his tenure of office. When he was appointed managing director, he succeeded three generations of the Kemp-Welch family, and found a company permeated with history and traditions and a lingering aloofness inherited from bygone days. Aware of the demands that would be made on the company in the post-war period, he set himself with characteristic zeal to bring about the changes which he saw were necessary. Along this road however the results of his policies within the organisation gave serious cause for concern to the board.

During the war years many difficult problems had been faced and solved, particularly within the S.D.I. Committee, where Joyce's skill, eloquence and pervasive personality, through which a warm and generous nature was often seen, had undoubtedly played a major part; but then unity of purpose was subject to compelling necessity. In peacetime conditions, bent on reasserting Schweppes' leadership in the industry, he conceded no time for a readjustment of attitudes and brooked no opposition. Those among the senior staff who were unwilling or reluctant to accept change came under severe pressure and some left the company. Others stayed on, casualties of the drive to establish the new order. Many of those not personally affected were disturbed by the march of events and the morale of the management was put in jeopardy. Towards the end of 1948 therefore the board decided that whilst giving full credit to his achievements during one of the most difficult periods in the company's history, the termination of his engagement as managing director was in the best interests of the company generally. Concurrently with the termination of his contract J. W. Joyce also resigned his seat on the board. Whilst some will remember Jimmy Joyce for the 'stripes' they received at his hands, many remember also the loyalty and affection he was capable of generating and his great power of leadership. After a number of years there was a reconciliation with the company when he was again invited to Connaught Place, and he lived on with his memories until the ripe old age of ninety-four.

The post-war illumination of the electric sign in Piccadilly Circus, delayed until 2 April 1949, brought scenes of great rejoicing

Chapter 10

Sir Frederic Hooper: Company and Image 1948–1955

The Freedom of Cirenschwepster awarded to F. C. Hooper

In May 1948, J. W. Joyce had requested the board to invite F. C. Hooper (later Sir Frederic Hooper) to investigate and advise on the selection and training of personnel, in his capacity of professional business consultant. Sir Frederic Hooper, then aged fifty-six, a West Countryman, had begun his working life as a botanist at London University. After serving in the Army throughout the 1914–1918 war, he worked for an Athens bank for two years before accepting the invitation of Lord Woolton (then Frederick Marquis) to join Lewis's at Liverpool. Twenty years later, he succeeded Lord Woolton at Lewis's as joint managing director. He resigned in 1942 and took over as director of the Political Research Centre in London, later becoming director of the Business Training Scheme, planned and operated by the Ministry of Labour to assist the re-settlement of returning ex-servicemen. He was a well-known broadcaster, writer and speaker on a wide range of subjects.

Sir Frederic quickly completed his preliminary sur-

vey for Schweppes and submitted a final report arising from his investigations. The board clearly considered that his expertise in management and experience of staff and labour problems, which had been amply demonstrated in the course of his career, were the attributes needed in the company at that time. In July therefore Sir Frederic was elected to the board and appointed joint managing director, and became sole managing director when J. W. Joyce resigned in the following November. Another boardroom change occurred in January 1949, when Lord Milford resigned owing to his advancing years after eight years in which his guidance on financial affairs had been so valuable.

Sir Frederic Hooper took office as managing director at a time when the stage was set for the full deployment of his talents. He took control of a well-established company which throughout all its vicissitudes had maintained, since its foundation, a consistent marketing policy, that of producing mineral waters of the very highest quality. Only during the period of anonymity under the Concentration Scheme had it consented in the national interest to manufacture to standard war-time formulae. Soft drinks were progressively increasing in popularity. What was once a luxury was becoming part of the generally accepted standard of living. The company was gearing itself to take advantage of the trend, and to do all in its power to foster it. Though by 1 January 1949 there had been eleven months of competitive trading, there was still difficulty in meeting demand. Fruit juices remained under Government control until October 1949. Schweppes secured its share, but not its choice of quality. In the face of a steadily rising demand for squashes, Schweppes refused to sacrifice quality and had to ration available supplies to customers. Sugar was still short and closely controlled. A prolonged and exceptional summer in 1949 boosted sales of minerals, but the rising tide was evidenced by the manner in which sales kept up after the hot weather had ended.

Reorganisation had already begun under J. W. Joyce. Production arrangements under a new chief engineer, H. A. F. Canfield, had gone ahead rapidly. Utilising the substantial financial reserves built up under Sir Ivor Philipps and during the Concentration period with guidance from Lord Milford, the company had placed very large orders for new machinery. There were big developments in production capacity, which was soon outstripping sales by a wide margin. Sir Frederic applied himself to rectifying this imbalance with great success.

He found the centralised system of managerial control to be over-complex and delegated authority in production and sales to branch managers, who were thereafter rewarded with a commission on their results. At head office the system of statistical controls was drastically simplified and a new system of cost accounting was introduced. The detailed operation of the business depended on the executive branch managers who were responsible directly to the managing director and controlled by him through the four head office departmental controllers of production, sales, accountancy and personnel. The thirteen branches thereby became self-supporting trading units in terms of production and sales, with the managers paid on results. The system stood up without strain to the period of rapid growth which followed.

During the period of Concentration the sales force had been seriously dislocated, for there had been little for them to do while all soft drinks were sold under a national label. The former sales manager had trans-ferred to branch management and a new appointment was necessary. Sir Frederic later said that, discarding more conventional conceptions, he decided that he wanted a thoughtful man with good judgement of men and matters and, since modern sales management was largely guided by trends revealed by statistical investigations, a first-rate grasp of figures and the ability to interpret them in terms of action. Just such a man was L. M. Alexander, a chartered accountant who had been secretary and accountant of Kia-Ora Ltd, where he had served many years under J. W. Joyce. He had held administrative office within Schweppes, after the merger of Kia-Ora, until Joyce had persuaded him to take charge of production with Alex Canfield. At a later stage LMA, as he was known to his colleagues, became general manager of Schweppes, carrying also the heavy burden of overseas development as this gathered pace. The appointment of LMA as sales manager served to demonstrate within the company that the emphasis which after Concentration had been heavily weighted on production had shifted to sales.

The sales policy took account of Schweppes' reputation for top quality and of the larger than ever number of people willing to look for quality when purchasing mineral waters. The market itself dictated an expansionist sales policy, as also did the internal need for sales to overhaul the production programme. The sales force was reinforced in numbers and a commission scheme introduced under which each man earned a bonus related to his increase in turnover over a basic year. Since the basic turnover remained constant, the system could, and did, provide an ever-increasing commission. With this spur and with good direction from sales management, an increasing number of new outlets was found and Schweppes' availability spread more widely than ever before. In 1948 it had been budgeted for sales to meet, by the end of 1951, the production potential of 80% over the existing volume of trade. The success of the new methods can be gauged by the fact that sales caught up with production capacity in 1950 when further machines were required.

Next Sir Frederic demonstrated his concern for the welfare of all those employed in the company. Schweppes had always been generous to their employees in the payment of sickness and retirement allowances. Sir Frederic was determined that these and other benefits granted on a discretionary basis should be bestowed as rights on the recipients. In collaboration with Arthur Deakin, then head of the Transport and General Workers' Union, and his officials, he drew up and implemented in the company a Code of

Sir Frederic Hooper

L. M. Alexander

Employment which was regarded as a model and frequently used as such by the union. The agreement was made in May 1950 between the company and the T.G.W.U. as being the union most closely appropriate to the company's employees, other than craft workers. It expressed the object of strengthening still further the spirit of co-operation and of goodwill which had always governed the relations between the company and its employees. The document, signed for the company by the Hon. Hanning Philipps and Sir Frederic Hooper, bore the signatures on behalf of the union of Arthur Deakin, General Secretary, and of Frank Cousins, National Secretary.

Similarly, in the matter of provision for sickness, he introduced a system called the Health Bank. Under this, all employees built up an entitlement for absence on pay, the amount depending on their length of service. The accumulated credit could be drawn on as of right, subject only to evidence of sickness being given to the company.

The Employment Code laid down working conditions and provided job security so far as possible; the Health Bank looked after people who fell ill. The third achievement was a significantly improved pen-sion scheme, introduced in September 1950, only a little over two years from Sir Frederic taking office.

There were thus newly-established codes for the fundamental terms of employment, sick pay and pensions, but Sir Frederic went still further in the area of personnel relationships. He introduced a system of joint consultation between representatives of the work-force and management, not without some initial misgivings on both sides. Consultation was at both branch level and company level. Every employee through his joint council was kept informed of what was going on at his branch, and managers were required to be really frank in what they told the workers' representatives about sales, production and branch profits. The elected representatives from branches and administration departments came to head office annually to meet the management at a time when the annual results were available but before they had been seen by the board. The representatives were shown the company balance sheet and the state of affairs was open for free discussion. Members of the Council understood that there must be no premature disclosure of information and no such leakage ever occurred. In addition to being kept far better informed than ever

H. A. F. Canfield

before, workers were able to add to their pay packet through incentive bonuses based on work study and these made a major contribution to the reduction of costs and increased productivity.

To meet the natural desire of most people to 'get on', a promotion course was started. Anyone below the rank of junior management could enter if, by taking a preliminary test, he could show that he had sufficient ability to profit by the course. In the first two years, twenty-two employees successfully completed the course and thirteen were appointed to junior managerial positions.

Sir Frederic was also concerned to give some reasonable guarantee of security of employment to every employee who had become 'established' under the Employment Code which gave permanent employee status after three months' probation. He therefore laid down that no branch manager or other executive might dismiss an employee without reference to him. As long as the company could afford to employ him and provided an employee did his job properly, he could only be dismissed for such reasons as serious breaches of discipline. Laying-off between seasonal peaks was no longer regarded as a reason for dismissal. The com-

pany had successfully set itself to solve the problems of seasonal peaks so that expensive high-output plant would be kept running as close to full production as possible throughout the year. A policy of vigorous advertising had helped to spread sales more evenly through the year; careful budgeting and production planning also played their part in arriving at the correct stock levels to meet peak sales. The result was the maximum utilisation of machines with constant employment for the operators, and consequent increase in their skill.

The personnel policy was increasingly understood and appreciated. The condition of guaranteed employment was put to the test in 1956. In 1955 there had been an exceptionally prolonged summer spell and the production lines, laboratories and the despatch and transport sections were unusually hard pressed. Representatives were called in to help ease the strain on the office staffs. Supervisory staff spread themselves over double shifts in the factories, with greatly extended working hours. During this severely testing period, the team spirit was everywhere in evidence and the company came through without a major breakdown. The enthusiasm generated by this experience led to some optimistic budgeting and production planning which built up stocks to a high level in the early months of 1956 in preparation for the summer. But in the event, there was no summer at all in 1956; it was in fact the worst for fifty years. As a result, sales fell heavily in the key months of July, August and September (though they finished well above the previous year) and there was not enough work for established staff in certain factories. Nevertheless no one was laid off.

In his annual address to shareholders in 1951 the chairman had said, 'We have striven to build up with our employees a pattern of living and of working which can form a single, satisfying whole, and in which labour, capital and management are capable of being regarded as partners, with common interests and a common stake in the profitability and stability of the company'. The results of the innovations were far reaching. They combined to strengthen the company and place its earnings on a stable basis. A new cohesion and enhanced spirit of goodwill towards the company and its policies were created in the post-war period among all sections of employees. Productivity rose considerably and there was a dramatic fall in labour turnover. In a period when the volume of trade in the soft drinks industry as a whole remained nearly static, Schweppes' turnover and trading profits in 1951 were more than double those of 1948. The momentum was maintained. In the following four years, turnover and trading profit doubled again. As an indication of the all-round increase in efficiency, during this period productivity increased by some 50%, the labour force producing twice the volume while only increasing by about a third.

A further development in personnel policy took place in 1956 when the annual bonus to factory and office employees, which until then had been decided by the board, broadly in line with the year's results, was with the help and conjunction of the unions turned into an official profit sharing scheme. The proportion of profits allocated to the scheme under the rules was distributed among the eligible employees on a scale settled by a small panel appointed by themselves.

With the passage of time and the further development of the company both from within and by amalgamations, some of Sir Frederic's schemes have been modified or absorbed in other arrangements more appropriate to the circumstances. However the effect of his policies in the field of personnel management cannot be overestimated. They created the stable background against which a great leap forward in the company's fortunes was able to take place.

In the management of people and in their motivation, as well as in organisation, therefore, Sir Frederic made a great impact for which he will long be remembered. In the world outside he was often thought of as the genial squire of 'Schweppshire', the man who added an extra county to the map of Britain. The idea was born during a snooker game at the Savile Club between Sir Frederic and Stephen Potter, the inventor of Oneupmanship, Gamesmanship, and Lifemanship. In the series of advertisements based upon it, Stephen Potter's words, with his special brand of humour, poked pure fun at everything British and the situations were initially illustrated by the artists Lewitt-Him. Schweppshire was in its very essence typical of Sir Frederic's flair for advertising and the idea was developed on the lines of his philosophy for advertising in general, and for advertising Schweppes in particular. He rejected advertising based on the kind of market research which regarded men and women as statistics. 'We advertise to human beings', he said.

While so much of interest was taking place in Schweppes' advertising, much was also astir in the field of design and display. Sir Frederic had brought into the company, to everyone's delight, the charming and gifted Grace Lovat-Fraser, widow of Claud

Map of Schweppshire in Piccadilly, 1954. In animation are seen racing on Schwepsom Downs, bird watching in Schwepping Forest, country dancing, the ghost of Lady Schwepstow, etc

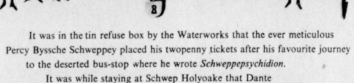

LITERARY
schwepping stones

All book-lovers know their Schweppshire..   It is difficult to
go far in this county — more than about two miles, say — without
stopping and lingering over some literary associations.
How far Hardy associated " Casterbridge " with Cirenschwepster
is not known, but there is little doubt that the creator of *Barschweppster Towers*
was literally soaked in its atmosphere.   No need to be reminded that
the lovely lyric, " When all the world was mad, lad ", from the
Schweppshire Lad, was written within a stone's throw of the lacrosse
ground of the Knitters and Needleworkers Federation Building.
The undrained field which forms the greater part of our
ornamental garden saw the birth of
the savage realism of
Spenser's *Schwepherd's Calendar*.

Municipal Museum at
CIRENSCHWEPSTER

SCHWEPPEY'S

Model of
TOMBSTONE

used by
R.W. SCHWEPPERSON

8

It was in the tin refuse box by the Waterworks that the ever meticulous
Percy Byssche Schweppey placed his twopenny tickets after his favourite journey
to the deserted bus-stop where he wrote *Schweppepsychidion*.
It was while staying at Schwep Holyoake that Dante
Gabriel Roschweppi was paid the signal honour of a visit from
Ralph Waldo Schwepperson, the American poet, who must, if this
tradition is accurate, have been nearly 110 years old at the
time.   He chaffed Dante for his *Schwepitaph on a Dead Poodle*.
" Where is the great schweppic we are waiting for?" he added.
D.G.R. retorted, as usual, with a long quotation
from *Marius the Schwepicurean*.

Written by Stephen Potter · Drawn by Lewitt-Him

SCHWEPPERVESCENCE   LASTS   THE   WHOLE   DRINK   THROUGH

One of the 'Guide to Schweppshire' advertisements which had their origins in a noteworthy snooker game. (See facing page)

Lovat-Fraser, the highly talented artist, best known for his designs for the costumes for *The Beggar's Opera*, who had died tragically young in 1921. Vital and enthusiastic, Grace produced, using outside artists chosen for their qualities and aptitudes, distinctive labels for new products, window displays, mobiles and sales aids as refreshingly different from those of the past as were the new advertisements. For Coronation year, 1953, the theme for window displays was 'Trooping the Schweppes colour' designed by Lewitt-Him. Using the window as a stage a full range of Schweppe's products paraded, dressed in pasteboard costumes, as Grenadiers, cavalry regiments, a Royal Marine band, State Trumpeters, Yeoman of the Guard and Scots pipers; bottles of Indian Tonic Water were represented as Indian Lancers and a squat ginger beer bottle made a formidable cannon. The next year the theme was 'Schweppes around the World' with elephants, Red Indians, Pacific cannibals and West Indian and other scenes. And so on. Grace's talents were always in demand for schemes of decor for offices or vestibules of new factories and she never failed to respond with enthusiasm.

In 1951, between May and September in the centenary year of the Great Exhibition, the whole of the United Kingdom was on show both to its own people and the world at the Festival of Britain. Whereas the concept of the Great Exhibition had been international, it was intended that at the Festival of Britain the United Kingdom and its people would be open to view, demonstrating our achievements and way of life. The activities were spread throughout the land and in London were concentrated in the Festival Pleasure Gardens by the Thames in Battersea Park. The Royal Festival Hall was built at the South Bank for an exhibition and as a permanent concert hall. Parallel with the more serious objects of the Festival, there was much gaiety in the nature of land and water carnivals, pageants, dances, fireworks, bonfires and sporting events throughout the country, providing a welcome relief from the austerity of the post-war period.

It was natural that Schweppes should want to contribute to this gaiety. Natural too that they should devise an up-to-date presentation of a traditional theme in the Schweppes Grotto. In the Pleasure Gardens at Battersea were constructed four caves representing Air, Fire, Earth and Water. Through Air, the first cave, one climbed a circular path passing niches for the four winds. With the north wind came the howl of wolves, the jingle of sleigh bells and the scent of pine forests; with the east wind, the sound

of temple bells, eastern music and the odour of spices. Jungle noises, with tom-toms and the scent of flowers, came with the south wind, while on the west wind was borne a breath of ozone and seaweed with the mewing of seagulls, sea-sounds and fog horns. The cave of Fire was suitably dramatic; a bridge spanned a crater of bubbling lava, while flames flickered around the walls and lit the cloud of smoke overhead. Earth was beautifully revealed by minerals with stalactites glittering in the changing colours, while fountains rose and fell to strange pulsating musical notes and the scent of peaty moors. Lastly the cave of Water, lit by rippling ultra-violet light, gave a sensation of walking through a coral reef with vistas of undersea life, moving fish and strange sea creatures. This piece of artistic fantasy attracted many visitors and the entrance fees (of over £9300) were donated to the National Playing Fields Association.

Parallel with a sustained high level of activity at home, an increasing effort was directed to the business overseas. Responding to a Government call to go all out for dollar earnings, the company had succeeded in 1949 in nearly doubling the value of exports to the United States achieved in 1948, which were themselves substantially in excess of the pre-war level. At the same time, fresh steps were taken to develop the important Canadian market and after a visit by Sir Frederic for discussions on distribution and advertising in both America and Canada, the company looked forward to increasing sales in these countries in 1950.

At that time, the sale of soft drinks through the grocery trade, on today's scale, was still years ahead. Grocers were reluctant to handle returnable bottles and the development of soft drinks sales in any volume through their outlets had to await the introduction of the non-returnable no-deposit bottle. Schweppes were dominant in the mixer trade through licensed outlets; mixers constituted about 85% of their business, but were themselves only about 25% of the total mineral water business. In mixers, therefore, where Schweppes business was mainly concentrated, saturation point seemed not far away and the obvious development was to extend the business still further overseas wherever possible. This could be done by adopting the American method of granting franchise bottling appointments to selected reputable firms, since it allowed expansion with a minimum outlay of capital and did not involve direct managerial responsibility in operations spread over the world. Franchised bottling also overcame the inevitable cost disadvantages of shipping overseas the finished pro-

Entrance to Schweppes' Grotto, Festival of Britain, 1951

ducts of which the greatest bulk was in water, glass and wood.

Therefore a significant step forward was taken by the completion of the first franchise agreement, given to Messrs Simonds-Farsons-Cisk Ltd, for the island of Malta. The results were encouraging and led to a great expansion of trade on this basis. While the holders of the franchise are responsible for the bottling and distribution of the products, Schweppes provide them with their secret ingredients and with such technical and marketing assistance as they may require. The quality of the products sold under the Schweppes name is under constant supervision, backed by the full technical resources of the company, to achieve a consistent world-wide standard for each of the franchised products. The Malta franchise was soon followed by others and today the company has many

franchise agreements with bottlers around the world. Throughout the American continent, in Africa and Asia generally, and in such important European markets as Spain, Bulgaria, Yugoslavia and Turkey, Schweppes' business has developed through franchises. Today some 60% of all Schweppes' volume sales originate in franchise areas.

Sir Frederic visited Australia in December 1951 for discussions on future policy with the resident directors. This resulted in 1952 in the formation of Schweppes (Australia) Pty. Ltd to take over the business which for so long had been operated from Sydney as a branch of the British company. 1952 was also memorable for two things. A 21.7% increase in the value of home sales with practically no increase in selling prices since 1948, and similar results for exports and franchises, brought the consolidated trading profit above the £1m mark for the first time in the history of the company; and in the autumn it was announced that the company had entered into negotiations with the Pepsi-Cola Company for two franchise agreements. Under one of these, the Pepsi-Cola Company would bottle and sell Schweppes' products in the United States and Canada. Under the other, Schweppes would bottle and sell Pepsi-Cola in the greater part of England, Scotland and Wales, though restricted to London and the South while sugar remained on ration. Both agreements became operative in May 1953. They were often spoken of as 'reciprocal' but they were in no way interdependent. In fact, while the English agreement is still operative, the American agreement was terminated by mutual consent in December 1957, enabling Schweppes to appoint bottlers other than Pepsi-controlled plants.

In America, to operate the agreement, Schweppes (USA) was formed as a wholly owned subsidiary of Schweppes (Overseas) Ltd (which had just changed its name from Schweppes (Colonial & Foreign) Ltd). Sir Frederic Hooper despatched Commander Edward Whitehead to take charge of the operation. At home, the Park Bottling Company Ltd was formed to operate the Pepsi-Cola franchise under the direction of Eric

E. G. E. Rayner

Rayner. Commander Whitehead became a director of Schweppes (Overseas) Ltd and Eric Rayner was appointed to the Schweppes main board. Both Commander Whitehead and Eric Rayner were to prove highly successful in their respective tasks of promoting Schweppes in America and Pepsi-Cola in the United Kingdom.

In the autumn of 1952, while the Schweppes–Pepsi agreements were being constructed, the whole of the soft drinks trade in the United Kingdom was beginning to look forward with some excitement to the lifting of control on sugar, which was now in sight. The national consumption of soft drinks, which had risen rapidly in the ten years before the war, had continued to increase steadily after the ending of the War Time Association controls in 1948. Production was still limited however by the level of the sugar allocation to the trade, related to 1938–39 consumption. The final release of control was certain to see a period of intense competition. Moreover, the stage was being set for a battle of the giants. The American beverage companies were moving into position. Canada Dry, 7-Up and Coca-Cola would be in the race, allying themselves with brewers and others who were keen to have a larger stake in the developing soft drinks market. By signing with Schweppes, Pepsi were able, at one stroke, to secure distribution facilities throughout England, Scotland and Wales. A few Pepsi appointments for relatively small areas had already been granted but eventually these were gathered into Schweppes' franchise.

Schweppes took over, through their subsidiary The Park Bottling Company, Pepsi's existing factory at Park Royal, covering the London area, and soon extended operations to the South Coast. Progressively Pepsi-Cola was bottled at all Schweppes plants throughout the United Kingdom. Eric Rayner took command and set to work to weld together a team which would stand up to the testing times ahead. So far as possible, he discouraged overlapping with Schweppes to create in Park Bottling a sense of unity and intrinsic loyalty. 1954 brought a poor summer and corresponding disappointment, but meanwhile plans to achieve national distribution pressed ahead. Next spring the situation was well stated by Park Royal's correspondent to the Schweppes' house magazine when he wrote, 'Early summer finds the Group's "biggest babe" in good heart and growing rapidly. Strong in spirit, gaining in confidence and making its presence felt, the babe, aided by the sunshine, which is bound to come this summer, will surely develop into an effervescent toddler before the year is out!' To

Photograph of a typical in-store display during the era of the David Ogilvy advertising campaign featuring Commander Whitehead

quote from the same correspondent later in the year, after the sun had indeed shone in no small measure in the first July instalment of a prolonged summer season, 'The pressure was intense; sales records were smashed, every vehicle was out delivering, hired transport was called upon, the factory stock melted away like "snow off a dyke" and before many days had gone, a night shift of volunteers, headed by the Managing Director (whose alertness was put to test by a humorist who slipped a "Coke" bottle among the "Pepsi" on the bottling line) were turning out thousands of dozens to add to the day and evening production of the untiring regular factory team. Not once did the organisation wilt, although it was strained to the limit, and we claim that few competitors stood the heatwave demands as successfully'. Such an account portrays the excitement of working for a soft drinks company in a heatwave, but it also epitomises the spirit of Park Bottling and those who served in it, in those days. Eric Rayner must have had good cause for satisfaction. But they kept their sense of humour and the apocryphal story was told, to dispose of any complacency or over-confidence, of the Pepsi salesman who, far from home and out of advertising aids, called on a village grocer, suggesting that he should stock Pepsi-Cola. Back came the shattering reply, 'No thank you, I buy all my vinegars from Crosse & Blackwell'.

From America the news was also good; it was estimated that in 1955 some 70 million drinks were mixed with Schweppes Tonic in the USA. Schweppes were publicly commended by HM Treasury for the manner in which they had tackled the American market and shown their readiness to accept the financial risks involved in an operation of such magnitude.

The launch of Schweppes, bottled in America, was also notable for the remarkable work and presentation achieved by the company's overseas director, Commander Edward Whitehead, in making Schweppes Tonic Water known throughout the USA and Canada. This was the subject of wide comment both here and in America as one of the outstanding efforts of British manufacturers launching their products in dollar markets. Commander Whitehead was hand-picked for this crucial task by Sir Frederic Hooper. It was David Ogilvy, the English head of the New York advertising agency, Ogilvy, Benson and Mather, whose inspiration created the advertising campaign in which the Commander became the central figure; one of the most successful campaigns ever waged, which won acclaim for Schweppes throughout America, the stronghold of soft drinks.

In the USA, therefore, and in Canada, where sales were also accelerating, the outlook was good. The large sums spent in merchandising however had inevitably to be regarded as a long-term investment and it was largely due to increased productivity at home, with its sound profitability, that temporary losses could be disregarded in building up such valuable overseas markets.

There were developments in Africa, too. The company had for some years been anxious to see its products manufactured in Rhodesia. The South African board having decided that it ought at that time to concentrate on its business within the Union, London announced in February 1955 that it had negotiated with the British South Africa Company to purchase their controlling interest in Spa Food Products Ltd of Salisbury, Rhodesia. Spa had been selling mineral waters and fruit crushes in Rhodesia for twenty years and had five factories in the territory. It changed its name to Schweppes (Central Africa) Ltd and was granted a franchise appointment covering the then Federation of Central Africa comprising Northern and Southern Rhodesia, and Nyasaland, thus considerably strengthening Schweppes' position in Africa.

SCHWEPPSHIRE, COUNTY OF

Arms—Quarterly: 1. or three bowlers sable, *for City;* 2. sable the battlements of a tower gules, thereon a ghoul ancestral also gules holding in the dexter hand a sword point downwards and supporting with the sinister arm a head truncated argent, *for Schwepstow;* 3. azure a cirro-cumulus therefrom issuing rain proper, *for Fog-schwepster;* 4. or a bend gobony azure and argent between two helmets Metropolitan azure, *for Schweppesminster.* **Inescutcheon**—vert Ye Olde Cottage proper, smoke passant sable, *for Isle of Schweppey.* **Crest**—Lion sejant guardant proper, armed umbrella sable, crowned bowler proper. **Supporters**—dexter: a batsman habited argent, capped vert, bearded gules, holding cricket bat proper; sinister: a Sherlock proper holding in mouth a meerschaum or.

The coat of arms of the famous County of Schweppshire. Designed for use as a colour advertisement in 'Debrett's Peerage, Baronetage, Knightage, and Companionage'; early 1960's
Overleaf: The first of the fascinating 14-year series of magazine advertisements that grew from the invention of the imaginary County of Schweppshire and two which followed, giving more essential information about Schweppshire. Press advertising 1951

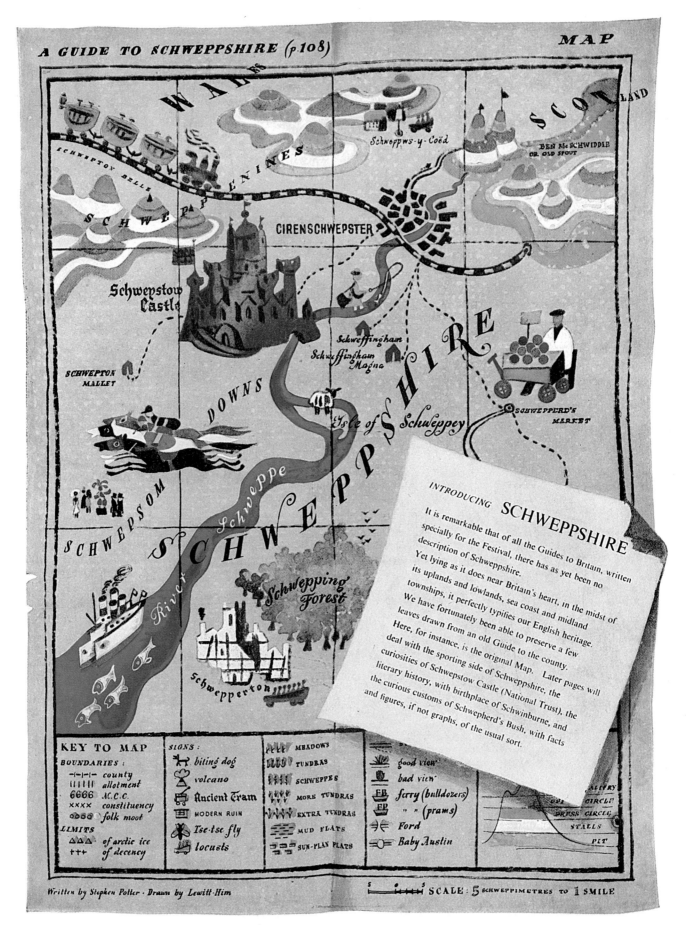

WALES

SCHWEPPENINES

SCOTLAND

SCHWEPTON BELLE

Schweppws-y-Coëd

BEN McSCHWIDDIE
OR OLD SPOUT

SCHWEPPENINES

CIRENSCHWEPSTER

Schwepstow Castle

S C H W E P P S H I R E

Schweffingham
Schweffingham Magna

SCHWEPTON MALLET

DOWNS

Isle of Schweppey

SCHWEPPERD'S MARKET

Schweppe

SCHWEPSOM

SCHWEPPSHIRE

River Schweppe

Schwepping Forest

Schwepperton

INTRODUCING SCHWEPPSHIRE

It is remarkable that of all the Guides to Britain, written specially for the Festival, there has as yet been no description of Schweppshire.

Yet lying as it does near Britain's heart, in the midst of its uplands and lowlands, sea coast and midland townships, it perfectly typifies our English heritage.

We have fortunately been able to preserve a few leaves drawn from an old Guide to the county.

Here, for instance, is the original Map. Later pages will deal with the sporting side of Schweppshire, the curiosities of Schwepstow Castle (National Trust), the literary history, with birthplace of Schwinburne, and the curious customs of Schwepherd's Bush, with facts and figures, if not graphs, of the usual sort.

KEY TO MAP

BOUNDARIES :
-·-·-·- county
||||||| allotment
6666 M.C.C.
xxxx constituency
oooo folk moot

LIMITS
△△△ of arctic ice
+++ of decency

SIGNS :
🐕 biting dog
🌋 volcano
🚋 Ancient Tram
🏚 MODERN RUIN
🦟 Tse·tse fly
locusts

Ɱ MEADOWS
TUNDRAS
SCHWEPPES
MORE TUNDRAS
EXTRA TUNDRAS
MUD FLATS
SUN-PLAN FLATS

good view
bad view
FB ferry (bulldozers)
FP " " (prams)
Ford
Baby Austin

GALLERY
UPPER CIRCLE
DRESS CIRCLE
STALLS
PIT

Written by Stephen Potter · Drawn by Lewitt-Him

SCALE : 5 SCHWEPPIMETRES TO 1 SMILE

THE LITTLE STINK (Odor odor). *Professor Fowler, with his class, secretly examines actual nest.*

Schwepping Forest

Schwepping Forest is of course the last remains of the natural forest which only five thousand years ago — yesterday afternoon in terms of geological schweppochs — surrounded the teeming suburbs of Cirenschwepster.

Every tree has its history. It was underneath this ancient acacia that the news was received for the forty-seventh time of the landing of the Danes by Ethelred the UnSchweppe.

The soil of Schwepping Forest is soil, lying above the sub-soil beneath which is the soil beneath the sub-soil. In geological section, it is seen that if you go fairly far down there are layers of rock — a layer on top with other layers beneath them.

Through glades once trodden by squires in the knightly dance, ornithologists like Professor James (" Beau ") Fowler now wander, and he has recently recorded (annals *Zool : Stud : Vol. :* CCCCCCX) that account of the Little or Bulgarian Stink which shows these birds proved to have bred 53 in May 1950, 784 in May 1951. Does this point to a new Stink migration?

Written by Stephen Potter
Drawn by Lewitt-Him

Variation of inferred STINK POPULATION in relation to Mean Female Display

MAY 1949

MAY 1950

SPORT in Schweppshire

Sport in Schweppshire is completely dominated by golf, where it was first played on the Border by Edward the Confessor. Football originated in the typical Schweppshire habit of kicking Opponent's ball into a bad lie.

Fishing devolved from the impoverished lads who dived for golf-balls in the stream guarding the first green at Royal Mid-Schweppshire: and Schwepsom Downs reminds us that horse racing stems from polo and that polo itself originated in the Schweppshire custom of playing golf on mules.

SOME FACTS AND FIGURES. Holes done in one: this feat has been performed 984 times but at the tenth hole only, which measures 6,012 yards. A putter is used from the 10th tee at the top of Ben McSchwiddie (or Old Spout) to push the ball to the soup-plate green at the bottom of the precipice.

RECORDS (the August Sugar-Tongs, 18 holes Medal). The record in 1485 was 128. This became 193 in 1760, when " Oh, do let me have that one again " was banned. In 1789, no play (French Revolution). But in 1803 the record was lowered to 102, when shuttlecocks were substituted for the old ball (composed of dried milk pudding in skin).

In 1926 the record was lowered to 72 (America discovers black and white golf shoes) and it became 62 in 1950 owing to imaginative interpretation of " Ball Deemed Unplayable ".

(New Rules, Royal and Senile). Our great source for early history is Samuel Schwepys, famous diarist of the Schweppenteenth Century.

Written by
Stephen Potter
Drawn by
Lewitt-Him

EDWARD THE CONFESSOR* FIRST TO PLAY GOLF IN SCHWEPPSHIRE

FROM BING C

✱ *He confessed, of course, after a medal round, that he took 9 not 6 shots in a bunker.*

Chapter 11

New Products and Acquisitions

1955–1962

Schweppes Bitter Lemon was introduced in 1957

The history of Schweppes is in part the story of a constant search for suitable new products. Under Sir Frederic Hooper's guidance the company had widened its scope through the Pepsi-Cola agreement, but the fifties saw a major development in its own range.

Early in that decade the whole soft drinks industry was affected by the introduction of comminuted citrus drinks. These products, though similar in appearance and use to traditional squashes, are made by entirely different techniques and have very different properties. The production of comminuted citrus base involves slicing up the whole fruit and immersing the pulp with the peel in sugar syrup. The slicing process not only releases the juice but also the aromatic oil contained in the peel. The process was not new but development had not been possible because of the war and also the fact that until 1953 the Soft Drinks Standards, first published in 1943, had not included a standard for comminuted orange. Considerable interest was aroused when J. Lyons & Co., through their subsidiary O. R. Groves, commenced franchising, through soft drinks manufacturers, both

the process and a small machine for manufacturing the comminuted base. The product was excellent; it was bottled as a concentrate for dilution and also sold at ready-to-drink strength in one-third pint containers. The question was: would this variant on the traditional squash really capture the public taste?

Schweppes' research laboratory was instructed to produce a similar orange product. Using its expertise on the extraction of flavours from citrus fruits, a product of similar character to and equally as good as Lyons' was developed. For processing the fruit, the laboratory decided to use commercial machines readily available and to match, as far as possible, the existing processing methods for squash, a decision which greatly facilitated the rapid expansion of production when this was required in the mid-1950s. In a pilot test of the diluted product, through a small number of cinemas in the spring of 1953, the acceptance of the product was so good that in the summer Sir Frederic Hooper ruled that full-scale production of Comminuted Orange should start as soon as possible for retail sale alongside the traditional squashes. It was launched as 'Suncrush' Orange Drink, through Kia-Ora. Later on 'Suncrush' was extended to lemon and other citrus drinks.

The knowledge gained from the development of 'Suncrush' materials and technique was of major significance for the creation by Schweppes of their phenomenally successful drink Bitter Lemon.

Since 1950 the laboratory had been experimenting in developing a sparkling bitter orange suitable for inclusion in the Schweppes range, but it was not until the 'Suncrush' comminuted base was available that they felt they had a fully satisfactory product of unique flavour. At about this time, Lyons introduced a new product which was basically a tonic water with the addition of a small proportion of lemon juice. As an answer to this, Schweppes' research laboratory quickly produced a Sparkling Bitter Lemon with a character similar to their experimental bitter orange. The Bitter Lemon however made use of new techniques, and a special comminuted base was developed similar to 'Suncrush' base though differing in important respects. Sparkling Bitter Orange and Bitter Lemon were launched on 1 May 1957 with budgeted sales till the end of the year of a quarter of a million dozen Bitter Lemon and a half a million dozen Bitter Orange. To the end of September, sales closely followed estimates. Then on 1 October, TV advertising began with immediate dramatic effect on the sales of both drinks. Against expectations, Bitter Lemon was the more successful. By the year-end Bitter Orange had reached its planned target but Bitter Lemon had sold more than three million dozen and sales were still rising. Some Bitter Lemon was drunk in substitution for Schweppes Tonic Water but mainly it was new business. So successful was it, however, that at one time its sales outstripped those of Tonic. After about two years other soft drink manufacturers realised the potential of Bitter Lemon and brought out their own products in competition, and Tonic then recovered its leading position in the Schweppes range. Bitter Orange has been discontinued but Bitter Lemon maintains its prominent position. In the year of introduction of bitter drinks, home sales of carbonated drinks rose by 19.7% over the previous year and this was followed by a further increase of 15.4% in 1958. It was a measure of the company's progress that the 1957 ten-year review showed a rise of only 2% in net selling prices in a period in which all prices rose on average by 51%.

A less successful innovation was the acquisition in 1955 of the British company owning the exclusive long-term rights for the sale and distribution of Apollinaris Spring Water for the whole of the United Kingdom, the British Commonwealth and the Americas. In the heyday of Apollinaris Water in this country, before the first world war, the rivalry of Schweppes with this imported spring water had been considerable. It seemed now as though the old scores were finally settled. It was perhaps a whim of Sir Frederic's that in addition to their century-old loyalty to Malvern Water for mixing with Scotch whisky, Schweppes should also have Apollinaris in its range. The product took its place in the list for several years but after having at an early stage disposed of the Apollinaris overseas interests, Schweppes finally surrendered the rights retained for the United Kingdom.

Yet another acquisition followed in March 1955 with the purchase of Jewsbury & Brown Ltd of Manchester, a fine old company, established in 1864, with a high reputation in the North West of England. Jewsbury & Brown continued to trade separately under its old name and trade marks until 1964 when it was merged in a soft drinks consortium under the Schweppes umbrella, in which Schweppes eventually sold their interests in 1977.

There was a breathing space in 1956 after these relatively small transactions but, in a sense, the theme of broadening the basis of the company could again be seen in that year in the completion of a new research and quality control laboratory at Hendon. The laboratory was planned to make a vital contribution to the company's development and earning capacity, particularly in the case of diversification into new and possibly different types of trade.

In July 1957 came Schweppes' successful bid for the old-established and world famous business of L. Rose & Co. Ltd. Sir Frederic Hooper used to meet Mr Lauchlan Rose, grandson of the founder of Rose's, over lunch from time to time to discuss matters of mutual interest. At one of these meetings he proposed a merger and Lauchlan Rose at once saw the advantages of such a move for both companies. The Rose's board also saw the inherent advantages of joining with the larger Schweppes organisation with its extensive facilities. Both companies were successful and expanding and it was not difficult for the accountants to arrive at the terms for the bid, worth £1.8m, on the basis of an exchange of shares.

Rose's was founded in the Scottish port of Leith by Lauchlan Rose, born in 1829, who abandoned the family business of shipbuilding to become a trader in

Late 19th-century advertisement of L. Rose & Co.

Lauchlan Rose

dioxide, obtained by passing the gas from burning sulphur through water – an adaptation of an existing method of preserving light wines by burning sulphur candles in the casks. Lime Juice Cordial, 'preserved by an entirely new process, entirely free from alcohol', was a practicable proposition, and a tall bottle, heavily embossed with an attractive design of lime leaves and fruit, with a trade mark of a lime branch, still used today, was registered.

The firm was under-capitalised and progress was slow, but the appearance of would-be competitors showed that the new product was winning acceptance. About 1870 Lauchlan Rose moved to a larger factory at 41 Mitchell Street, Leith and in 1875 made London his headquarters in premises at Curtain Road, Finsbury. He died in 1885 at the early age of fifty-six, leaving a widow and nine children. His grandson, the present Lauchlan Rose, has described life at work and in the home in those days – 'No telephones, everything written by hand, a long wait for a reply to a letter sent overseas, no motor cars, no tube trains, no electricity. The absence of these "modern amenities" made for a more peaceful life. Family life ran on well ordered lines to which my grandfather conformed. Prayers for all, including the staff, before breakfast, and church without fail, usually twice, on Sundays.'

From its beginnings the company had either imported lime juice from the West Indies or bought it through brokers in London. In 1895 however it purchased the Bath estate near Roseau, the principal town of Dominica in the Windward Islands; its crop of 10,000 barrels of fruit each year was soon doubled by better cultivation, and other estates at Soufriere and St Aroment were acquired. The great bulk of the crop was destined for the manufacture of citric acid, a relatively small quantity being exported as green fruit to the USA and Canada or as juice to the United Kingdom. The citric acid market was so important that Rose's began in 1906 to export from Dominica citrate of lime instead of concentrated juice, thus cutting out a process and commanding a higher price from the acid manufacturers. This was a successful move, but it led to an unfortunate venture, around 1920, into making the finished article, citric acid, in Dominica. The process was unsuited for the local facilities and climate and in any case a new technology developed which used molasses instead of citrus fruits as the raw material – a devastating blow to the lime plantations in the West Indies.

The first Lauchlan Rose's three elder sons had run the business since his death; John and Hugh retired during the first world war, leaving Charles as sole

grain and flour before establishing L. Rose & Company in 1865 as a 'Lime and Lemon Merchant'. It was very much a maritime business, since it had been customary for years for all British ships to carry a supply of lime or lemon juice on all but the shortest voyages as a preventative against scurvy; indeed in 1867 it was made compulsory by the Merchant Shipping Act – hence the nickname for British sailors, particularly in America, of Limeys. Although it was not known that lack of Vitamin C caused scurvy, a rampant shipboard disease for centuries, it had been found that it did not occur on ships supplied with lime or lemon juice.

Lime was preferred to lemon because it contains hardly any sugar, whereas the sugar in lemon led to fermentation and hence spoilage unless it were preserved when absolutely fresh. The juices were supplied unsweetened, and fortified by 15% of rum as preservative; this was then the normal method of preserving fruit juices, with the result that there was no such thing as a non-alcoholic fruit drink available to the consumer.

Lauchlan Rose saw this as an additional market and patented a process for preventing fermentation by adding to the juice very small quantities of sulphur

managing director, to be joined by his son Lauchlan on returning from the war in 1919. His war service had an unforeseen consequence. Before the Somme offensive in 1916, he had been involved in running a light railway as near to the front line as possible, working under Sir Gordon Guggisberg. He met Sir Gordon again in 1924 at the British Empire Exhibition at Wembley. By this time Sir Gordon was Governor of the Gold Coast (now Ghana) and he suggested that Rose's should grow limes there. Despite the surplus of limes in Dominica, the company agreed to sponsor the planting of several hundred acres by native farmers, to buy their fruit and to build a factory to process it. In such a fortuitous way did Rose's presence in Ghana begin.

In 1924 Charles Rose retired and Lauchlan Rose became general manager, to face a decade of severe difficulties. Bottled lime juice was having to compete with the rising popularity of other fruit squashes; modernisation plans were halted by the onset of the depression; the now loss-making plantation business in Dominica was hit by a disease of the trees and by two hurricanes, in 1928 and 1930; the Admiralty switched from lime juice to synthetic ascorbic acid. In short, everything seemed to have gone wrong, and it was a long haul back to prosperity. But it was achieved by the mid-1930s, partly owing to the introduction of lime marmalade, and the popularity of gin and lime which helped to make lime juice an all-the-year-round drink. Lime juice, too, was demonstrated by research to be good at eliminating 'hangovers' – whence the light-hearted advertising campaign featuring Gerald and Hawkins, which enjoyed a long run well into the post-war period.

Only foresight enabled Rose's to survive into that period. Their factory was very close to two London railway stations, and highly vulnerable to bombing; accordingly, they found alternative premises at St Albans, moving there during the 'phoney war'. On 7 September 1940, three days after the start of the blitz, the old premises were almost totally destroyed. Like all other members of the industry, Rose's submerged its identity from 1943 to 1948 in the S.D.I. which has already been described; Lauchlan Rose was a member of the committee of Twenty-Four.

Immediately after the war the company began to re-develop its export markets, with marked success. At home, too, new sales records were achieved, profit figures reflecting this growth, achieved by good organisation and hard work by a loyal and dedicated staff.

The link with Schweppes in 1957 can fairly be said

C. F. J. Barker

to have fulfilled expectations in all important respects and to have benefited both parties. Arising from this merger of the two great leaders of the industry, the Rose Kia-Ora Sales Company was formed. The Rose and Kia-Ora companies together provided a sales force large enough to meet strong competition and to promote expansion. Rose's trade was fairly equally divided between the licensed and grocery trades, a fact which significantly increased Schweppes' awareness of the potential of the grocery trade where in a few years it was to become deeply involved.

C. F. J. Barker, managing director of L. Rose & Company, was appointed managing director also of the new company. Lauchlan Rose, with his immense knowledge of the industry, became for five years a welcome and valuable member of the Schweppes board. He retired from Rose's at the end of 1969 after fifty-one years as a director, for thirty-six of which he was chairman of the board. He continues his association as Honorary President of the company which bears his name.

The happy outcome of the Schweppes-Rose amalgamation was in contrast with Schweppes' failure in 1958 in a struggle with the Beecham Group for a merger with Thomas & Evans Ltd of Porth, a well-managed, prosperous and expanding mineral water company based in Wales, selling 'Corona' beverages. The opening bid had been made by Beechams. Whilst some shareholders of Thomas & Evans felt that it would be better that the company should remain independent, and Welsh, a strong tide ran in favour of a link with Schweppes, if a take-over was inevitable. Unfortunately when the votes were counted, Schweppes had an insufficient number in their hands to justify them in proceeding.

However, 1958 ended on a happy note with the group trading profits exceeding £3m for the first time. To keep pace with the growth of sales a sustained effort was needed to expand production, which meant a heavy investment in buildings, plant, machinery and equipment of the most modern design. Alex Canfield, the chief engineer, and his staff of engineers and architects carried a heavy load in those years. In eleven years six major new factories were commissioned at Aintree, Fareham, Birmingham, Bristol, Gateshead and, finally, Sidcup, the largest and most technically advanced soft drinks factory anywhere in Schweppes. This factory, which was in production from January 1961, was given the signal honour of a formal opening ceremony on 11 April 1962 by HRH The Princess Margaret and the Earl of Snowdon, who devoted half a day to the visit and made a tour of the factory to see it in normal operation. During the same period, major extensions were carried out at Leeds and Hendon and even to the recent additions at Aintree and Birmingham. The new factory at East Kilbride followed a few years later in 1966. In parallel, the network of distribution depots was greatly extended.

The installation of progressively higher speed plant had been made possible by a reduction in the number of sizes and varieties of products, coupled with increasing sales, so permitting the longer runs for each size without which the economy of the higher speed units would have disappeared. The heavy capital commitment in those units was such that they had to be kept running for a minimum number of hours to show a reasonable financial return. Accurate sales budgeting and careful production planning were necessary so that the right level of stock was built up in slack seasons to be cleared during peak selling seasons, thus making the optimum use of plant throughout the year. It was necessary to calculate levels of plant installation and programme expansion some five years ahead so that at all times the continuous output of the plant was equal to the rising annual sales.

A big increase in productivity was brought about

by mechanised handling, based on a standardised package which would stack uniformly on a standard size pallet. Apart from its economy in the use of labour, it enabled the cubic space of depots and factories to be fully utilised by the higher stacking of palletised goods.

Work study also played a great part in reducing costs by rearranging production processes to give maximum output with minimum labour and effort and in providing a basis for the application of incentive bonuses for increased productivity in a given time. The effect of all these measures by 1962, in terms of productivity, was to reduce direct and indirect labour costs from 4d to 2.84d per dozen bottles over a period of about fourteen years, during which basic wage rates had risen 1.85 times and working hours had been reduced from 44 to 42 hours a week. Canfield stressed however that increased productivity based on complex and expensive high speed plant, with its increased depreciation charges and higher operating and maintenance costs, required that the higher level of sales for which it was designed be maintained at a constant or expanding level, if commensurate returns were to be secured. This warning had particular relevance as the great buoyancy experienced by the company in the fifties gave way to the distinctly more difficult trading climate of the sixties.

In spite of a long wet spell in the summer of 1960 there had been a good overall increase in sales in that year. Canned bitter lemon had been introduced, sales being mainly through the grocery trade, particularly self-service stores. These were complementary to bottle sales through the licensed trade, and a new market was opening up for Schweppes' products. A larger canning plant had been ordered to cope with other flavours and to give national distribution. The expansion of factory facilities generally was still in full swing.

But the effects of the 'wind of change' in the market place began to be felt in 1961. Acquisitions of smaller brewers by the larger, and the growth of multiple wine and spirit merchants, was altering profoundly the whole of the licensed trade. 'Free houses' were declining in number, as more and more pubs were placed under management by breweries and fewer run by tenants. In the grocery trade, large multiples and superstore chains strengthened their share of the market. The effect on Schweppes, as on other manufacturers, was that an increasing proportion of its trade was concentrated in the hands of fewer and larger buyers who expected to receive more favourable terms for the same volume of trade; in consequence its margins were continually squeezed. To meet the new situation Schweppes reorientated their sales forces so that Schweppes' salesmen sold all brands of drinks handled by the Group to the licensed trade, while the sales force of the Rose Kia-Ora Sales Company sold all brands to the grocery and allied trades. This concentrated the expertise of each sales force in its own field and improved the service and personal contact with buyers, who welcomed the arrangement.

One consequence of the intense competition in the sale of squashes and comminuted drinks was a decision by Schweppes and Lyons, who for generations had enjoyed friendly relationships, to join forces against other big brands in the market place, which they did by cross-shareholdings in the appropriate subsidiary companies. Both took legal advice to ensure their agreement did not violate the Restrictive Trade Practices legislation, but the Registrar of Restrictive Trading Agreements thought otherwise, which started an eleven-year legal wrangle. The Registrar finally won his point of law that the agreement should have been registered, but failed on other points against the companies (who were thus able to recover a major part of the very heavy legal costs involved). The offending agreement was cancelled, and Schweppes and Lyons made a new one which met their purposes until it was eventually terminated by mutual consent for commercial reasons.

It is arguable that the tougher trading conditions of the sixties added to the problems which Schweppes encountered in its first major diversification outside the soft drinks industry. This took place in 1959 when within a few months, and at a cost of £5m, it extended its interests into jams, marmalades and canned fruits and vegetables by the acquisition of three well-known businesses: Chivers & Sons Ltd of Histon, Cambridge, Wm. P. Hartley Ltd of London and Aintree, and Wm. Moorhouse & Sons Ltd of Leeds. In doing so, Schweppes gained a considerable share of the very competitive market for these products, as well as an established goodwill in the trade built up over three-quarters of a century and more.

A mutual interest in citrus fruit had already led to co-operation between Schweppes and Chivers extending over many years and both companies had respect for each other's policies and standards. It was in 1873 that Stephen Chivers made the first boiling of jam in a barn at Impington. His father and grandfather, both farmers and fruit growers before him, had sent their crops laboriously to markets in London or Bradford but he had decided to turn the fruit into jam in the

place where it was grown. History was in the making at that moment. A relative, a chef at Pembroke College, Cambridge, provided the recipe and a local grocer offered to dispose of all the jam that could be produced. The quality of Chivers products has always stood high, and the business prospered in meeting the demands of city dwellers in days of rapidly rising population. Table jellies were made as one of a number of other products to provide employment out of the fruit season. To Schweppes' technical knowledge of fruits and fruit flavours was added the accumulated experience of the Chivers research laboratories. These laboratories had rendered outstanding service to the country in the field of nutrition during the second world war and the high standard of their work was widely recognised in industrial and academic circles in Great Britain and abroad.

The birth and growth of Hartley's was closely linked with the life story of Sir William P. Hartley, its founder, born in 1846. As a boy he worked in his parents' retail grocery business in Colne but soon began to develop a wholesale trade. By great personal effort he found himself, while still a very young man, controlling one of the largest wholesale businesses in Lancashire. He decided to make his own preserves and began to build up the high reputation for quality ever since associated with the name of Hartley. In a remarkable career inspired by Christian convictions, Sir William was prominent as Justice of the Peace, Liberal and Methodist. He was knighted for his public services in 1908 and he was a great philanthropist. He died in 1922. His liberalism was reflected in his business principles. In Hartley's, as in Chivers, there was a long tradition of thoughtful care for the welfare of workers and pensioners. The Hartley Village, at Aintree, built in 1886, was one of the first villages for employees to be built by an industrialist.

Like Hartleys, Moorhouses started as grocers, in a remote Yorkshire village. The firm traces its history to a day in the early 1880s when, it is said, William Moorhouse was delivering orders in the dales and was invited to take tea in a farmhouse. The lemon cheese he was given was so good that he asked for the recipe and persuaded his wife to make some for sale. Its subsequent popularity was the foundation of the firm's success. Commercial production of lemon cheese began in 1886. The product range was widened to include preserves, and Moorhouses became the first big manufacturers of mincemeat in 1891.

A large scale diversification by Schweppes at this juncture in its development was almost inevitable when the opportunity occurred, as it did then. With limited room for expansion for its mixer drinks, and the take-home trade still some years ahead, Schweppes had first expanded strongly overseas. It had then entered the 'pop' trade, through Pepsi-Cola, but a further broadening out at home seemed an obvious step. Schweppes' skilful and experienced team of managers and technicians had already achieved most of the improvements in organisation and productivity that were possible in the Group at that stage, and could accept new challenges. The three companies acquired provided considerable scope for integration of manufacture, distribution and accounting, on which Schweppes' resources in the areas of research, methods study and advertising could be profitably brought to bear. The research laboratory's basic knowledge on fruits, fruit juices and flavours could be applied to preserves and jellies; the bottling and handling techniques developed for soft drinks were also capable of adaptation to other kinds of food packaging. The board was confident that within a few years the three businesses could be combined into a highly efficient and profitable whole, and their exports as well as their home trade further expanded.

To act as a management company for the combined companies, a wholly owned subsidiary was formed under the name of Connaught Food Products Ltd. But the way ahead was long and hard, taxing the skill and ingenuity of management most severely. A period of intensive effort in reorganising and consolidating began in 1960, to which it sometimes seemed there would be no end. Overlapping production activities, with consequent under-employment of production facilities and personnel, had to be cut back, involving the closure of plants, in particular Hartley's massive factory at Tower Bridge. Compensation to redundant employees was paid on a generous basis. Canning factories at Huntingdon and Hereford were disposed of. Farming operations of Chivers, around Cambridge, were hived off. There were heavy write-offs of stock. A distribution service consisting of some twenty-four depots and two hundred modern delivery vans to cater especially for a service to the grocery trade was created, similar to Schweppes' extensive service to the licensed trade. A new marketing organisation for Chivers and Hartley labelled products, combining the sales staffs of both companies, was formed, to be effective from 1 January 1962, backed up by the new transport organisation. Moorhouse continued to expand its business, which was largely to the catering trade.

1961 was a disappointing year, in which only Chivers (Ireland) Ltd and Moorhouses traded successfully and substantially increased their profits, Chivers UK and Hartley both making losses; but 1962 brought a substantial measure of success. The new Chivers-Hartley Sales Company had settled down and was well accepted by the trade. Further economies in production still had to be made but these would flow gradually as plans materialised to make the Chivers Histon factory a modern preserve-manufacturing unit. Here a new high speed vacuum-pan jam-boiling plant was installed, and satisfactorily proved, and in March 1963 the first output was marketed in a range of 'Hartley's New Jam' of exceptional flavour and quality. This 'New Jam', made by a process unique in this country, went on to become an outstanding success and within a period of ten months had become the second largest selling brand of jam, with $12\frac{1}{2}\%$ of the market, and still expanding.

By 1964 therefore, Chivers-Hartley was on an even keel with turnover increasing, while Moorhouses maintained their special position in the catering trade. Less advantageous sugar prices and intense competition however were eroding profit margins. The process of rationalisation had been more difficult and taken longer than had originally been expected and altogether had been a sobering experience.

Another business was purchased in 1961, in the drinks field, that of R. Fry & Co. Ltd of Portslade, Sussex. The main purpose of the acquisition was to secure their well-positioned factory premises on the south coast near Brighton. The impact of a 15% Purchase Tax imposed on soft drinks in the Chancellor's budget of April 1962, however, meant postponement of that plan. On its own, Fry's business became unviable and their brand name 'Fryco' was sold, the premises being used partially as a distribution depot. The old-established business had become the first victim of the 1962 Purchase Tax on soft drinks. Fry's subsidiary, Ingram & Royle Ltd, which for long years had been the well-known importers of high class continental table waters, was retained in the Schweppes Group.

Sir Frederic Hooper's term of office had been expected to continue until the end of 1962 when it was hoped he would be succeeded as managing director of the Schweppes Group by the Rt Hon. Viscount De L'Isle, V C. Lord De L'Isle had been a director since 1949 except during the period from October 1951 to December 1955, when he held ministerial office as Secretary of State for Air. He was appointed managing director of Schweppes (Home) Ltd in January 1960 but in the following year it was announced that

Viscount De L'Isle, VC

Her Majesty The Queen had approved his appointment as the future Governor-General of Australia and he would take up that post in the summer of 1962. While his colleagues felt proud of his distinction, they knew that they would greatly miss his inspiring leadership. The chairman therefore persuaded Sir Frederic to carry on in order to help the company in its unexpected position. Sir Frederic agreed and soon after Lord Watkinson (then Mr Harold Watkinson) was invited to join the company to succeed Sir Frederic in due course, and he became a director on 1 October 1962.

In his latter years in the company, when he was handing over responsibility to younger men, Sir Frederic had been able to devote further time to public service. It was 'for services to Government Departments' that his knighthood was bestowed on him. It is rare for one man to be able to perform services deserving honour to more than one Department of State. He had served on important Royal Air

Force Committees inquiring into organisation in 1954, and in 1955 into serving aspects of the RAF. In 1956 he was a member of the Committee on Employment of National Servicemen in the UK; from 1957 chairman of the Advisory Board to the Regular Forces Resettlement Service, Ministry of Labour, and from 1960 adviser on recruiting to the Defence Minister. It was through Sir Frederic's collaboration with him in this last assignment that Harold Watkinson was invited to succeed him at Schweppes. He was appointed a managing director on 1 January 1963 and spent the greater part of that year preparing to take over the complete direction of the company's affairs.

In September the company suffered a sad loss in the death of Alex Canfield after a protracted illness. The building of the new factories at Aintree, Bristol and Sidcup and the re-equipment, expansion and organisation of production in the post-war period were his monument and the company owed him much.

But further sadness was to follow. The half-yearly management conference, attended by managers from all parts of the country, was held as usual in October, to be followed by dinner and dancing at the Dorchester Hotel in the evening. It was the last of such meetings that Sir Frederic would attend. At the close of the morning conference session, he paid tribute to the team of managers that had served him – a team, he said, which he now handed over with pride to Harold Watkinson. The doctors had advised him to rest and he expressed his regret that he must therefore miss the afternoon session and also the dinner that evening. The following morning, when managers gathered at Connaught Place, they heard with a sense of profound shock and sorrow that Sir Frederic had died during the night.

Little or nothing has been written here of Sir Frederic Hooper's early career, of his work in public life, his patronage of the arts, his success on television and many other distinctions. These were recalled in tributes which appeared in the Press and were spoken of in the address given at his memorial service at St Martin-in-the-Fields by Sir William Emrys Williams CBE, who concluded with the apt words 'Let us salute the memory of a friend whose effervescence lasted his whole life through'. This history recounts only those facets of Sir Frederic's work by which his influence was most reflected in Schweppes. Here surely the extent of his achievement shows that, once again, Schweppes had been fortunate in having at its helm a man uniquely suited to match the needs of the times.

Chapter 12

Viscount Watkinson
1962–1969

Viscount Watkinson

The Rt Hon. Harold Watkinson, CH, MP, had joined Schweppes after a distinguished political career. He represented Woking from 1950 to 1964, serving as a member of the Cabinet for five years, first as Minister of Transport and Civil Aviation and then as Minister of Defence from 1959 to 1962 when he resigned from the Government – having previously told the Prime Minister that he wanted to return to business life when opportunity served – and joined Schweppes. In the Birthday Honours list of 1964 he was created Viscount in recognition of his political and public services.

He was no stranger to industry. From King's College, London, he had gone into the family business, later being associated with a number of technical and engineering journals. After active service in the war with the RNVR, he became managing director of a machine tool company, a position he resigned on joining the Government as Parliamentary Secretary to the Ministry of Labour. During the four years he held that office he established a very close relationship with many trade union leaders, Arthur Deakin in particular

being a personal friend until his untimely death.

His introduction to Schweppes was a testing time in several ways. 1963 started with ten weeks of the hardest weather of the century when the difficulty of moving about and the sheer expense of keeping warm severely hit the licensed trade. The physical effort of shopping reduced food sales. After this set-back the sales and management team fought back well and recovered most of the lost ground by the end of the year. The recovery was also helped to an important degree by the completion of a reorganisation, begun the previous year, of the management structure of all the principal operating companies of the Group on a functional basis. A simplified structure was seen by Lord Watkinson as an essential requirement following the dramatic period of post-war growth under Sir Frederic Hooper, though in achieving this it was important not to lose the vitality and original marketing concepts that had done so much to build up Schweppes in the past. The growth of the business had been due, in a heartening degree, to the expansion of trade in the United Kingdom and overseas. Combined with the extensive diversification into food products by acquisitions, the result was a complex structure of trading companies which had become too large to continue to be controlled overall by the managing director, as it had been in the past.

Three market-orientated trading divisions were set up, each under the chairmanship of a main board executive director. These divisions were directed to the licensed and catering trade, with Eric Rayner as chairman; to the food trade, with James Barker as chairman; and to overseas, where Lord Watkinson himself undertook the chairmanship. As a focus for day-to-day management a group executive committee was established, under Lord Watkinson, on which were represented the top management of the operating divisions and the heads of service departments.

1964 proved another good year over most activities of the Group, the consolidated trading profit exceeding £5m, a record figure for the eighth year in succession. The board again affirmed its determination to continue its policy of vigorous expansion overseas notwithstanding what it felt to be an unreasonable burden of taxation on earnings remitted home.

The year saw the retirement of L. M. Alexander whose fine achievements have already been spoken of. The chairman's description of him as a skilled solver of difficulties was an apt summation recognisable by all who knew him. As group general manager he had been one of a triumvirate with Sir Frederic Hooper and Alex Canfield and in that capacity his unusual talents had had their fullest scope, to the immense advantage of the company.

In the summer of 1965 Schweppes launched their new range of low calorie 'Slimline' sparkling drinks. These drinks contained cyclamate, an artificial sweetener which gave a much better balanced sweetening taste than saccharin, and a more palatable product. Cyclamate had been in use in the United States and Japan for some fifteen years when, in 1965, British soft drink manufactureres were allowed to use it. Schweppes' 'Slimline' range was immediately successful and when in the summer of 1966 the full impact of TV advertising was felt, sales leapt ahead.

1966 again saw excellent progress, achieved against the background of the most competitive conditions at home and abroad the group had yet experienced. The company's determined efforts overseas were reflected in the overseas division's profits which had doubled in the previous four years.

1966 was also memorable for the introduction of the non-returnable bottle. This entirely new form of packaging for soft drinks was immediately welcomed by the industry and by the public. The innovation became possible when, after a great deal of effort and research, the glass industry developed a lightweight screw-topped bottle which could be filled with carbonated drinks at the high pressures traditionally used for mixers. The new technique was a breakthrough as previously bottles of the weight of glass that could withstand normal mixer pressures would have been too costly to use as throw-away containers. The specially hardened glass used in the production of these lightweight bottles was strong enough to stand up to the rigours of the filling process and of the distribution chain from the factory to the home.

In general, self-service grocers and supermarkets were, for very practical reasons, reluctant to handle returnable containers. The administrative burden of receiving and sorting, storing and transporting empty bottles, the additional work of refunding deposits and dealing with VAT, would inevitably have meant higher costs and increased delays at checkouts. Moreover, food retailers, always concerned to maintain hygiene standards, would not have wished to have quantities of unwashed bottles stored on their premises.

The bottle became the subject of fierce opposition from ecologists, although not until 1971, five years after its first appearance. The objections were principally the use of scarce world resources on a throw-away article, the extension of the litter problem, and the cost to the community of dealing with the ultimate disposal of the bottle. Although the bottle was adopted generally in the soft drinks industry, and there were, of course, numerous other food products sold in discardable glass containers, Schweppes was made the prime target for criticism.

The arguments against the bottle were presented, understandably, solely from the ecologists' point of view. There are, however, many valid off-setting arguments on the side of the non-returnable bottle, in addition to its convenience to the grocery trade and the public, which are not obvious at first glance. Non-returnable bottles use about half the glass needed to make a returnable bottle. They cost less to make than returnables and use less fuel in the manufacturing process. Unlike returnable bottles they do not have to be stored after use while awaiting collection, transported back to the bottler's factory, sorted and checked for condition, washed and sterilised in four different stages, each requiring large quantities of hot water, creating a correspondingly high volume of effluent requiring treatment. There is no shortage of raw

"That's funny! They always used to go SCHWEPPE-S-S-S-S-S!"

Cartoon inspired by the appointment of former Minister of Defence Lord Watkinson as managing director

materials for glass making, the main constituents being sand and crushed glass or 'cullet'.

Also, to keep the matter in perspective, far more soft drinks are sold by Schweppes in returnable bottles than in non-returnable, through pubs, clubs, and the catering trade, where the products are consumed on the premises. The campaign was directed at Schweppes as the leaders of the industry and likely to be most influential in reversing the trend. Schweppes are considerate of local amenities in areas where they operate and have in other ways demonstrated their concern for the environment. They accepted that further research was desirable on the subject of packaging and the environment. They encouraged and co-operated with various initiatives involving packaging material manufacturers, industrial users and central and local government, believing that the answer to the more efficient use of packaging and energy resources lies in reclaiming and re-utilising (not necessarily as containers) a wide range of non-returnable materials of which lightweight glass is only one. Today, local authority 'bottle banks' for the collection of used bottles are increasingly popular. The glass industry is effecting a major saving on energy in recycling the waste glass, but there is a further benefit to Councils through the diversion of glass from refuse.

On 24 January 1968 it was announced in the Press that an agreement had been reached between the boards of directors of Schweppes Ltd and Typhoo Tea (Holdings) Ltd on the terms for a merger. Both boards were convinced that their companies had much to gain from joining forces. Typhoo had long been a household name in the country, synonymous with the highest standards of quality. It had operated with a high degree of efficiency based on the marketing of a single product in a single pack and at a single price. Its directors saw the need for diversification but realised that with their slender organisation the launching of new products in the highly developed United Kingdom grocery market would be extremely difficult. A merger with Schweppes would give their shareholders an interest in a group with a range of famous brands which were marketed successfully throughout the world. Schweppes' directors saw the proposal from a different viewpoint. Trading overseas was a tradition in their company dating back well over one hundred and fifty years to the times of Jacob Schweppe. The tradition had never been forsaken and through the years had been pursued with ever-increasing vigour. For some time the Schweppes board had been concerned at the need to broaden its base in Britain as a means of underpinning future overseas developments. This would be secured by a major merger with a soundly based British company whose products offered export possibilities and whose United Kingdom operations would merge satisfactorily with theirs.

The story of Typhoo is of an idea which grew into a great business. It began in 1820 when William Sumner purchased the eighteenth-century business of Pratchett and Noble, druggists and grocers, of the Bull Ring, Birmingham. William Sumner's sons divided the business in 1863, William taking the druggist's business and John the grocery. In 1891 John, in partnership with John junior, moved the business to Hutton House, High Street.

John Sumner junior founded Typhoo as a result of a simple domestic incident. His sister had indigestion and someone sent her a packet of very special tea, saying it would cure it. It was a small leaf tea and, as almost all tea sold in those days was large leaf, she looked at it doubtfully, but she tried it and, against expectation, found relief. She gave some to her gardener, and to other sufferers, all of whom benefited. 'Why don't *you* sell this tea?' she asked her brother one day.

John had been looking for a specialty, and his sister's remark made him think seriously. He told an old friend in the wholesale trade that he was thinking of importing thirty chests of the tea, a choice leaf-edge tea from Ceylon, to try it out. The friend was sure the public would never buy so small a tea and would call it dust: but the thirty chests were bought, and £200 found for advertising. The next thing was to hit on a name – it had to be distinctive; it had to roll off the tongue and be capable of protection by registration. Many names were thought of and discarded until 'Typhoo Tipps' was hit upon. It sounded oriental, it was alliterative and, most important, Typhoo could be registered. 'Tipps' could not, so it was later abandoned when many imitators copied it, even to the eccentric spelling which originated in a printer's error.

The first customers received an inducement in the shape of a generous jar of cream with each pound of Typhoo, but its flavour and wholesomeness were enough to widen its sale. The higher price proved no deterrent, since it went half as far again as ordinary tea. Soon another grocer asked if he could buy Typhoo on wholesale terms, since his customers were asking for it. So began the agency trade with retailers which by 1926 numbered over 16,000 agencies.

Typhoo's rapid progress called for additional capital, but the heavy stocks carried by the old-established grocery business locked up most of John Sumner's money. A crisis arose when a new bank manager decided to call in the firm's overdraft. With immense courage, Sumner decided to sell the grocery business, which had an excellent credit standing, and stake his future on Typhoo. When he failed to find a 'going concern' buyer, he shut the shop, sold off the stocks, then went to the bank and paid off the overdraft, at the same time closing the account and offering some advice to the bank manager!

With some friends he formed Sumner's Typhoo Tea Ltd, and by 1909 felt confident enough to refuse an offer of amalgamation with a wholesale tea house, and to leave his staff to run the business while he made a three-month trip to Ceylon. Here he was able to arrange a buying and blending agency which led to great economies in prime cost, passed on in a lower price to the public and a better margin for the trade.

The 1914–1918 war all but brought about the ruin of Typhoo when, in 1917, all supplies of tea were placed under Government control. In vain did the company plead that it did not deal in ordinary tea; as a last resort, the public was asked, in a circular put in every packet of Typhoo tea, to write direct to the Tea Controller. He was deluged with so many letters that the permit was granted, supplies assured, and Typhoo saved.

Packing and warehousing capacity was steadily ex-

tended, a private bond being established to save time over dock clearance, and an interest (later to become an outright purchase) taken in a London firm of tea merchants, in order to buy at the Mincing Lane auctions the additional quantity of Ceylon tea demanded by the ever-growing business. The second world war naturally brought difficulties over supplies, and also disaster when more than two-thirds of the Typhoo premises in Birmingham were destroyed in an air raid in 1941.

After the end of tea rationing, Typhoo entered on another great phase of expansion, becoming a public company in 1949. Sales maintained a steady record of growth until Typhoo became a market leader in its field. Interestingly, credit terms were first granted to a few selected customers in 1963, with all customers being granted monthly credit terms by November 1964. On the merger with Schweppes in 1968, H. C. Kelly and J. P. Tustain, who had been the architects of Typhoo's post-war expansion, joined the Schweppes board. The former, who was over seventy, retired the following year, though J. P. Tustain continued to make a valuable contribution until 1976.

There were other changes on the Schweppes board in 1968. Lord Rockley, deputy chairman, retired after serving for twenty-three eventful years, and a sad loss was the death of the Hon. Richard Greville; both had been held in great affection in the company. Lord De L'Isle's increasing responsibilities led to his resignation. The year brought notable strengthening of the board by the addition, as non-executive directors, of Lord Carrington and Donald Methven (for long a legal adviser to the company) and of Basil Collins as an executive director. Basil Collins had served in L. Rose & Co. under Lauchlan Rose and came into Schweppes after the merger with Rose's. His role had been as export director until he was chosen for the demanding task of general manager after L. M. Alexander's retirement.

The merger with Typhoo brought about in one stroke the major step in the enlargement of the United Kingdom company which was desired; in the following year the Group's trading profit rose from £6m to £10.8m. Other steps were taken to widen the business, including the purchase of Goldhanger Fruit Farms (a fruit and vegetable canning business), an interest in Cantrell and Cochrane – both since sold – and the acquisition of the Kenco Coffee Company. This last was to bring impressive results, particularly in hotel and catering outlets, with an increasing presence in the grocery market.

The history of this company goes back to 1934 when

The Beatles in the Prince of Wales Theatre, London

it was founded as a specialist coffee business by coffee planters from Kenya. They had a shop in Sloane Street, London, and also developed a mail order business. The business was acquired by one of its chief customers just before the second world war. After the war it grew rapidly and bought new factory premises at Earlsfield, in which, with necessary extensions, it still manufactures today. The factory was equipped with a semi-automatic roaster, a great advance on the open flame roasters which were still being used by competitors. A second similar machine was added in 1958 to meet the continuously increasing demand. The company had then grown to the point where it could no longer specialise in Kenyan coffee. The original name of The Kenya Coffee Company Ltd was changed to The Kenco Coffee Company, signifying the fact that high grade Kenyan coffee continued to be used extensively in the high quality blends. The next important stage was the development of protective packaging to replace the conventional greaseproof paper bags. For this the breakthrough came from an entirely novel process, invented by their director R. C. Champion, for which Kenco were granted a patent in 1962. This dealt with the basic problem of controlling the CO_2 gas in roasted coffee and opened the way to the development of sealed packs which protected the fresh condition of the coffee. Kenco were therefore able to sell roasted and ground coffee in

really fresh condition on a national basis. By the end of 1968, when Kenco was bought by Schweppes, its factory was again under great pressure and a larger and improved machine was installed to keep production going until the two old machines could be replaced. The company is still achieving record sales and profits.

As the base of the Schweppes Group in the United Kingdom was broadened, it took another step in pursuit of its aim of further expansion overseas. The company had acquired a share interest in Canada in Powell Foods Ltd at St Catherines, near Niagara. This was a growing business, built up by Clifford Powell and his family, which provided the company with opportunities for marketing not only Rose's, Chivers and Hartley products, but also Schweppes' mixer lines. In July 1968 Lord Watkinson and Basil Collins spent some time in Canada with Clifford Powell and Commander Whitehead and put in train negotiations which led to the formation of a new Canadian company, Schweppes Powell Ltd. The company marketed the same range of products as were sold in the United Kingdom, plus certain important specialities, such as Welch's Grape Juice.

At home, the Drinks Division were disturbed by the rumblings of a mounting campaign against the use of cyclamate as a sweetener in food products. By the end of 1967 rumours of conceivably harmful effects of cyclamate had been causing public disquiet after highly preliminary and unauthenticated findings of researchers were picked up by the Press and other opinion-formers. When a Sunday newspaper published the names of users of cyclamate several soft drink manufacturers gave up the use of this sweetener straight away and soon after three leading food retailers also stopped using cyclamate in products made under their names. The campaign continued. In October 1969 the U.S. government heard of new research findings linking cyclamate with cancer in animal experiments and four days later cyclamate was banned in that country. Governments in many other countries followed suit and the major British companies, including Schweppes, effected their own voluntary ban even before the British government spoke. The Minister's statement prohibiting use in the United Kingdom said that there was no cause for alarm and no evidence whatsoever that cyclamate had caused cancer in humans. Other work carried out on the toxicology of cyclamate had given no cause for concern. Nevertheless in view of the new evidence there could not be certainty about the safety of cyclamate without further investigation and until the results of such investigation were available cyclamate should not be added to food and drink of any kind. In Western Europe cyclamate survived only in Spain, which limited its use to carbonated soft drinks and diabetic foods, and in West Germany and Switzerland, which limited it to diabetic products only.

The brief heyday of cyclamate had a lasting effect on Schweppes' business. Sales of the 'Slimline' brand doubled between 1966 and 1970 and even after the reformulation with saccharin growth continued at a rate which outstripped the performance of the carbonated soft drinks market as a whole. The taste for low-calorie mixers had been established and when competitors joined the battle in the mid-seventies 'Slimline' held a dominating lead.

Although the Group had been strengthened substantially by the acquisition of Typhoo, and other smaller businesses, and its products, led by Schweppes Tonic, enjoyed considerable success in overseas markets, it was still small when compared with the international giants of food and drinks with which it was competing. Its assets were having to sustain increasing demands for further investment abroad. This situation was paralleled in the Cadbury Group which had an even higher proportion of its sales overseas, mainly in chocolate. Cadbury's too had brooded deeply on the future and had a mental picture of the type of company with which it might consider

merging, which Schweppes matched to a remarkable extent. A catalyst was needed to bring these two famous companies together into a whole which would be greater than the sum of its parts.

1968 had already proved an eventful year in Schweppes but the final and perhaps most auspicious hour arrived in November, when Lord Watkinson and Adrian Cadbury were both speakers at a marketing conference in London. Having listened to one another's contribution on overseas and home marketing, they were struck by the similarity of approach of both their companies. This led to informal talks on scope for collaboration at home and abroad. The discussions brought a growing conviction that each company had much to offer the other and that a merger of their operations would result in the creation of a strong international group ranking high among world companies. As the talks went on, both companies felt increasingly confident that in the future they could make more profits together than separately and that a more detailed examination was fully justified. An intensive study therefore began, at board level, both in London and in Birmingham, which extended over six weeks. An announcement that the two boards had reached agreement on the terms for a merger was made on 29 January 1969 and the proposals were finally blessed by the shareholders on 29 March. Lord Watkinson was the first chairman of the newly named Cadbury Schweppes and Adrian Cadbury the deputy chairman and managing director.

During the progress of these momentous events another milestone was reached for Schweppes in the course of its long history. This was the retirement of the Hon. Hanning Philipps, chairman of Schweppes for as long as most people in the company could remember. The influence of Hanning Philipps' chairmanship is incalculable. He joined the board as a young man in 1930 when his uncle, Sir Ivor Philipps, had already been chairman for twelve years. With great skill, Sir Ivor had brought Schweppes through to a position of strength after its first difficult days as a public company. Hanning succeeded to the chairmanship when Sir Ivor died in 1940, though it was five years before he returned from active service to take up his task. He is a descendant of a family of great antiquity in South Wales, where his links are strong; he was Lord-Lieutenant for Pembrokeshire from 1958 to 1979. He served in North-West Europe during the war as ADC to General Alexander. His chivalrous character is felt by all who meet him, and in Schweppes he was regarded everywhere with affection, respect and trust. At his side, Lady Marion Philipps, the daughter

The Hon. Hanning Philipps

hand-fillers in multi-storey factories to our present-day high speed production lines, computers and other electronic devices; from a Company one-twentieth the size of the world-wide organisation of 1968.

At this point, inevitably, I ask myself how did it then look to me; what were my special hopes? How have they fared? Of course, I looked forward to being the head of a successful and growing Schweppes Empire with exciting new fields to be conquered. Who wouldn't? Then I saw myself as a trustee for the already widely accepted Schweppes reputation for quality and service to its customers. Not least, I saw myself in due time handing on not only a large and prosperous firm, but a firm in which, despite prodigious and rapid growth, all could remain both proud and happy to work.

The growth came; partly through expansion of our basic Schweppes business; partly by joining forces with willing partners in other allied fields. In quality, despite all our expanded output, no rivals anywhere put us in the shade. Within the House of Schweppes, with rights and duties clearly defined and freely accepted I believe not only do we form a unified and contented team ourselves, but to others in British industry we have set an example as pioneers in many aspects of industrial relations.

That this should be so reflects the greatest credit on our Chief Executives and on you all and this applies not just at home, but far and wide, wherever Schweppes is known. For as my wife and I have visited our many overseas associates, we have consistently found what I can only describe as this 'Schweppes family spirit'. It seems to be world-wide and remarkable. And even looking beyond our own Companies and our franchise friends, we have only had to mention the magic word 'Schweppes' to be assured of the warmest of welcomes wherever we have been. This is surely something to be prized. Despite its size Schweppes must be a business with a soul.

My wife, whose long interest in our Company and whose help on my many world-wide journeys have contributed so much to any success I may have had, joins me in offering you all, whether still in harness or long retired, our thanks for all you have done for us and best wishes for the time that lies ahead of you.

of a noble house of Scotland, graced many Schweppes' occasions at home and abroad. In the long history of Schweppes, no one served the company more truly.

At his retirement he looked back for a moment on the past and wrote a farewell message to everyone in Schweppes. It is just as apt today for all of us in the company, and as a final glimpse of the Schweppes family for all those friends throughout the world for whose enjoyment we have the privilege of making superlative sparkling drinks. He wrote:

We have come a long way in my thirty-eight years with Schweppes, twenty-eight of them as your Chairman. From

These words epitomise the best things in the continuing story of Schweppes – quality and service to customers, progress, pride and pleasure in one's job, the Schweppes family spirit around the world – and, the sum of it all, the magic of the name of SCHWEPPES.

Facing: One of a series of international magazine advertisements, circa 1965

Overleaf: The famous U.S.A. Schweppesman in two of the long-running, and internationally respected, series of advertisements created by David Ogilvy, left circa 1961, right: circa 1954

SCHWEPPES  completes the picture

How many can afford to buy Schweppes <u>Ginger Ale</u>?

GREAT NEWS! *Everybody*—man, woman, and child—can afford the new Schweppes *Ginger Ale*.

In this picture you see Commander Whitehead, a lover of the Grand Gesture, acquiring it by the *case*. The Commander's old family retainer (a thrifty Scot) is watching with approval. He knows that even though Schweppes is the emperor of *all* the ginger ales, buying it will put nobody in the poorhouse.

Incredible as it seems, Schweppes—made from *imported* elixir—costs no more than domestic brands!

Schweppes even *looks* different from ordinary ginger ales. It's a pure sunny amber, with a brilliant sparkle that the proud English refuse to hide in green bottles. (Schweppes Ginger Ale is bottled in crystal-*clear* glass.)

Your whole family will adore Schweppes flavor—a true *ginger* flavor, dry and bracing. The grown-ups will say Schweppes is a terrific mixer, because Schweppervescence *lasts the whole drink through.*

So ask for Schweppes Ginger Ale wherever you go. It's worth making a scene if you don't get it.

"You kin get Schweppes over in Lone Pine, stranger!"

ABOVE you see a heart-warming photo of Schweppesman meeting Schweppesfan.

At right, gazing thirstily towards Lone Pine, is the Schweppesman, Commander Edward Whitehead, President of Schweppes, U.S.A.

At left is Allen MacConnell, devoted Schweppesfan, who picks up a case of the stuff on every shopping trip.

Everywhere the Schweppesman travels in our country these days he meets constituents. Admirers of Gin-and-Schweppes Tonic. Devotees of Vodka-and-Schweppes. And purists, who drink Schweppes *straight*.

No wonder Schweppes has taken the U.S.A. by storm. Only Schweppes gives a drink Schweppervescence — little bubbles that last your whole drink through. *Curiously refreshing!*

Yes, you can get Schweppes in Lone Pine these days. And in Peoria and Palm Beach and everywhere else from sea to shining sea. So get the real stuff — insist on the authentic Schweppes Tonic.

In London, they speak Schweppes

His Royal Highness Prince Philip unveiled an Emett model of Schweppes Bitter Lemon during his visit to an exhibition of British goods in Chicago in 1966. With him are Commander Whitehead and Lord Watkinson, then chairman of the Committee for Exports to the USA

Her Royal Highness The Duchess of Kent on the occasion of her visit to Fareham factory on 20 April 1982 to open the new bottling line. With her is Mr Basil Collins, Deputy Chairman and Group Chief Executive

Facing: The international language of Schweppes. French press advertisement circa 1960

Automated production at Schweppes' largest UK bottling plant, at Sidcup, Kent

Chapter 13

Overseas Companies

Drivers of five wagons exhibited at Sydney Agricultural Show, 1905. At ease!

AUSTRALIA

When the first white settlers in Australia were landing at Sydney Cove in January 1788, Jacob Schweppe had already been occupied for some eight years in the manufacture of artificial mineral waters in Geneva. The date of the first arrival of Schweppes' mineral waters in Australia is a matter for conjecture but if it could be established, it would probably be surprisingly early in the nineteenth century. The firm first had an appointed agent for importation in 1850. This was Edmund Monson Paul (who was in no way connected with Jacob Schweppe's partners in Geneva, Jaques and Nicolas Paul); in later years E. M. Paul's son Edmund Sheffield Willoughby Paul was also destined to play a significant role in the history of Schweppes in Australia. By the 1870s the trade in Australia justified the opening of a warehouse in Sydney for direct distribution. This was in Margaret Street, a strange coincidence, as one of the firm's early addresses in London had been for many years in Margaret Street, Cavendish Square. The warehouse was under the control of E. M. Paul.

Soon the decision was taken to manufacture in Australia and by 1877 a plant was set up in premises in Foveaux Street, Sydney. From the Liverpool factory in England a young man called Sawell, whose father before him had also worked for Schweppes at Liverpool, was sent out to open the Sydney factory in a way which would keep faith with home traditions. Two later generations of this family were also destined to serve Schweppes in Sydney. In 1885 a second Australian factory was opened at Abbotsford in Melbourne which, as the business continued its steady development, was itself rebuilt in the 1920's and later replaced by new and larger premises in Moorabbin (1962) and Tullamarine (1973). Means of distribution were meagre and with the start of the new century a number of agents were appointed in the country districts between Sydney and Melbourne at such places as Albury, Wagga Wagga, Hay, Narandera and Goulburn to mention but a few. Subsequently additional agents were created in the West, North West and North; some of them over five hundred miles from Sydney, so that orders were railed in eight-ton trucks.

E. S. W. Paul, who had worked under his father for a number of years, succeeded him as manager of the Sydney and Melbourne branches in 1902. He had received training in Schweppes in England, working at the company's factories at Colwall, Liverpool and Hendon. He was an able and resourceful man. He was also a qualified solicitor – and had a propensity for litigation! He was elected to the new board of Schweppes in 1919 and the directors respected his judgement and regularly congratulated him on the Australian results. In a faraway land he enjoyed a very free hand, at least from 1919, and he ruled – it could be said that he dominated – Schweppes in Australia. In London his name was legendary, and many were the stories told of his idiosyncrasies. His autocratic style, however, tended to discourage initiative in others and to perpetuate methods and systems where change was desirable. His era closed when he retired in 1947 having, like his father, dedicated fifty years to the company, and having fulfilled his pledge to the shareholders in 1919 that so long as he lived he would do everything he could to further the company's interests. He left the company's name standing first in the country for quality in mineral waters and with tremendous active and latent goodwill on which to continue to build and develop.

The early 1900s were important years in the development of Schweppes' Australian business. Interstate deliveries were commenced and very large quantities of mineral waters were shipped to Queensland, South and Western Australia, and to Tasmania. Schweppes' waters and fruit juice cordials were to be found in all the leading hotels on the West Australian goldfields, which represented a distance between factory and consumer of over two thousand miles. When in 1906–7 Schweppes began the manufacture of fruit juice cordials they were one of the earliest firms in New South Wales to do so, and that area of the business expanded considerably.

In the years immediately following the first world war, the products of the gold mining and copra industries in the Pacific Islands were largely shipped to Sydney, where Schweppes' branch participated in the increase in trade which resulted. Schweppes' waters were consigned to various islands all over the South West Pacific, and could be obtained at the leading centres in the Philippines and the Dutch East Indies. A new departure was also made when the firm ventured into the cash-sales market, and began to supply countless small shops on a cash on delivery basis. This greatly extended the distribution of their products among the public.

At about the peak of the Australian company's prosperity and expansion in the inter-war years, an arrangement was made with Tooheys, Ltd, one of the leading breweries in New South Wales, for the supply of mineral waters to their various houses. Schweppes also purchased the plant and freehold property at which Tooheys' mineral water business was carried on. Tooheys' controlled about 95% of the whole of the licensed hotels in New South Wales, so the arrangement was of the first importance.

The world-wide depression in 1932–5, however, affected Schweppes Australia in common with countless other firms. Unemployment and scarcity of money depressed sales. The beginning of World War II in 1939 naturally brought a general disruption of trade, which became intensified when from 1941 onwards the tide of conflict reached the Pacific itself. All manufacturing requirements were in short supply, rationing was introduced, transport grew chaotic and manpower and government regulations seriously affected output. Those conditions continued up to 1945.

The post-war period was a time of spectacular development for the whole Australian continent and for Schweppes within it. To preside over this development, A. J. Byron was appointed general manager in 1947, with the task of rehabilitating the Australian and New Zealand businesses. The New Zealand branch had been opened at Wellington in 1935 but activities were suspended during the war, when it became impossible to import the Schweppes essences. Manufacture was recommenced in 1948; factories were later built at Auckland and Napier. The New Zealand company eventually came to be 51% owned by Schweppes (Australia) Ltd, that interest now being owned by Cadbury Schweppes Hudson Ltd of New Zealand.

John Byron had joined the company at the age of fourteen in the Sydney despatch office. Promoted to Melbourne branch manager in his early twenties, he held that position for twenty-five years. He was appointed a director of the company in 1950 and was later managing director in Australia. He retired in 1965 after fifty years' service. How well he succeeded can be summed up by comparing the three branches operating in 1947 with the seven in Australia and two in New Zealand, and numerous franchise bottlers throughout both countries, in 1965. Turnover increased sevenfold during those eighteen years.

In December 1951, Sir Frederic Hooper (then Mr Hooper) visited Australia for discussions on future policy. As a result, in 1952 the Australian business was transferred to a newly formed Australian subsidiary company, its territory including New Zealand and Indonesia. The new company was formed with the objective of inviting investment by the Australian public, which was fulfilled in 1960.

Development had continued apace in the post-war era. A factory was opened in Adelaide in 1951 and the following year another was acquired in Brisbane. The distribution problem was solved by the establishment of bottling franchises with well known firms at strategic locations. Further expansion was achieved by a series of acquisitions of well established soft drink companies in principal towns of Australia. The old multi-storey Sydney factory in Foveaux Street, though much extended and improved over the years, had become unsuitable for modern production methods in the soft drinks industry, which demand a smooth flow on one floor through all the operational departments. A new factory was therefore built at Alexandria which, covering four and a half acres, was then believed to be the largest in the southern hemisphere. It was officially opened on 10 September 1957 by Lord Rockley, deputy chairman of the London board, in the presence of two hundred representatives of business and Government.

Eighty years of personal effort of countless men and women contributing to the success of Schweppes in Australia are enshrined in the history of Foveaux Street. The new Sydney factory at Alexandria turns the page of a new chapter for some future historian of a new company; for in 1971 Schweppes (Australia) Ltd was merged with Cadbury Fry Pascall Australia Ltd to form Cadbury Schweppes Australia Ltd.

BELGIUM

With the formation of Schweppes (Belgium) Ltd at the end of 1923 began the association of Schweppes with John Martin and his family which happily still continues. John Martin had set up as a manufacturer of aerated waters in Antwerp in 1910 at a time when the prospects seemed favourable. Within four years however the Kaiser's troops were moving into Belgium. John Martin and his young family were among the passengers on the last train out of Antwerp to Holland. After distinguished service during the war, he returned to Antwerp and with determination and enthusiasm began to rebuild his shattered business. It was in November 1922 that he approached Schweppes with the proposal that he should bottle their products in Belgium. Because of the duties on imported mineral waters and the formalities and costs associated with the return of empty bottles and cases, Schweppes were exploring the possibility of manufacturing their waters

in Belgium and marketing them at a price more closely competitive with local brands. As a result an agreement was reached with John Martin for the formation of Schweppes (Belgium) Ltd with the right to bottle Schweppes and use the Schweppes trade marks and also to continue John Martin's own business of mineral water manufacturer and bottler and importer of English beers.

The manufacture of Schweppes minerals began in Antwerp in 1924. The joint business grew and the spread of its activities helped it to weather the difficulties of the world-wide depression of the early thirties. No one had a greater appreciation of the qualities of Schweppes or showed greater tenacity in maintaining its traditions than John Martin. Belgium has many natural spa waters and not a few manufacturers of soft drinks and in relation to these, Schweppes' products were still expensive. John Martin knew however that their unrivalled quality and the cachet of the firm's great traditions would command a market among the discriminating. This air of distinction he carefully fostered both in production and in advertising.

In 1933 however, the quality of the water supply was seriously threatened by the construction of the Albert Canal, the waterway linking the Port of Antwerp with the River Meuse at Liège, in the making of which the course of certain rivers had to be diverted. It was John Martin's wish to acquire a first class natural spring for manufacturing purposes, and at this juncture by great good fortune the British company owning the famous Genval Springs near Waterloo decided to close down. The concession of the Springs together with the buildings was taken over by Schweppes (Belgium) in 1934.

The Genval property lies in a delightful wooded valley, about twelve miles from Brussels on the fringe of the Forest of Soignes. Formerly a wild marshy area, it had been converted by the previous owner into a beautiful lake by the side of which a bottling factory had been picturesquely housed in a reproduction of a Norman abbey. The bottling plant from Antwerp was transferred to this monastic setting and although the design of the building had been based on aesthetic rather than on industrial lines, the installation was accomplished without a single blemish marring its romantic beauty. The Antwerp premises were entirely turned over to the bottling and maturing of imported British beers. The surroundings at Genval were then remodelled, with sweeping lawns and mixed borders creating a garden of English character and a glorious setting for the imposing building. To the tourists and

Schweppes at Genval

visitors to Genval, the name of Schweppes has become associated with this beautiful 'very English' scene.

From the beginning John Martin's policy for Schweppes was to keep out of the general large scale competition in low cost mineral waters. The principle of quality was put before quantity, and in return a premium price was expected and obtained. In this policy the Belgian company was eminently justified, to the extent that no place would be considered in the front rank unless Schweppes minerals were stocked.

Soon war came again and for the second time, on 10 June 1940, John Martin had to leave everything behind. As soon as the Germans occupied Antwerp, the company was placed under the authority of a German administrator who at once decided that the works at Antwerp and at Genval should operate primarily in the service of the German armies, the former bottling beers supplied from Germany and the latter producing mineral waters for consumption by the armies of occupation or for despatch to the various fronts. The company's personnel decided that they would not be willing collaborators and throughout the occupation did everything in their power to protect the interests of the business. This attitude on the

part of the staff was attended, of course, with constant and considerable personal danger which they endured courageously.

In September 1944 John Martin, when on a mission for the British Government, was the first Allied civilian to re-visit Antwerp, which he found in a fever of liberation. Fortunately damage to the company's property was slight, for in spite of the heavy bombardment suffered by Antwerp the factory building escaped. Genval was not quite so lucky. It had been occupied successively by British, German, American and Belgian troops. Anti-aircraft guns were placed on the factory roof and the passage of tanks across the stretches of lawn, paths and borders turned the lovely gardens into a wilderness. Rehabilitation of the business was long and laborious, with raw materials, such as sugar, in short supply. John Martin steadfastly refused to resume the manufacture of Schweppes lines until they could be made to pre-war standards of quality. No effort was spared either to restore to their original glory the buildings and plant and the marvellous Genval gardens.

The original term for the duration of the company under Belgian law came to an end after thirty years and in 1954 the term was renewed and a reorganisation effected. Under this the old company was re-named John Martin Ltd and a new company formed, Schweppes (Genval) Ltd, which was granted the Schweppes franchise for Belgium, Holland, Luxemburg and the Belgian Congo. This operation was jocularly referred to as 'separating the water from the beer'. Meanwhile, recognising John Martin's achievements in Belgium, Schweppes transferred to him in 1954 control of Schweppes (Paris) Ltd and the franchise for the whole of the French and French North African territories. His younger son John J. Martin then moved to Paris to become managing director.

It is appropriate here to pay tribute to John Martin, who contributed so much to Schweppes' prestige on the Continent and who died in 1966 at the age of eighty. He triumphed over the devastating effects of two world wars in which he was forced to leave the country of his adoption. He left a legacy of progress which was a monument to his sense of purpose. His work in Belgium was continued by his elder son Andrew who has now delegated the daily business to his nephew John Charles Martin, joint managing director. Andrew remains on the board, a true bastion of Schweppes tradition.

SOUTH AFRICA

It is believed that Schweppes were trading in exports to the Cape as far back as 1820 or even earlier, though for the remainder of the century they took no steps to manufacture in South Africa. When the Boer War had ended, a plot of land was purchased in Durban for the construction of a factory which was never built, unfortunately, as the straitened finances of the company in London caused the scheme to be suspended in 1903. Nevertheless, the board continued to discuss the possibility of a South African company from time to time and in May 1924 asked one of their number, W. J. Barnett, to visit South Africa to assess the possibilities. During his travels Barnett met W. G. Pegram, with whose old-established mineral water business he had been greatly impressed. The meeting soon bore fruit and detailed discussions followed. At that time Schweppes were holding an option to purchase a combination of manufacturers in Johannesburg; they also still held the building site in Durban. W. G. Pegram was convinced therefore that Schweppes were determined to open up somewhere in South Africa. The chairman of his board, Sir Harry Hands, who had been connected with the company for many years, strongly favoured the proposals, as did Gerald Orpen and the other directors. They saw the wisdom

of safeguarding the future of their company and at the same time consolidating its interests with the extensive resources, experience and prestige of Schweppes.

The founder of the firm which eventually became Schweppes (South Africa) Ltd was a Cornishman, Samuel Wordon, who started the first soda water factory in the Colony in Cape Town in 1852. Other firms followed and soon he had five rivals. His son, also Samuel, carried on the struggling business, and in 1891 took into partnership a recent immigrant from England, Thomas Henry Pegram. Things looked up, aided by the gold discoveries in the Witwatersrand, and Thomas Henry's young brother Wallace went out to the Cape to work for Wordon and Pegram. The old name was retained when Samuel Wordon retired and Wallace Pegram took his place in the partnership.

By the time of the Boer War sales had outgrown capacity, so the old Albion Ice Works was secured, at Rondebosch in the Cape Town suburbs, together with the right to pump 100,000 gallons a day from the famous Albion Spring. The property and spring were later purchased outright. A new plant was installed to produce a range of beverages which included ginger beer and fruit syrups, though the firm's winner was their Club Soda, which was immensely popular with the military. In 1916 the name of the firm – by now a public company – was changed to Pegrams Ltd, and two years later, on T. H. Pegram's death, Wallace Pegram became managing director. He it was who met and talked with W. J. Barnett in 1924 when the latter made his foray to South Africa on behalf of Schweppes.

The name of Pegrams Ltd was changed to Schweppes (South Africa) Ltd upon its acquisition by Schweppes. Soon after this the South African company formed a subsidiary called Schweppes Transvaal Agency Ltd to take over Mineral Waters Ltd of Johannesburg which was given the right to sell Schweppes mineral waters in the Transvaal. In 1928 Schweppes (South Africa) succeeded in acquiring control of the Van Riebeek Natural Mineral Water Company Ltd which placed under its control the water from the celebrated spring marketed under the name of Van Riebeek Water, well known and appreciated for its high quality. Ill health then prompted W. G. Pegram to resign as managing director, though he remained on the board, and A. Gordon Hogg, already a director, was elected to succeed him. For many years, until 1969, successive representatives of Ohlsson's Cape Breweries sat on the board and were always of great assistance in forwarding the interests of the company throughout South Africa.

The transport fleet of Pegram's Ltd after repainting in Schweppes' livery, 1925

The depressed conditions of Europe and America had begun to affect South Africa, and consequently the company, in 1930. Notwithstanding, it was then that a formal pension scheme was introduced which embraced all permanent employees, talking the place of the previous voluntary arrangements. The slump deepened and Schweppes' trade was severely affected. The turn of the tide came late in 1932 when South Africa abandoned the Gold Standard, although the effects of the revival which followed took time to show themselves. By 1934 however the outlook again looked bright; the company had weathered the storm and was in sound condition, little suspecting that a second world war lay ahead.

Immediately after the outbreak of war the company's men began to join the forces. The many troopships and other vessels calling at Cape Town and the general massing of soldiers, sailors and airmen created a large increase of sales; moreover neighbouring countries cut off from European supplies became important customers. All this imposed a great strain which everyone accepted cheerfully. There were inevitably problems and worries, many arising from Government controls over glass, fuel, tinplate for crown corks, sugar and other ingredients, notably of course quinine. With the improvement in the position of the Allies and the opening of the Mediterranean, traffic round the Cape diminished though sales remained at record levels. The sustained demand made it necessary to alter and add to factory and warehouse. Deliveries of new plant

were becoming possible and orders were placed in America. Eventually the end of the war with Germany brought a rapid easing of the supply position and, in spite of the chilling prospect of the final campaign against Japan, the company looked forward with optimism to the future. After the war A. Gordon Hogg retired as managing director, making way for John Harvey who had been company secretary and then successfully reorganised the Transvaal company.

In the post-war period, John Harvey addressed himself to a range of subjects including conditions of employment and improvements to the pension fund, the completion of the merger with Schweppes Transvaal Agency to unify the management, and the general consolidation of the company's facilities throughout the Union.

Another landmark was passed in December 1948 when the ordinary shares of the company received an official quotation on the Johannesburg Stock Exchange. Rondebosch factory was rebuilt and the new plant was in operation by April 1949. Another major project was the building of an exceptionally handsome new factory in Durban, which came into production in 1952.

It was now fifty years since the incorporation of the company as Wordon and Pegram Limited and a hundred years since Samuel Wordon set up the first soda water factory in the Colony at Cape Town. The unexpected imposition of an excise duty on mineral waters early in 1952 brought about the closure of

mineral water factories in various parts of the Union, through falls in turnover, but at the annual meeting marking the historic anniversary, Gerald Orpen reported that the tax had resulted in little or no change in the company's sales. 'Your Directors', he added, 'feel that our long-established policy of producing and offering to the public only the very finest quality and most wholesome mineral waters is bearing fruit, and that we can look forward to the continued success of your company.' A modest claim indeed for a company which had every reason for pride in its achievements and an honourable record extending back, as one historian of the company remarked, to a time when not a mile of railway had been laid in South Africa, and the Great Trek was a recent affair.

The board wished to extend production to other centres in the Union and in 1954 the company was able to acquire, on favourable terms, the old-established mineral water business of Makepeace & Son (Pty) Ltd in the fast-growing city of Port Elizabeth. When reorganised for the production of Schweppes' products the factory afforded scope for large savings and improvements in efficiency.

1960 ushered in a decade of rising sales and profits, the all-time record profit for 1968 exceeding the half million Rand, after tax, for the first time. During the period however, there had been a sad but inevitable thinning of the ranks of the 'old guard'. Gerald Orpen, the Grand Old Man who was friend and adviser to Field-Marshal Smuts and who had succeeded Sir

Harry Hands as chairman ten years before, had died aged eighty-three in 1958. In a short space of seven months in 1966–1967 came news of the deaths first of A. Gordon Hogg after forty-eight years with the company, then of Wallace G. Pegram, one of the founder members of Wordon and Pegram from the 1890s, and finally of Aubrey N. Payne with forty-one years' service to the board to his credit.

But events did not stand still. A first experiment in the granting of a bottling franchise in January 1968 came to a premature end in May 1969, at the request of the franchisee, as too many customers for his own lines switched to Schweppes' products!

A welcome visit to South Africa by Adrian Cadbury in March 1968 presaged momentous changes to come. Shortly afterwards the merger was announced between Schweppes and Cadbury. Within a year this had resulted in a proposal for the amalgamation of the Schweppes and Cadbury Fry interests in South Africa under the name of Cadbury Schweppes (South Africa) Ltd which came into effect on 3 July 1970.

FRANCE

It is likely that by 1790 Jacob Schweppe's artificial mineral waters had found customers in French towns close to Geneva as they had in Swiss towns bordering the lake as far at least as Lausanne. The first certain knowledge of Schweppe's waters in France, however, is of the case of Seltzer sent to Paris in 1790 for distribution there by Dr Belcombe. Thereafter records cease for nearly a century when it becomes clear that Schweppes had a consistent trade in France, particularly in Paris and on the Riviera. An advertisement in a London periodical of January 1878 reminded readers that visitors to Paris would find Schweppes' waters at all the leading hotels, cafés and restaurants. At the International Exhibition held in Paris that year Schweppes received the highest award for their mineral waters.

In 1927, two years after the purchase of Pegrams Ltd in South Africa, Schweppes' director W. J. Barnett, who had figured prominently in those negotiations, was in Paris. He was there to consider the establishment of a mineral water factory in France, a brave enterprise in the land of vineyards and fine wines and of many famous spa waters. John Martin of Schweppes (Belgium) Ltd lent his assistance and became an original director of Schweppes (Paris) Ltd which was formed early in 1928, as a subsidiary of Schweppes (Colonial & Foreign) Ltd. The new company was established in the small village of Gonesse some ten miles north-east of Paris where a search had found premises with an excellent supply of spring water from an artesian well suitable in all respects for the manufacture of mineral waters. To ensure that the waters were the true Schweppes, Jack Hill from Hendon crossed the Channel to take charge of production. Deliveries of the first Schweppes bottled in France began in Paris and the surrounding districts in October 1928.

The company had been launched at an inauspicious time. A great effort was made through advertising in the Press and on the hoardings of the capital to bring the name of Schweppes effectively before the French public. Bars and cafés were called on personally, no mean task in a city such as Paris. A notable event in the annals of Schweppes' advertising took place with the presentation of a review at the Folies Bergère, starring Josephine Baker, where in a southern scene set amid lemon groves labelled 'Schweppes' the fruit was picked from the trees and thrown into the auditorium by the ladies of the chorus. But poor summers, the world financial slump and the worsening political situation in the 1930s prevented real progress.

After little more than a decade came the war with Nazi Germany culminating with the occupation of France. The Schweppes factory was completely taken over by German troops in June 1940 and it was not until the following September that permission was obtained for re-entry into part of the premises. The factory had been devastated and looted by anyone with

a thirst. Bottles and cases were recovered from the surrounding countryside for miles around.

With communications with London severed, a temporary director was appointed under an Order of the French Courts. Under the watchful eye of the invader production was restarted as far as possible and throughout the remainder of the German occupation Schweppes goods were made and distributed in Paris.

The hero of the war years, and the man who it is said 'saved the company' was Mons. Arthur Corthals. A Belgian, with a fine record from the 1914–18 War, he had joined the company at its formation, and was chief accountant and secretary when the Germans entered Paris. With the help of colleagues, he carried on the business and guarded the company's interests in the most exemplary way. He succeeded in preventing the deportation of any of the office or factory workers to Germany, although they had orders to go on no less than six occasions. His disregard of personal risk is exemplified by his action when ordered by the Germans to declare all stocks of fruit juice. He replied that there were none, though there were in fact nearly 15,000 cans of pineapple, orange, grapefruit and tomato juice on the premises. Realising the danger of their discovery, he rented a small store where the cans of juice could be hidden under sacks of potatoes. In reply to police enquiries as to what had become of the company's juice stocks, he replied that they had all fermented and been thrown away. His statement was, for the time, accepted. Meanwhile the owner of the store became anxious and the juice had to be removed elsewhere. Soon after, he received a warning that the police were still suspicious and he found a buyer for the juice which then commanded three times its original value. Payment was made in cash which was used to purchase much-needed materials for manufacture.

Guy Linay, the pre-war manager from London, who remained in Paris at the outbreak of war, took his family to central France and obtained employment at a hydro-electric plant as a means of lying low. He joined the French resistance movement with which he worked until he returned to Paris in 1944 to hard times and shortages which for some years hindered production of Schweppes to a standard acceptable to the board. Possibly due to the privations he had endured, his health failed and he died in 1952.

On the lighter side, it can be recorded that for a period of many months towards the end of the war, the French management, lacking a supply of electricity, ran the bottling machines from the rear axle of an old war-battered camion driven by wood fuel; the

Paris plant was very probably the only mineral water factory in the world ever fitted with three forward speeds and one reverse! Production ran at some 18,000 bottles a day in top gear. There was not much need for reverse!

As a result of such resourcefulness, courage and loyalty, Schweppes (Paris) Ltd emerged from the war in a satisfactory, though understandably somewhat straightened, condition. The future of the business gave London food for thought but a solution was at hand. John Martin of Antwerp, who bottled Schweppes in Belgium in such impressive style and who commanded a deep insight into the continental market, was asked to take over the French company and accept a franchise for the whole of France and other French territories. He agreed and his younger son, John J. Martin, was appointed managing director in Paris in 1954. The new approach, coupled with the old faith in Schweppes, insistence on the highest quality and skilful marketing and advertising, transformed the outlook in France in the space of a few years. The main problem concerned production to

meet the ever increasing demand. The promotion of Schweppes Tonic Water was so successful that sales leapt ahead, in some years doubling those of the previous year. In 1957 the production of some lines was suspended to enable all energy to be directed to the production of Tonic. Dry Ginger Ale and Ginger Beer were imported from Schweppes in Belgium. By 1966 the continued growth required the construction of a new factory at Chateauneuf-de-Gadagne, near Avignon, and extensive enlargements and modernisation at Gonesse. The combined production approached one million bottles per day on single shift working and often in the summer sales well exceeded that figure.

Everywhere in France, Schweppes can be found; in any good class café or hotel from the smart districts of Paris to the hotels of the countryside and even to climbers' huts in the Alps. The French were the leaders in drinking 'Straight Schweppes', and to vast numbers of French people, an aperitif means a 'Schweppes Tonic'. To be 'with it' in France, you must say Schweppes.

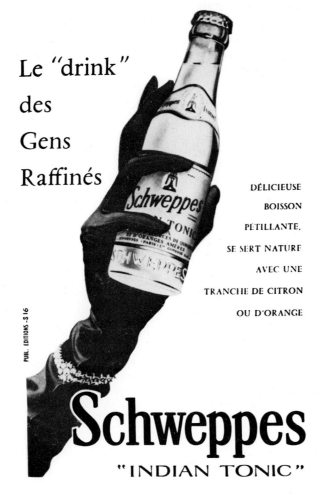

Le "drink" des Gens Raffinés

DÉLICIEUSE BOISSON PÉTILLANTE, SE SERT NATURE AVEC UNE TRANCHE DE CITRON OU D'ORANGE

PUBL. EDITIONS -S 16

Schweppes

"INDIAN TONIC"

Artificial Mineral Waters.

J. SCHWEPPE and Co.

Beg Leave to acquaint the Nobility, Gentlemen of the Faculty, and others,

That on Account of the increased Demand for their

Artificial Mineral Waters,

At Bath, Bristol, and the Western Parts of England,

They have been induced to commence the Manufacture of them at

No. 18, Corner of Philadelphia-Street,

Bristol,

MR. CORNELIUS HACKETT,

HOSIER,

WINE-STREET, BRISTOL,

Being appointed the sole Agent,

Of whom they may be had of equal Quality as at their Establishment in *London.*

LIKEWISE OF

Mr. WEBB, Apothecary, Cheap-Street, Bath;

At the under-mentioned Prices.

N.B. J. SCHWEPPE and Co. also intend to impregnate the BRISTOL HOTWELL *and* SPA WATERS *with fixed Air.*

	Stone Jars.	Glass Bottles.	
Soda and Seltzer Water, in Pints, -	0 7 6	0 8 6	per Doz.
Ditto ditto Half-Pints, -	0 5 0	0 5 9	
Spa and Pyrmont, in Pints, - -	0 8 6	0 9 0	
Ditto ditto Half-Pints, -	0 6 0	0 6 9	
Bristol Hotwell Water, impregnated, Pints,	0 8 6	0 9 0	
Ditto ditto Half-Pints	0 6 0	0 6 9	
Rochelle Salt Water, in Half-Pints.			

Allowance for Stone Jars, Pints, returned, 10d. per Doz.
Ditto for Glass Pints, ditto 15d. ditto.

* Orders from the Country must be accompanied with a Reference for Payment.

An Allowance will be made to those who retail the Waters, by C. HACKETT.

Printed by J. MOORE, No. 21, Small-Street.

Press announcement of the commencement of production in Bristol in 1803

Chapter 14

Schweppes Advertising

Anthony Thorncroft

Onomatopoeic advertisement, c. 1940.

THE EARLY DAYS

Advertising encapsulates the public image of a company. On top of its ability to sell goods and services, it conveys how a company sees itself and how it wants to be seen by its customers, work force, suppliers and competitors. Schweppes has always had a reputation for excellence in its advertising: it has continually used it to add value to the product. Certain of the qualities in the advertising – confidence, sophistication, humour – stretch back many years to the time when Schweppe's consumers viewed themselves as gentlemen; but the qualities have been retained and built upon in the last generation when the company has seen the marketing opportunities in the dissolving of social barriers and has sold happily to millions.

One of the more remarkable achievements has been the exploitation of the name. No one attempting to devise a name for a new brand would pause over Schweppes, but this strange, foreign word not only ideally suits the product range but lends itself to imaginative advertising. From the early slogans like 'Thirsty – take the necessary Schweppes'; to that word

which so perfectly summed up post-war euphoria, 'Schweppervescence'; through the imaginative delights of 'Schweppshire' to the TV impact of 'Schhh ... you-know-who' and to the current adoption of 'Schwepping' to express the sparkle of the brand in worldwide markets, Schweppes has married its name to the visual image of the product. And this continuity is not a tradition of fifty years; it stretches back two centuries. Schweppes has always been proud of its goods and more than ready to publicise them.

The first advertisements appeared in the London newspapers soon after Jacob Schweppe started to produce his mineral water. In a letter to the Government seeking assurances that the war with France would not affect his residence in London, he mentions that he is advertising in the Press; and in the same year a competitor is also buying space to complain of a new Seltzer water available in large quantities and at a low price. Within a decade it was Schweppe who took the offensive. In an advertisement in the *York Courant* of July 1803 the firm was forced to state, 'Caution: There are other Mephitic Waters sold,

*Commendation of Schweppes' Ginger Ale by Professor
John Tyndall, the famous Irish physicist*

IV   THE SKETCH.   Dec. 13, 1893

NEW PATENT SYPHONS FOR USE IN THE SICK ROOM.

Schweppe's Table Waters

Can now be obtained in the New Patent Porcelain-lined Syphons, precluding all possibility of metallic contamination.

CARRIAGE PAID to any address in the United Kingdom if ordered through an Agent of the Company. A List of the Leading Agents in any Town sent on application to the Secretary, 51, Berners Street, London.

SCHWEPPE'S

Soda Water
Lemonade
Sparkling
Malvern
Potass Water
Ginger Ale
dry & sweet

GOLD MEDAL

These Waters have always had the patronage of Royalty & continue to be supplied to Her Majesty
THE QUEEN
Every bottle of the genuine is protected by labels bearing the "Fountain" Trade Mark

CAUTION

TABLE WATERS.

RETAIL OF ALL CHEMISTS WINE MERCHANTS & GROCERS

"DRY" GINGER ALE.
Professor TYNDALL writes:

"Hind Head House, Haslemere,
"December 28, 1890.
"Gentlemen,—On the recommendation of an eminent London physician, I some time ago tried your Ginger Ale. . . . The supply of your Ginger Ale which I found so good came through Messrs. Savory and Moore, of Bond Street. . . .
"Yours very truly,
"JOHN TYNDALL."

"Hind Head House, Haslemere,
"July 27, 1893.
"Gentlemen,—My opinion of your dry Ginger Ale is so favourable that I am this day requesting M. Pictet, of Geneva, to forward a supply of the Ale to my cottage in the Alps, which I hope to reach by the end of next week. . . .
"Yours very truly,
"JOHN TYNDALL."

J. SCHWEPPE & CO., Limited,

Purveyors by Special Warrant of Appointment to the Queen and H.R.H. the Prince of Wales.

Head Office: 51, BERNERS STREET, LONDON, W.

which the public may imagine are Schweppe's. No one is appointed in this City for the Sale of Schweppe's but at the above Warehouse', a warning repeated in the advertising of the 1970s when new competitors again appeared in force.

Another echo of the future from the initial decade is a handbill published in 1798 which says that Schweppe's Seltzer and Soda Waters can be mixed with milk, wine or spirits, the first indication of their qualities as mixers. But for the most part Schweppe's was publicising itself throughout the country with 'tombstone' advertisements in the Press, and by the 1820s was already linking its quality to tradition: in *The Times* of 5 July 1820 the company offered 'their acknowledgements to the Public for the continued preference given to their SODA WATER and beg to assure them it continues to be prepared with the same scrupulous care and attention as has been observed so many years...' This idea of a conspiracy between

Handbill, c. 1880

The design of this price card was adapted from a delicately coloured bar poster of 1899 in art nouveau style

Schweppe's and its consumers as to the quality of the product has survived in the advertising to the present day. By 1838 the company was again having to warn, through the *Lincoln Gazette*, of imitations: 'none is genuine but such as have a label over the cork'. The advertisement also pushed two new lines, Potass Water and Effervescing Lemonade – and there was a word that was to reappear over a century later.

Schweppe's business grew steadily in the second half of the nineteenth century, stimulated by the catering concession at the Great Exhibition, which must have been worth a fortune in promotional terms alone, linked as it was in the public's mind to the Royal Warrant granted in 1837. By 1900 Schweppes advertising had started to become visual, although there is no record of the employment of an advertising agency before 1931, when Winter-Thomas took on the account. One, not perhaps unexpected, result of hiring professional advisers was a substantial rise in the

Piccadilly Circus, in the early 1900s

Schweppes advertising budget. In 1900 the company spent £10,000 a year; by 1931 it was £100,000 and it remained at this level throughout the thirties.

The advertising in the first three decades of the century reflects the certainties of the age. Schweppes was buying space in sporting and glossy magazines; in theatre programmes (sharing the bill with Sarah Bernhardt at the Coliseum in 1913); on board liners – wherever its market, at that time the socially secure middle classes, might be reached in a relaxed and convivial mood. The advertisements were backed up with show cards for bars and clubs and with a whole range of promotional offers – trays, barometers, golf score books, matches, playing cards, menus, all carrying the Schweppes brand name. The company enthusiastically embraced art nouveau. A retail price list of around 1900 shows a beauty decorated like an Inca princess. Pin-ups of glamorous (but wholesome) girls advertised Schweppes until the second world war, usually decorating bars but sometimes used in full page ads in theatre programmes or society papers.

Although in the early years of the twentieth century Schweppes knew that its market was the middle and upper classes, its name was already being promoted to a mass audience. Its horse-drawn vans, some pulled by magnificent greys, were a celebrated sight in London and meticulously maintained to enhance the company image; the new premises at Connaught Place, hard by Marble Arch, acquired in 1920, were chosen at least in part because of the public prominence of the situation; Schweppes, after its success in 1851, was always quick to tender for catering contracts at

Facing: A 1966 press advertisement from the famous U.K. campaign:-'The Secret of Schhh.... by You-Know-Who'

Overleaf left: A classic example of the enjoyable 'conspiracy' between Schweppes and its public – one of the famous 1965 U.K. press advertisements. Right: A typical 'product-as-hero' U.K. press advertisement of the late 1960's

Britons—be proud!
The French are stealing the secret of *Schhh...*

This particular tonic, they think, adds a je-ne-sais-quoi to the spirit.

Who are we to object if now the Paris sidewalks ring to the cry of "Gin et tonic, vodka et tonic – and let the tonic be par Vous-Savez-Qui!". For, in our imperial way, we stole the gin from the Dutch and the vodka from the Russians. Now, if the French steal our tonic, is this not justice?

(True, it was we who first raised these two naïve spirits to the heights of sophistication by adding the brilliant effervescence, the subtle blue bloom of our own native tonic; and perhaps – like the Romans – we should congratulate ourselves on having thus civilised the entire Western world – but Schhh . . . self-congratulation is out of date.)

Tonic Water by You-Know-Who

Issued in the interests of Anglo-French relations

You'll find the secret of *Schhh*
in everything made by You-Know-Who

But is it that simple?

It was clever of You-Know-Who to disperse the secret of Schhh into millions of bottles of Tonic Water, and sell it in pubs and off-licences like any ordinary drink. And it *might* have been a master-stroke, if the secret were not so laughably apparent by its brilliant effects on gin or vodka . . . It leads one to wonder — if the secret of Schhh has this effect on spirits, what must its ultimate effect be on whatever it was designed for (on you, for instance).

Tonic Water by
You-Know-Who

This whispering campaign is issued in the public interest.

The Tonic glints and glitters in the glass,
You see a rumour of a rainbow pass
Among its bubbles, or a flash of blue…
Were opals liquefied by You-Know-Who?

By Julian Orde who claimed to have found the Secret of Schhh …
in a dream, which she later forgot.

I always think the sipping of a gin and bitter lemon enhances a woman

I like to keep a woman company. When I've poured one bottle of You-Know-Who's Bitter Lemon I always pour another for myself; it's quite the most sociable way to get lemon into gin.

This particular mixture bubbles so freely with the Secret of Schhh . . . and the fine mist of crushed lemon caught up in its sparkle.

We both feel a lot better for it.

**Bitter Lemon by Schhh...
You-Know-Who**

exhibitions; in 1911 Schweppes sent promotional display cards on the first official mail-carrying flight;
and it advertised consistently on the sides of buses.
Most striking of all, in 1909 the company took a sign
at Piccadilly Circus, in the prime position at the
corner of Shaftesbury Avenue. This must have publicised the name worldwide on hundreds of millions
of postcards of this most celebrated of London land-
marks. There were jubilant scenes when the lights were
switched on after the war and it continued to lighten
London until 1949. Then a new Schweppes sign, one
of the largest in the country, took its place with neon
tubes representing 200 rising bubbles against a brilliant background of ice blue light.

But in the main Schweppes advertising was more
sophisticated and selective. In another pointer towards
the future, and the company's sponsorship of the
County Cricket Championship, Schweppes was advertising in *The Cricketer* in 1935 in the form of a

*Schweppes' name and slogans on bus sides have been part of
the London scene since before the first world war*

*Facing: William Franklyn, the famous U.K. Schweppesman of the 'You-
Know-Who' campaign, best known from T.V. advertising, sometimes
appeared in press advertisements such as this. (Late 1960's)*

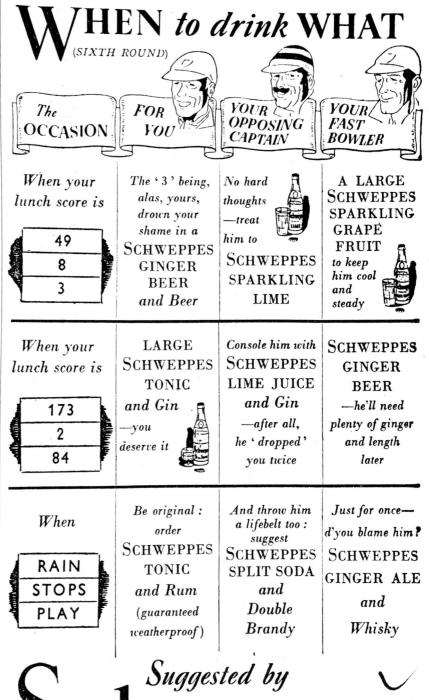

A press advertisement from a series based upon which variety of Schweppes is most appropriate for the multifarious social occasions with which life faced the British public. (Just prior to the second world war).

limerick, a theme returned to after the second world war. We read of 'A harmonium player of Leicester, When the zest of Schweppes Tonic posseicester, Used to stand up and beat, On the keys with her feet, Till the Vicar and Sidesmen suppreicester'.

The same qualities of gentlemanly humour and literary cleverness are revealed in a campaign of the immediate pre-war years in which colourful drawings show how foreigners try to cope when Schweppes is not available. 'In Arabia one drinks Sabzi when one cannot get Schweppes', the copy runs, with an informative note on what Sabzi is. This proved a rich seam and other advertisements in the campaign touched upon the Peruvians stuck with Chica, the Paraguayans with Maté, and the inhabitants of Guiana with Piwarri. One imagines the writers at Winter-Thomas as Oxford graduates proud of airing their knowledge. Apart from the period charm of the advertisements, the magazines where they appeared read like a nostalgic roll call – *The Courier, Hunting Diary, The Illustrated Sporting and Dramatic News*. Alongside this campaign Schweppes was running slightly more worldly advertising in the *Daily Mail* and the *Sunday Times*, a series of humorous cartoons showing readers how to cope (with the help of Schweppes, of course) 'when the local bore calls' or 'when it's a boy'.

This lighthearted education was to make way for a more serious approach at the outbreak of war. But just as the real fighting did not start for some time, so the main effects of the hostilities on Schweppes advertising were not felt immediately. It was only in December 1941 that the company explained to its consumers that Schweppes had to be rationed; then in 1943 came the disappearance of the brand altogether, along with its competitors, in the War Time Association, not to re-emerge until February 1948. But a little matter like the loss of its brand identity was not going to stop Schweppes from advertising. The public had to be reassured that one day their established favourite would be back, and life would return to normal.

So Schweppes advertised throughout the war, sometimes stressing the lack of the product; indeed making a virtue of it by linking the current desperate situation with other crises in the national history which were also part of the history of Schweppes. 'Since the Battle of the Nile...'; 'Since the Battle of Valmy...' started typical advertisements; Schweppes identified itself with a country under siege. The advertisements stressed 'the duty to make sacrifices towards victory'; that, as part of the war effort, it must 'disappear from the market until triumph is achieved'. At the same time

Example of a press campaign linking Schweppes with important events, c. 1943

a less serious note kept breaking through. An advertisement in the *Daily Telegraph* just before Christmas 1943 showed a couple of topers proposing a toast: 'here's to the day when we drink it in Schweppes'.

Advertising without a product was not Schweppes' only problem. The severe shortage of newsprint meant that advertisements tended to be tiny – when you could cajole space in a newspaper or magazine. The rationing not only of insertions but also of space encouraged a brevity of expression which, matched with Schweppes' traditional wit, produced some effective advertisements. One nostalgically read: 'If we had some gin we'd have a gin and tonic if we had some Schweppes'. But occasionally Schweppes advertisements burst before austerity-burdened readers with colour and impact. Some quite cheerful advertisements appeared, reminiscent of more relaxed times, in particular a series on drinking toasts through the ages, which allowed Schweppes and its consumers to forget the war and indulge in traditional light-hearted

The Origin of the "Toast"

Although healths have been drunk from time immemorial the custom of giving "toasts" dates only from the 17th century and the origin of the phrase is curious. Pieces of toasted bread were frequently placed in wine in the belief that it improved the flavour. The story is told that at Bath in the days of Charles II a celebrated beauty being immersed in the water an admirer dipped a goblet in the bath and drank her health. Whereon a fuddled gallant offered to jump into the bath saying though he liked not the liquor, he would have the toast. From that time the custom of toasting a famous beauty in the belief that it improved the flavour of the drink became the regular custom.

Schweppes*

Table Waters

famous since 1790

★ Temporarily giving place to the standard war-time product
but Schweppes quality will return with victory.

The Loving Cup

The loving cup and the grace cup are sometimes thought to be much the same thing. So they are in the ceremony of the drinking but their origins are very different. The true loving cup had a lid and the one about to drink would turn to the neighbour on his right who would remove the lid with his right (or dagger) hand and thus keep it innocently occupied. The grace cup which also passed round the table, was instituted by a Scots queen who conceived the idea of keeping back a bumper of specially choice wine until after grace had been said and thus keep the diners in their places.

Schweppes*

Table Waters

famous since 1790

★ Temporarily giving place to the standard war-time product
—but Schweppes quality will return with victory.

Two of a Mid-1940s series of press advertisements which kept the Schweppes name before the public in readiness for its post-war return

erudition. The Wassail Bowl, The Loving Cup, Greco-Roman customs, were all recalled with well-researched copy and comfortable illustrations. This campaign later developed a more patriotic theme, depicting the drinking traditions of the armed services based on a series of paintings by the distinguished artist Fortunato Matania; the naval officers remaining seated, the Gloucestershire Regiment allowing only two officers to join in the loyal toast (a painting which was later presented to the regiment).

But when victory had been achieved, though the miseries of the war continued – the shortages, the bleakness, the rationing – Schweppes advertising became tougher, not hiding behind nostalgia but looking towards the future. 'Schweppes will return', the ads said: 'Life will have more sparkle with the return of Schweppes'. The moment was ripe for the first great Schweppes advertising campaign aimed at the general public and one that has influenced the company's advertising down to the present day. The weary post-war world was ready for Schweppervescence; in fact it was just what the doctor ordered.

SCHWEPPERVESCENCE

'Schweppervescence' was dreamed up at a brainstorming session between Leonard Garland and his father Sidney, who ran the agency which had acquired the Schweppes account in 1945. In a manner which was to become a tradition in Schweppes advertising, Sidney Garland had become friendly with the company's managing director Jimmy Joyce, and it was on the basis of this friendship and mutual respect that he was entrusted with the account. When his son Leonard returned from war service he was given the responsibility of devising the advertising for Schweppes, a tricky proposition since there was no product available at the time. 'We had to create a characteristic instead,' remembers Leonard Garland, 'but one that we would be able to apply to any product that eventually came along,' for in those optimistic days it was taken for granted that Schweppes would be developing new products for the peace-time market.

Garland also appreciated that the post-war world would be less class-conscious and that Schweppes would be selling its products to a wider public. Schweppervescence was the perfect word both to portray the Schweppes brand and to promote its flavours throughout society. It suggested their liveliness, vivacity and sparkle, and it got away from the masculinity of previous advertising.

When the catchline that 'Schweppervescence lasts the whole drink through' was added Schweppes had

Two early examples of press advertisements introducing the word 'Schweppervescence', c. 1946

the perfect all-purpose slogan. Garlands was careful never to define Schweppervescence – it defined itself; it was the quintessence of a Schweppes drink. It was also perfect for the time. The word was introduced to the public on 8 June 1946 when London was packed with celebratory crowds for the Victory Parade. As they arrived at the main railway stations they were greeted with banners proclaiming the new word. It instantly reminded everyone of something that was not yet available but would be one day – in the meantime it summed up the national mood. Schweppes had always been big users of outdoor sites; the name was painted on countless railway bridges and proclaimed from poster sites as well as from bus sides and the Piccadilly Circus beacon. So such a barrage was not entirely novel, although the banner draped across the

Piccadilly Circus 1947, as seen in a Schweppes cartoon advertisement in Punch

Edgware Road from Schweppes' Connaught Place headquarters was rather eye-catching.

After the initial bombardment Schweppervescence showed its versatility by appearing in the Press. It was an unusual word so it looked at its best alongside other unusual words. 'When rations threaten contabescence, Then more's the need for Schweppervescence' ran one advertisement. 'Intumescence' was another rhyme unearthed by the agency, which was maintaining the literary tradition of Schweppes advertising. Newsprint was still hard to come by and when space was available the fact that poor quality paper married to antiquated printing presses often produced badly smudged advertisements persuaded Garlands to come up with clear, simple campaigns, like the Schweppervescence poems and small cartoons from David Langdon and Hewitt. An early advertisement shows two men at a bar and the comradely slogan, 'We have been friends together In sunshine and in rain', with just the word 'Schweppes' boldly at the bottom.

Not only was simplicity a sensible precaution given

poor printing, but it also enabled Schweppes advertising to stand out from the competition, for advertisers were usually limited to just 'four inch double' insertions, often placed one on top of another. The instant recognition of a word like Schweppervescence helped the advertising to be seen. In the immediate post-war world the quantity of advertising media was very limited. An advertiser was fortunate if he could get an insertion in a national newspaper once a month and in the fight for exposure any newspaper, even the communist *Daily Worker*, would be included on the schedule. Schweppes was fortunate to have in Garlands an agency that had been started by a former *Daily Mail* advertising director. The memory of Sidney Garland helped his son get at least his fair share of any advertising space going.

After the impact of Schweppervescence the company and its agency prepared for another exciting venture – the return of the brand in 1948. The public was teased with a series of cartoons by David Langdon which set the scene for this happy event. One shows a gentlemen's club, one member whispering to another, 'Have you heard that Schweppes is coming back soon?' with the answer coming from a bust perched on the library shelves, 'And I know the date – it's February 1st'. But Schweppes could not take its market for granted. For many years customers had not had the bother of asking for drinks by name; they must be made Schweppes-conscious again, or rather aware of Schweppervescence and its lasting qualities. So colourful cartoons appeared, drawn by Langdon, one both reminiscent of previous Schweppes advertising and of advertising to come. It depicted a cricketer going to bat half way through his Schweppes tonic and finding plenty of sparkle left in it on his return to the pavilion.

Leonard Garland's belief that Schweppes would be broadening its appeal in peace-time was soon confirmed, so Schweppervescence was also aimed at housewives and at home drinking. 'Who can think of entertaining without thinking of Schweppervescence?' ran one advertisement, adding the new key marketing fact, 'Most grocers and wine merchants stock Schweppes. You will find the larger bottles more economical'. In effect the advertising was returning to its message of a hundred and fifty years earlier when Schweppes had been consumed in the home, but instead of 'tomb-stone' ads there were now strip cartoons in colour, one showing the householder, significantly wearing a black tie, being forced by his wife to pop out to the bunker for more coal while she reassures him that 'Schweppervescence lasts the whole drink through', and that his whisky and ginger will keep its fizz.

But the traditional clubland market was not being forgotten. A series of humorous advertisements played upon the long history of Schweppes and its military associations. 'All Sir Garnet' started one, explaining that the phrase originated in Sir Garnet Wolseley's attention to detail, and ending 'Sticklers steadily stickle for Schweppervescence'. Another advertisement, very Schweppesian in its witty and erudite history lessons, links the Iron Duke of Wellington's cry 'Detail, Sir, Detail' with the product, and the slogan 'Schweppervescence, Sir . . . . thirst things first!'.

Garlands' advertising spanned the past of Schweppes with its amusing, literary approach, while pointing to the mass market future. A campaign which included elements of both introduced the Schweppigram (yet another clever exploitation of the name). A typical 'gram' reads: 'How many Income Tax inspectors, Save the State for Me and You, Never has so much been owed, by so many to so few'. The attraction of the Schweppigrams was that they could be adapted to any seasonal occasion or news event. Garlands encouraged the general public to join in the fun, offering £5 prizes for the best Schweppigrams about the 1950 General Election through advertisements in the Press. 'A Schweppigram is a sort of epi-

Schweppes and its part in history. A typical quality magazine advertisement of the late 1940's.

"Call me a Cab!"

We like to think of the late Jos. Hansom. When he had completed the vehicle which bears his name he stroked his chin with anticipatory pleasure, secure in the knowledge that Disraeli would, in the fullness of time, christen his invention 'the gondola of London.' Once launched upon the gas lit streets, this graceful fleet of hansoms conveyed the Peerage, Gentry and Toffage about their nocturnal occasions, cigar smoke wreathing opulently through the skylight.

"A sovereign if you drive me to a botttle of Schweppes, Cabby!"

Clip-clop, clip-clop. For Schweppes, too, was part of the London scene. The selfsame Schweppes which has gone on building up its bubble reputation for more than a century and a half. And still today the cry rings out over misty London squares:

SCHWEPPERVESCENCE . . .

and don't spare the syphon

FIVERS for ELECTION SCHWEPPIGRAMS

£5 PRIZES will be paid to all major or minor poets who write Election Schweppigrams that are published in Schweppes advertisements in the "Daily Mail" between now and Election Day, February 23rd next.

The examples below give an idea of Schweppigrammarian technique. Rules of scansion can be schwepped aside, but brevity is still the soul of wit; four lines is the outside limit—and, of course, your Election Schweppigram should have some direct or indirect bearing on the Election, but keep out any reference to Schweppes and its products.

The sooner you send in your Schweppigram on a postcard—the better your chance of winning a fiver. Address to SCHWEPPIGRAMS, 4, CONNAUGHT PLACE, LONDON, W.2. Don't forget to add your own name and address. All entries must be received by or before first post on Friday, Feb. 17th.

NOTE: *All prize-winning entries become the copyright of Schweppes Ltd. The decision of Schweppes' judges is final. No entry will be accepted that reaches Schweppes' offices after first post on February 17th, 1950. Proof of posting cannot be accepted as proof of delivery.*

A Schweppigram
Is just a poetic epigram—
Not heavy or depressing
But schweppervescing.
So a schweppigrammarian
Is a poet (a light and airy 'un)
Who finds fivers acceptable
For verses not too
　　　　　dischwepputable.

SCHWEPPERVESCENCE LASTS THE WHOLE DRINK THROUGH

Examples of a very substantial series of 'Schweppigrams' which were used in UK national and local newspapers in 1950

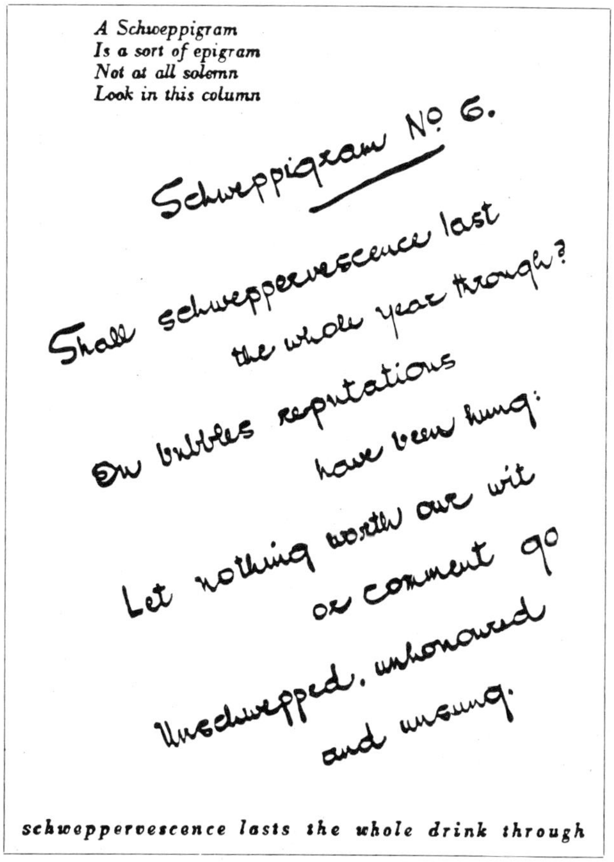

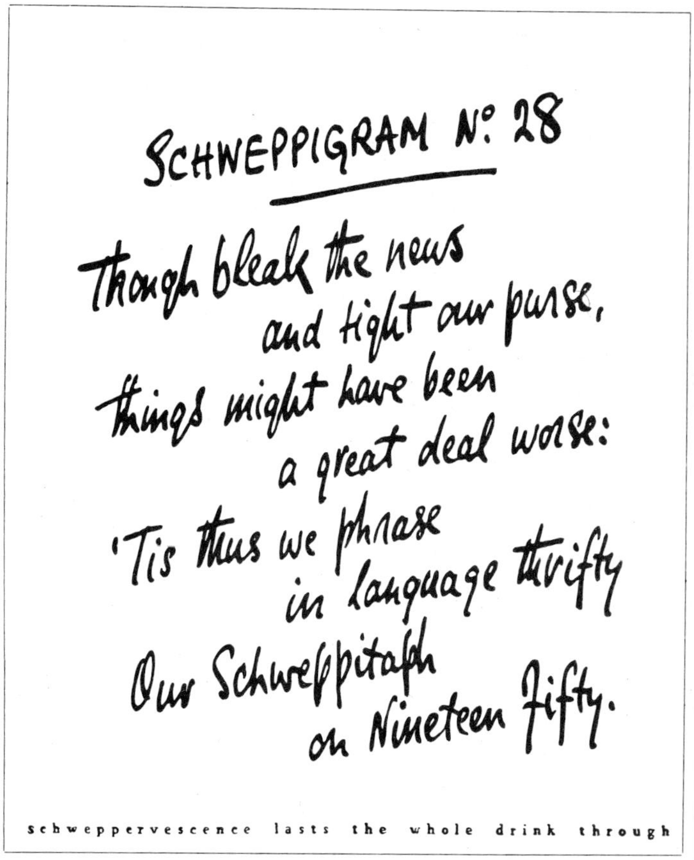

A Schweppigram
Is a sort of epigram
Not at all solemn
Look in this column

Schweppigram No. 6.

Shall schweppervescence last
　　　the whole year through?
On bubbles reputations
　　　have been hung:
Let nothing worth our wit
　　　or comment go
Unschwepped, unhonoured
　　　and unsung.

schweppervescence lasts the whole drink through

SCHWEPPIGRAM No. 28

Though bleak the news
　　　and tight our purse,
things might have been
　　　a great deal worse:
'Tis thus we phrase
　　　in language thrifty
Our Schweppitaph
　　　on Nineteen fifty.

schweppervescence lasts the whole drink through

gram, not at all solemn, look in this column', ran the competition. Such a democratic approach was a sign of the times.

Perhaps Garlands, boosted by the success of Schweppervescence, was running slightly ahead of Schweppes. In 1949 Frederic (later Sir Frederic) Hooper took over as its managing director. He took a great deal of interest in the advertising – in the past Garlands had dealt almost exclusively with the advertising manager – and although he agreed that Schweppes' future lay in the mass market, he was anxious to retain the more sophisticated campaigns aimed at Schweppes' traditional customers. It was basically a question of timing; both sides could agree on clever humorous advertising that was increasingly to appear in popular newspapers as well as in quality magazines. In the event, the advertising confirmed Schweppes products as being of the highest quality, chosen by the rich and discerning. It was no bad image to have as they became steadily available in a wider range of outlets.

Garlands had seen Schweppes through the difficult post-war years. When it took on the account the budget had declined from £100,000 in 1939 to around £55,000. In its six years it grew to £300,000 a year, the extra cash being used to promote Schweppes to millions more potential consumers while retaining all the old entertainment values which had already been built into the brand. Indeed while at one stage Garlands was experimenting with beer mats for pubs carrying the Schweppervescence slogan it was also producing advertisements, like the Schweppigrams, which it hoped would be collected. The cartoons too, especially the series by Langdon, were of a class so far above the general level that they were cut out and preserved by readers.

When Schweppes and Garlands parted company Sir Frederic paid the agency the compliment of ensuring that its great contribution to the company's post-war re-establishment, Schweppervescence, should continue to live by buying the rights to the word from Garlands for £150. He was determined that there should never be any legal quibbling over such a valuable property. And, of course, Schweppervescence continued to survive and is still appearing in advertisements in many parts of the world. There was another happy legacy from the Garlands years. Schweppes' current UK agency, Saatchi & Saatchi, is the direct successor of Garlands.

SCHWEPPSHIRE AND TV

In 1951 a new agency assumed the responsibility of creating the advertising for Schweppes – Bloxhams. Sir Frederic Hooper had known Clifford Bloxham during his years with Lewis's of Liverpool, so it was not surprising that when Bloxham set up his own advertising agency, concentrating on bright creative ideas with a small and select workforce, Sir Frederic should entrust him with the Schweppes account. For the next fourteen years Bloxhams lifted Schweppes advertising to even greater heights. This was the period which introduced the imaginary county of Schweppshire and launched the brand onto a new and exciting medium, television, which was to ensure that Schweppes products were promoted to the entire British population.

As the years progressed Sir Frederic's interest in advertising seemed to grow. He did not interfere in the day-to-day preparation of advertisements, but he presented Bloxham with a series of guidelines which were far-reaching for the period and indeed still seem innovatory. For a start, he did not want the agency to produce the creative work internally; its task was to secure the best talent available on the open market. He believed that if an agency became too closely involved with creativity the advertising would get into a rut. Sir Frederic was ahead of his time in recognising what, in today's marketing jargon, would be seen as the importance of 'exclusive advertising positioning' and he was determined to have advertising quite unlike any other.

A striking consequence of this approach was an advertisement placed by Bloxhams inviting applications for an account director to work on the Schweppes advertising: the first requirement was that the applicant should have no experience of Schweppes or of advertising; talent and a fresh approach was all. Naturally the advertisement attracted a great deal of interest and the final selection, Micheline (Mickie) Matthews, proved a great success. She had to work within the rules that Sir Frederic had prepared for Schweppes advertising – it must entertain; it must be different from any other company in whatever field; it must be noticeable; and it must inspire affection for the brand, for in that way the public would come to like the company and all its works. This very original approach did not always delight the resident agency creative team but it had one tangible advantage – it worked. John Holmes, now responsible for international advertising strategy at Schweppes, was then a junior account executive at Bloxhams. He recalls that Clifford Bloxham transferred him to work on the

Schweppes account in readiness to support the new account chief, when appointed.

It was a busy but enthralling and Schweppervescent time and my earlier upbringing in the ad agency business via production and administration stood me in good stead! During that time, and subsequently as Schweppes U.K. marketing manager in the 'You-Know-Who' era, I learnt many lessons about how Schweppes should be advertised. Three basic lessons have since been personal guidelines. Firstly, recognition that outstanding advertising needs to be preceded by an outstanding brief. Secondly, it is extremely important to help to generate and sustain real enthusiasm in those who are going to make the creative contribution. Finally, the campaign will only be a great one if it builds a bridge of affection between the brand and its consumers. It is essential for 'Schweppes' (both the brand and the company) that people should really like us and they will only do this if they love our ads even more than our products.

The originality of the approach paid off and throughout the 1950s and the early 1960s the advertising continued to be famous and the company prospered.

Among Bloxhams' first advertisements introduced in 1951 was the 'How many Schwepping days to Christmas?' campaign which lasted to the mid-1960s. This was easily adaptable, the days tailing down to just one Schwepping day left. Perhaps the most memorable advertisements on this theme appeared on the sides of buses, especially the London buses. Schweppes advertised on only 300 of the 6000 buses then operating in London, but the impact (outside of Christmas time the advertising concentrated on the Ssssound of Schweppes) lasts still. Another early campaign which proved to have great staying power was built around the phrase 'Curiously refreshing' to describe a well photographed bottle of Schweppes. This was still being used in the American advertising twenty years later.

But it was the Schweppshire campaign which represents the peak of Schweppes advertising in the 1950s. Once again Sir Frederic played a dominant role. The idea of this imaginary English county was born, as we have seen, during a snooker game between Sir Frederic and the humorist Stephen Potter, and the map of Schweppshire was unveiled in the Spring of 1951. For fourteen years Potter annually produced six fresh insights into this idiosyncratic county, much assisted by an artist, usually George Him.

Schweppshire was in the great tradition of Schweppes advertising – quirky, gently humorous, very English, reassuring. Gradually over the years readers of quality magazines such as *Vogue*, *Punch*, *Illustrated London News* and *The Tatler* learned a great deal about Schweppshire and its inhabitants, among whom were Samuel Schwepys, Percy Byssche Schweppey,

and Dante Gabriel Rosschweppi. The exact location of Schwepping Forest and Schwepstow Castle (Queen Elizabeth schwept there) could be pinpointed, and the latest developments discovered from *The Schweppshire Post* which tended to carry headlines like 'Councillor collides with cow, escapes with slight abrasions'. The main activity in Schweppshire would seem to be golf – football was just catching on: its origins apparently had sprung from a golfer kicking an opponent's ball into a bad lie. Such behaviour could bring the culprit before the Supreme Court, other courts, and Wimbledon. Later advertisements featured the University of Schweppshire; its stately homes; and its vital statistics – the birth rate fortunately was 'quite good'.

Sir Frederic predictably also laid down the rules for the Schweppshire advertising. It was not to be corrosive, caustic, or to provoke bitter smiles. While it could touch on British weaknesses, it had to be 'heartwarming' and if the fun was nostalgic, it could never conjure up feelings of 'loss or regret'. Each successive advertising manager at Schweppes, and each agency account director, during the fourteen years of this famous campaign was charged with the task of ensuring that Sir Frederic's deceptively simple rules were followed.

Schweppshire proved to be extremely adaptable. Each year saw a new theme. In 1962 the six advertisements parodied television under the guise of a new TV station, Television Schweppsicolor. A year later the Traditions in Schweppshire were examined; they included 'Killing nothing out of season', 'The preservation of Cosiness', 'Insistence on Getting in the Sun' and 'Kindness to Children'.

Stephen Potter was very popular in the early 1950s through his Gamesmanship books, which taught people how to behave badly in the nicest possible way; Schweppshire was equally inspired. It touched on the foibles of the nation in a sympathetic way, was nostalgic without being maudlin, and never mocked itself. Above all it was civilised, very much the humour of the middle classes who had traditionally been Schweppes' best customers. But Sir Frederic saw Potter as widening the appeal of the company throughout the social scale while retaining all the old values.

Schweppshire was that wonderful thing – brilliant individual advertisements that built up into a longrunning and developing campaign. Eventually Schweppsylvania was born, which introduced British readers to a little-known state of the Union and some of the more amiable of American weaknesses. As talk of

The Schweppshire Post

A TRIUMPH & AN OPPORTUNITY

The more than international interest aroused by the Guide to Schwepp-shire demands a response. We hope, during 1952, to be able to reprint pages from our daily organ, THE SCHWEPPSHIRE POST, thus vividly pin-pointing, uniquely, SCHWEPPSHIRE'S LIFE TO-DAY.
But opportunity shatters schedules. A General Election has given new meaning and fresh urgency. Here, then, is a preview of POST'S policy.

THE SCHWEPPSHIRE POST'S ELECTION MANIFESTO

It is addressed to YOU

This is a message. A message for YOU. For you, because YOU are one of 2,371 guaranteed SCHWEPPSHIRE POST readers, and though YOU diminished at first, now YOUR number is increasing daily. YOU will be bigger after October 25th. And why?

POST policy is YOUR policy. Politically, POST is for progress; yet realises that tradition plays its part. Internationally, POST is fearlessly for Peace, remembering war's honoured tradition. The country must remain alerted for defence, always recognising that the bogey of the atom bomb must not allow us to be ruled by scaremongers. We stand for Britain first, always remembering that the English-speaking peoples play their part, with the coloured peoples as their inseparable adjunct. For agriculture, the farmers must be absolutely free, and we must guide them to this freedom with the full co-operation of the Advisory Committees. POST is if possible even more for Youth; with maturity standing shoulder to shoulder with Age. POST is for our heritage of health, is for our national heritage, this realm, this diadem, this moat.

POST is for YOU.

Stephen Potter

. . . for ye that fare further,
longer is the way . . .

SCHWEPPERVESCENCE LASTS THE WHOLE DRINK THROUGH

A 'Schweppshire' advertisement written by Stephen Potter and published in a number of UK magazines late in 1951

Britain entering into closer political and economic ties with Europe grew more widespread, there was 'Europe in Perschwepptive' informing us about the habits of continentals. Potter's imagination rarely flagged and those bright colourful advertisements became one of the most talked about and admired campaigns of the decade. Remarkably for the time, Schweppes was shrewd enough to avoid all brand promotion in the advertisements. At the foot of the page the familiar slogan 'Schweppervescence lasts the whole drink through' was enough for the public, just a gentle reminder of the popular favourite.

While Potter amused Schweppes' traditional consumers, the popular Press, both national and provincial, was starting to carry advertisements by another distinguished artist of the time, the French cartoonist Siné, whose tiny drawings of animated bottles with punchy slogans like 'Thirsty – take the necessary Schweppes' perpetuated the brevity and wit developed by Schweppes during the war years when newsprint and advertising space had been rationed. A feature of Schweppes advertising has always been that however minor the advertisement in terms of cost or coverage, be it a page in the programme of a company sports day or a hotel menu card, the artwork and the creative idea must be of the quality of a colour page in a glossy magazine. Often the artwork would be more expensive than the price of the advertising, and a Siné drawing could flourish unseen by the general public. A magazine like *Chief Steward*, which circulated among the few hundred stewards on luxury liners, would merit a specially planned cartoon showing a sailor playing with a model boat in the bath, Schweppes' name on the bath mat, and a caption, 'Where there's a ship there's Schweppes'.

Stephen Potter, George Him, and Siné were not the only major creative people engaged through Schweppes' determination to use the best available talent. Loudon Sainthill also contributed drawings and the Swiss artist Leupin created for the 1961 Christmas campaign, always the key period in sales terms, a very memorable Christmas tree design, the foliage consisting of labels from Schweppes products. Each year Baron, the leading photographic studio, provided the prints for the annual Schweppes sporting calendar. When the association with Potter eventually came to an end Schweppes looked for a young humorist to continue the tradition. The man approached was Jonathan Miller, coming to public notice through his contribution to the review *Beyond the Fringe*. Unfortunately a link was not forged but the very idea is a good illustration of the Schweppes eye for fresh talent.

Two examples of a long-running series of humorous advertisements used in the 1950's and 1960's and associating Schweppes with its tradition of consumption aboard the many ships of the world; both conventional and less conventional

Four of the many Schweppes UK newspaper advertisements published throughout the 1950's

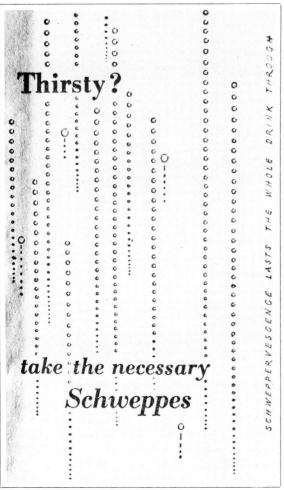

But the most significant advertising development of the 1950s was Schweppes' wholehearted appreciation of the importance of television advertising in reaching a mass market. Sir Frederic Hooper was determined to sell Schweppes products to all sections of the community but without sacrificing the high standards of the advertising. So in the Press, Siné's cartoons were introduced to the *Daily Mirror* and other mass circulation newspapers and television time was bought in the week that ITV transmissions began, initially in the London area and then gradually throughout the country. Sir Frederic himself provided the introductory voice-overs for the first series of commercials – a suggestion made by the agency rather than self-aggrandisement – and every week for several months the Schweppes name was projected through a cartoon character, a learned professor continually searching for Schweppes as he explored the world. One week we would find the professor in darkest Africa looking for Schweppervescence (what else?), the next discovering that Schweppes played its part in the building of the pyramids.

After the professor, Hermione Baddeley was used in a series of commercials in which she played cameo roles, usually gently mocking the product. Then Elsie and Doris Waters took a turn. The objective, as with the professor, was always to entertain, and it was this continuous search for a new humorous approach which inspired Bloxhams to ask Benny Hill, then a new and original comedian, to appear in some commercials. He proved such a success that from 1959 until 1964 Schweppes' television advertising was built around Benny. He was a great perfectionist and jealous of his talent. He would develop and refine each characterisation with great care well before the film shoot and he, and Schweppes, insisted that no commercial should be seen more than six to ten times with the consequent chance of viewer boredom. Every year he would make several commercials for Schweppes and six of them won awards at the chief international competition for television commercials, held each year alternately at Venice and Cannes. In 1961 Schweppes carried off the top prize for the best commercial of the year against competition from twenty-three countries.

A typical commercial would show Benny as a highbrow writer boasting of his literary specialty – which turns out to be composing rhymes for Christmas crackers. Then he would be a midget, shrunken by a witch doctor, standing helpless beside a giant can of Schweppes Bitter Lemon; or a gardener whose prize exhibit is a bottle of Schweppes Tomato Juice. Burglar, farmer, astronomer, piano tuner – it was in his Schweppes commercials that Benny Hill perfected the characterisations that were later to bring him vast audiences in the UK, and on American television. But there was satire along with the acting. Fashions of the day were gently sent up, as were other advertisements, the popular films of the period, and new developments like street interviews. They made very distinctive advertisements and, although some of the topical allusions may pass us by, they have aged very well; the prizes were obviously deservedly won. But by the mid–1960s Schweppes was facing tougher competition in the market place and a campaign which projected the product more forcefully, rather than one which offered an amusing comic interlude, was thought to be the answer to the increased competition. There was also the criticism that while the Benny Hill commercials were distinctive and, individually, of a very high quality, as an idea they were hard to build upon. But it was perhaps outside administrative changes which tipped the scales towards a fresh approach.

During the 1950s and early 1960s, the organisation of advertising inside companies changed dramatically. The old system of an advertising manager dealing with an advertising agency was superseded by marketing departments and managers with responsibility for individual brands and their advertising. Sir Frederic Hooper found the new methodology unsympathetic to his idiosyncratic and individual approach and it was only after the coming of Lord Watkinson in 1962 that Schweppes developed a marketing department. Not until 1960 did Sir Frederic pass on to Bloxhams sales figures, which he regarded as private to the company and likely to inhibit the creative ideas of the agency. Once the advertising formula was developed – Schweppshire for the up-market magazines, Benny Hill for television and cartoons for the popular Press – it was persevered with year after year. The advertising expenditure also changed only gradually, the budget rising from £300,000 in 1951 to £325,000 at the advent of television nationally in 1956, to around £450,000 by 1964.

What also remained unchanged during this period of rapid progress were the basic beliefs behind Schweppes advertising. The striving for excellence was there, as was the determination to use the best talent available to produce advertising which was enjoyable. If people enjoyed the advertising they would enjoy the product; if the product was of the highest quality, so the advertising had to maintain the same standards. Some of Sir Frederic Hooper's views may have been quirky, but his success in achieving confident adverti-

Two of the world's most famous advertising personalities of the 1960's meet; both known through outstanding USA campaigns from David Ogilvy. Commander Edward Whitehead of Schweppes and 'the man with the eye-patch' from the Hathaway shirt advertisements

sing that was also unusual, that involved the consumer in a conspiracy of fun, and that embraced the whole community in the traditions of Schweppes, never faltered.

COMMANDER WHITEHEAD AND THE USA
The great challenge for any ambitious British company is to sell its products successfully in the US, the home of mass marketing and consumer choice. This is a challenge that Schweppes met in the early 1950s and

its subsequent success owed much to one of the most effective advertising campaigns ever mounted, a campaign built around the very different skills of two British men – advertising agency chief David Ogilvy and the head of Schweppes in the US, Commander Edward Whitehead. The two men had much in common and it is not surprising that they should become the closest of friends.

David Ogilvy had gone to New York in 1949 with the expressed intention of representing British advertisers in the massive American market; he went with the encouragement of the Chancellor of the Exchequer, Sir Stafford Cripps, and the British Government which allowed him to take out extra capital to finance the project. By coincidence the man selected by Frederic Hooper to represent Schweppes in the US, Commander Edward Whitehead, had worked in the Treasury under Sir Stafford Cripps, after six years' service in the RNVR, and had the same high ideal that the future prosperity of the UK depended on the effective development of overseas markets. At first Ogilvy met some opposition from British advertisers in the US, who wondered what a British executive could know about the American market, but by some imaginative campaigns he soon represented the leading British prestige names – Rolls Royce, Peninsular & Orient Lines, Guinness, British Travel.

So it was not surprising that he should be visited by Commander Whitehead and Frederic Hooper and asked to work on Schweppes advertising. Perhaps the most famous and successful of the Ogilvy campaigns of the time was for Hathaway Shirts, which featured a distinguished looking man wearing a black eye patch. As soon as Ogilvy saw Commander Whitehead, a tall, handsome, English gentleman who still sported an imposing red naval beard, he realised that the Schweppes chief executive in the US would make the perfect ambassador for the product. For almost twenty years the Commander carried the Schweppes advertising in the US. It made him the second most famous Englishman in the country (only headed by Sir Winston Churchill) and, more to the point, established Schweppes as an expanding and profitable brand in that vast and prosperous market.

Commander Whitehead was at first reluctant to assume the role but soon appreciated the logic behind the campaign and over time thoroughly enjoyed his second career as the symbol for the company. It tapped in him remarkable dormant talents. He became a witty and distinguished public speaker; a skilled actor; a public personality. He discovered that he enjoyed being a celebrity and played the part to

WARNING
to Gin Lovers

A lot of Americans have started drinking gin-and-tonic in the last year or two. This is all to the good —there is no more refreshing drink, particularly when the weather is hot.

But in all seriousness we must warn you that gin-and-tonic does not taste the same unless you mix it with Schweppes original Quinine Water, imported from England.

That is our unshakable conviction, and the conviction of millions of Englishmen who have been drinking Schweppes since long before you were born. They *insist* on Schweppes. They avoid substitutes. They abhor imitations. Schweppes is a *sine qua non*, a sine *quinine* non, for an authentic gin-and-tonic.

HEUBLEIN FOOD IMPORTING CO., INC.
730 FIFTH AVENUE, NEW YORK

Two advertisements which appeared in the New Yorker, c. 1950, in the relatively early days of popularising gin and Schweppes tonic in the USA

'It says here that you can't make an authentic Gin-And-Tonic without Schweppes Quinine Water.'

perfection, always ready to acknowledge the approaches of strangers and fully aware that as he became better known, so Schweppes grew in awareness and popularity. For not only was Commander Whitehead recognised throughout the US; he was also liked and admired by Americans. At the start it was the beard, a rare sight in the America of thirty years ago, that attracted the popular imagination; later it was the integrity of the personality.

But like all brilliant advertising ideas the use of the Schweppes chief executive as the advertising model was much more than clever casting; it perfectly fitted the marketing task that Schweppes had set itself. For many years Schweppes had sent bottled products, basically its Quinine Water (it was then not allowed to to described as Tonic in the US), across the Atlantic. But in 1952 it signed the deals with Pepsi-Cola whereby the giant American company would bottle Schweppes in the US while Schweppes would produce Pepsi in the UK. As a result the price of a 10-ounce bottle of Schweppes came down from the 40 cents charged in the rather exclusive shops which sold it to around 18 cents and available in a much wider range of outlets. Commander Whitehead was the ideal person to convince the American consumer that the lower price and the fact that Schweppes was now produced in the US in no way affected its traditional quality and taste.

The first advertisement, in colour, appeared in *The New Yorker* magazine and showed Commander Whitehead descending from a BOAC plane wearing a black Homburg hat, holding in one hand a rolled umbrella and in the other a despatch case containing 'the original Schweppes elixir'. The headline read 'The man from Schweppes is here' and the advertisement was designed to assure Americans that the Commander would personally ensure that the high standards of Schweppes would be scrupulously maintained even though 'You can now buy Schweppes Quinine Water for about the price of ordinary mixers!' Familiar advertising slogans like 'Schweppervescence lasts the whole drink through' were incorporated in the copy. The whole impact was very British, very confident, very Schweppesian.

For almost two decades the advertising approach changed little. Colour advertisements, mainly in up-market journals, showed Commander Whitehead on a fine horse under the caption, 'The British are coming again – this time with reinforcements'; in hunting pink at a meet with 'Hunting for a new drink? Try vodka and Schweppes'; exploring the US – in Hollywood, the Rockies, the Western plains,

bringing the magic of Schweppes to all America; then he is back at the New York docks supervising the unloading of another consignment of the 'Schweppes elixir'.

The advertisements were sometimes informative, sometimes evocative. He is shown on the beach (supported by a Rolls Royce) with the caption 'I claim this land for Schweppes'; teaching a smart lady in an exclusive bar how to pronounce Schweppes: ' "It's monosyllabic" says the Schweppesman'; giving instruction on how Schweppes should be poured: 'Slowly – into a tilted glass – and don't stir'; preparing a gin and tonic on stage for dancer Beryl Grey with the slogan 'Prima ballerina takes her first Schweppes (in America)', a familiar exploitation of the variety in the word. All in all the chief executive of Schweppes in the US would spend a month of his year as an actor in advertisements – for which he was well paid, with the bonus, which very much appealed to him, of keeping all the smart clothes that he wore on the sets.

Perhaps the main reason why the advertising was so effective was the personality of Edward Whitehead. He was not playing a part. He was very much the man in the advertisement, and the man in charge, and as time went by he grew even more into the character portrayed. By the end there was hardly any exaggeration. For example, he was a great outdoors man who loved hunting and sailing, and the advertisements depicting him at these activities found him completely at home. An advertisement showing him driving through the snow with his box of Schweppes led Commander Whitehead to take up skiing and he became very adept. He was also a perfectionist in the advertisements. After a tiring day under the television lights filming a commercial, David Ogilvy remembers that only a hand shot was required the next day to complete the film. Whitehead insisted on returning to ensure that it was *his* hands that were screened. He had the vanity that is part of showmanship.

At the start the Schweppes advertising budget was quite small, around $250,000, and it never rose above $1m a year. But David Ogilvy reckons that the free publicity that Commander Whitehead attracted through his appearances on television and radio shows and in newspaper interviews brought Schweppes around $20m worth of free advertising in a year. A particularly effective ploy was for an advertisement to appear in the major local newspaper when Schweppes appointed a new bottler. It would invariably show the Commander arriving at the airport to be met by his new business partner. The bottlers loved to appear in the advertisement because they enjoyed working with Schweppes and with Commander Whitehead, the epitome of the English gentleman. Whitehead would spend most of his year travelling the US, speaking at dinners, appearing on local television stations, helping to glamorise the lives of regional bottlers. No wonder the Schweppes sales increased by over 500% in ten years.

There was a bonus for David Ogilvy. 'It was hard for the client to disagree with the advertising if he was appearing in it'. In fact the two men became the best of friends, their families spending much time together. This had its advantages. Mrs Whitehead sometimes objected to the extent to which her husband had become a public figure, constantly in demand, constantly being approached by strangers. David Ogilvy suggested that she should appear in some of the advertisements, to great effect. 'Who's the woman behind the Schweppesman?' read the slogan.

Commander Whitehead adapted to television with great ease. He was filmed superintending the arrival of his vintage car in the US; on his yacht; at parties. He had a perfect public school voice and, dressed in white tie and tails, and charming a lady, he perpetuated for Americans the image of the Englishman created by the British movies of the thirties and forties. He even aged in a most distinguished fashion, his beard flecked with white, his athletic bearing intact. Sometimes the very fame of Whitehead worried his colleagues at head office in London. 'You have created a Frankenstein's monster whom I cannot control', Sir Frederic Hooper once snorted to Ogilvy; but throughout his years of fame Commander Whitehead remained amiable, charming and very kind. He was also very brave. One commercial showing Whitehead delivering some more Schweppes by helicopter required the door of the 'copter to be left open: a very dangerous manoeuvre.

But eventually the time approached for Commander Whitehead to retire. His role in the advertising became less prominent. In the commercials he might just appear in the last frame remarking that Schweppes was 'curiously refreshing', a slogan revived by the agency in the US. In some later magazine advertisements the Commander has to be searched for among the crowd of Schweppes drinkers. Finally David Ogilvy produced thirty new approaches to succeed the Commander, ranging from using his son Charles, who considered but finally declined the invitation, to employing another bearded personality, the actor James Robertson Justice, in the role. But a new chief executive for Schweppes in the US

wanted a new approach and Ogilvy's agency lost the account in 1971. The advertising in the US in the subsequent decade never managed to repeat the eye-catching style of the Commander Whitehead years. But then David Ogilvy maintains that it was 'one of the half dozen most memorable campaigns in the history of advertising'. He includes in this list another that his agency, this time in London, prepared for Schweppes, 'The secret of Schhh ...' campaign.

Commander Whitehead and David Ogilvy established Schweppes in the very competitive American soft drinks industry. Their impact extended far beyond the advertising. Perhaps the main long-term commercial benefit was the high quality of local bottlers that could be signed up because they liked the idea of a partnership with Commander Whitehead and Schweppes: the public relations work done year in and year out by Whitehead was his greatest contribution. But the power of his personality could only be brought to bear when his face and form were made known through the advertising.

His role in the advertising and his subsequent fame probably gave Commander Whitehead the extra confidence required to do his job well. He became an expert on marketing, lecturing on this 'new' subject at the Royal Albert Hall as well as to American business seminars. This again improved the reputation of Schweppes in the US. In reality, Ogilvy believes, Whitehead always ran the operation by hunch and rarely applied the marketing techniques he publicised. But as always his image was first class. Perhaps the only criticism of the Commander Whitehead advertising is that it was such a perfect fit between the personality and the marketing task that there were bound to be problems when Commander Whitehead retired. It was an impossible campaign to follow. But if great advertising is to be rejected because it so stands above the competition, all the advertising agencies and marketing departments in the world might as well pack up.

SCHHH...

The arrival of Lord Watkinson as chief executive in 1963 replaced one strong-minded man by another and in his searching reappraisal of the company it was not surprising that the advertising and marketing should be re-examined. The Benny Hill campaign had been running on television for over five years and while undoubtedly popular it had certain weaknesses – it concentrated attention as much on the comedian as on the Schweppes brand name and it lacked a strong underlying theme. All the other great Schweppes campaigns had built upon an imaginative slogan: the television commercials retained the humour of the company tradition but hardly added a new word to the language. Perhaps more decisively, in a growing soft drinks market Schweppes' market share, although still dominant, was under increasing pressure. So, just as the advent of Sir Frederic Hooper heralded a change of agency from Garlands to Bloxhams, a new chief executive led quickly to another new agency.

Lord Watkinson decided to ask the most famous advertising man of the day, David Ogilvy, to review all of Schweppes' advertising. It was Ogilvy, of course, who had seen the potential in using Commander Whitehead to spearhead Schweppes advertising in the US and the success of that idea provided him with a track record for the company. Ogilvy found a chaotic situation. The rapid acquisition programme of Sir Frederic Hooper had added numerous brands to the Schweppes stable and their advertising agencies had tended to come along too. There were seventeen different agencies. Ogilvy recommended a drastic rationalisation, to bring all the Schweppes brands together into one agency to be promoted as a unified product range. Lord Watkinson accepted much of Ogilvy's advice and gave his London agency, Mather & Crowther, the prize of the Schweppes account.

Out of this rather abrupt and unscientific change of agency was born perhaps the most famous of all the Schweppes advertising campaigns, 'The secret of Schhh ... you-know-who'. But it was not an easy birth. Mather & Crowther, later to become Ogilvy & Mather, was a very different agency from Bloxhams. While the latter prided itself on its creativity, David Ogilvy took a scientific approach to advertising. He encouraged his agency executives to prepare advertisements in line with a set of rules. The headline must included the brand name and a benefit for the consumer, plus something to whet his curiosity. As it happened, the Schweppes advertising broke most of these guidelines but another part of the Ogilvy approach – detailed research – proved vital to the eventual acceptance of the agency campaign.

Tubby Pitcher, now President of Ogilvy & Mather, was given the Schweppes account to look after. His first task was to find out about the market, no easy task, for in those days soft drink sales through grocery outlets were a small part of Schweppes' business and it did not take the widely accepted and authoritative Nielsen sales data. In fact, it had very little hard information about its markets. So it was by the more time-consuming, but infinitely more pleasurable, path of visiting key account customers in pubs, clubs and hotels with Schweppes' sales reps that Tubby Pitcher built up his knowledge of his agency's important new client – important as much for the prestige of its advertising as for its expenditure.

Although Mather & Crowther did not have to make a competitive pitch for the Schweppes account it still had to satisfy the board with its campaign, and initially this was difficult. The agency devised a series of cameo pub scenes in which the characters in different alcoves of a bar asked for different Schweppes flavours – a tonic group, a posse of ginger ale drinkers, a bitter lemon bunch. The Schweppes board thought it lacked fizz and the agency went back for second thoughts, dividing its resources into two teams for double creative input.

It was Royston Taylor, now creative head at Dorlands, who eventually devised the 'Schhh ... you-know-who' campaign. He had only been in the agency for two years, which is perhaps why he ignored David Ogilvy's rules as he doodled away at ideas. It was obvious that the advertising must appeal to the mass market while maintaining Schweppes' superior quality image. 'I thought that whatever we did had somehow to be part of the contemporary popular atmosphere which at that time was dominated by James Bond and spy novels. I was also imagining how you could advertise the product without mentioning the name.' Playing around with the whispered secrets of spies, Taylor came up with 'you know what', later changed to 'you know who', placed in an espionage context. It was then passed on to the art department for a visual treatment. The vital 'Schhh ...' came later as Taylor tried to add the product advantage to the advertising. Inevitably his mind went back to Schweppervescence; 'the secret of Schweppervescence'; 'the secret of Schhh ...'. The two ideas were put together and the slogan that was to work for seven years and to endure until today was created. The fact that the 'Schhh ...' sounded like a Schweppes bottle being opened was an unexpected bonus.

With the slogan and the spy setting the rest was easy. At that time Patrick McGoohan was a popular television actor as Dangerman. He was asked to appear in the pilot commercial but filming commitments and some disagreement over creative control scuppered that idea. So the agency approached William Franklyn, not nearly so well known but a leading character in another spy series, *Top Secret*. A commercial was made showing Franklyn slipping into a room through a secret panel, raiding a cache of Schweppes Tonics hidden in a grandfather clock, and adding the mixer to a glass of spirits held in the clenched fist of a dead man sprawled across a desk. The script contained all the later hallmarks – the secret; the enemy out to get it; the avoidance of the brand name. It also contained an imaginative touch from the producer of the commercial, Roger Adams. He suggested that dead body – the first ever seen in a commercial, but not the only time that he added his own visual twist to a Schweppes advertisement.

When the commercial was shown to the Schweppes board there were doubts about the risk taken in not naming the brand – only Guinness had dared to run advertising that credited the public with the intelligence to fill in the product. But then Mather & Crowther was able to show its marketing skill by producing research conducted a day or two previously which proved that over 90% of the public was well aware that Schhh... was Schweppes. The pilot commercial was soon on air and over forty others were to follow with conspicuous success in the course of the ensuing years.

Apart from keeping the Schweppes name before the public in a context which stressed its superiority over the competition, the advertising was also designed to persuade consumers to ask for Schweppes specifically by name. Research confirmed that less than 10% of customers asked for a specific mixer – the fact that a brand of whisky, gin or vodka was specified no less infrequently was little satisfaction. The Schweppes advertising improved brand specification as well as brand awareness by making a joke of it. 'You-Know-Who' soon became a catch phrase. The Schweppes sales reps were able to leave cards stating, 'You-Know-Who called with the Secret of Schhh...'; point of sale posters could proclaim, 'You-Know-Who is inside'; Lord Watkinson became Lord 'You-Know-Who'. Cheques were made out, not to Schweppes, but to 'You-Know-Who'. While the actual naming of the brand in pubs only improved slightly (the British are so averse to being specific), Schweppes successfully penetrated the public consciousness and sales rose. It even gained market share, a remarkable achievement for such a dominant brand leader, for marketing history suggests that really strong market leaders attract a constant stream of competitors and have difficulty in maintaining overall dominance for long.

The commercials were never unduly expensive to make. They relied upon good creative ideas and skilled film-making for their effect. The same production company, Illustra, was employed, ensuring that all who worked on the films acquired special knowledge about what was possible and right for the product.

To begin with the three leading flavours – tonic, ginger ale and bitter lemon – had different creative approaches (Patrick Campbell was the spoke-spoke-spokesman for ginger ale) but the success of William Franklyn soon ensured that he became the salesman for the entire Schweppes range. But the use of Franklyn changed over the years and also the selling task that was demanded of him.

For the first few years he was the man on the run trying to protect the secret of Schhh... from unspecified rivals. By the end of this period the character was beginning to suffer from paranoia. In the early commercials he could be awaiting a call from a contact in a telephone box which was snatched up by an enemy helicopter and lifted over London; but soon he was hunted down on a beach persecuted by children in dark glasses as threatening as Midwitch Cuckoos. Fortunately, before the idea became an excess of the creative team's soaring imagination, it was appreciated that the audience's enjoyment of Franklyn was such that he could sell the product on the strength of his own sophisticated personality; anyway, spy-mania was over.

The emergence of Franklyn's social superiority and sang froid – protecting his Schweppes as a house was knocked down around him, for example – coincided with new selling tasks. Schweppes was aware that its position in the licensed trade was threatened by mergers and the appearance of brands owned by the major brewing groups. Franklyn had to fight off this parvenu opposition. Some Schweppes marketing executives think that some of the advertising paid too much attention to the competition. In one commercial Franklyn was shown having to get rid of some inferior tonic water foisted upon him at a party – he pours it into a parrot's drinking water and the bird immediately topples from its perch. Franklyn had by this time *become* Schweppes, completely identified in the public mind with this rather special mixer. He could even undertake such a hard-nosed marketing exercise as selling the new non-returnable bottle. He was discovered in the Crush Bar at the Royal Opera House with some mixers hidden in his dress tails prepared for the dire discovery that the Covent Garden bar might not sell Schweppes. This commercial also included another inspired touch from Roger Adams. The soignée lady accompanying Franklyn let loose a broad Liverpudlian accent when she spoke – a 'Lorraine Chase *Luton Airport*' touch ten years in advance.

Looking back on this stage of his career William Franklyn attributes the success of the campaign to the

WHEREVER YOU GO-DRINK SCHWEPPES

UNITED KINGDOM Schweppes Ltd Connaught Place London · AUSTRALIA Schweppes (Australia) Ltd · BELGIUM Schweppes (Genval) Ltd SA · CANADA Schweppes (Canada) Ltd · CANARY ISLANDS Establecimientos Industriales Añaza SL · CEYLON Ceylon Mineral Waters Ltd · CENTRAL AFRICA Schweppes (Central Africa) Ltd · EAST AFRICA Schweppes (East Africa) Ltd · FEDERATION OF MALAYA Union Ltd · FRANCE Schweppes (Paris) Ltd SA · GERMANY Landskroner Getränke GmbH · GIBRALTAR Saccone & Speed Ltd · HONG KONG International Beverages Co Ltd ‡ITALY S·I·L·V·A di V Bianchi · JAMAICA Desnoes & Geddes Ltd · JAPAN Japan Soft Drinks Ltd · MALTA Simonds-Farsons-Cisk Ltd · NEW ZEALAND Schweppes (New Zealand) Ltd · NORTHERN IRELAND Cantrell & Cochrane Ltd NORWAY Nora Fabrikker A/S · PORTUGAL Sociedade Central de Cervejas SARL · PUERTO RICO Orange Crush of Puerto Rico Inc · REPUBLIC OF IRELAND Schweppes (Ireland) Ltd · REPUBLIC OF SENEGAL Tonic Afric SA · SINGAPORE Union Ltd · SOUTH AFRICA Schweppes (South Africa) Ltd · SPAIN Rioblanco SA · SWEDEN Apotekarnes Mineralvattens Aktiebolag · SWITZERLAND Weissenburg Mineralthermen AG · UNITED STATES OF AMERICA Schweppes (USA) Ltd · VENEZUELA CA Embotelladora Caracas *and exported to all parts of the world*
‡*The Colosseum, Rome*

One of a series of advertisements created as a campaign for use in multi-national media

fact that the commercials were largely made by a triumvirate – Roger Adams, the director Douglas Hickox (later to move on to feature films like *Entertaining Mr Sloane*) and himself, with no interference from the client and very little from the agency. So a great esprit de corps developed, with everyone encouraged to make suggestions. It was Franklyn, a keen sportsman, who suggested the commercial featuring Rod Laver, the Wimbledon champion of the time, and it was Mrs Franklyn who contributed the punch line to the ad, 'anyone for tonic?'. Franklyn also got Fred Trueman to appear in a commercial apparently filmed on a traditional English village green, but actually shot in the West Indies – the most appropriate spot for cricket in November.

The commercials for the year, generally about six, would be completed in three weeks or so, usually in the UK, but occasionally abroad. A shoot in Spain caused problems. It was to feature a desert island, but a suitable island was not forthcoming. Franklyn suggested that a reef of rocks could be converted into an island by covering them with tarpaulins and some imported sand. Unfortunately, bad weather in-

tervened and the production team had to fly out to Spain three times to complete the film. Then a scene showing Franklyn sending off a note in an empty Schweppes bottle aroused the anger of the anti-litter lobby and thirty-odd letters of complaint were enough to persuade Schweppes promptly to remove the commercial from the screens. But this was exceptional. The commercials were invariably made quickly, easily and happily, and none was rejected.

Working for Schweppes gave Franklyn financial security for the first time in his life (he was paid £2,000 for the first batch of commercials and much more later) and a public personality which he has never lost; he is still greeted with 'Schhh...' as he walks down the street. He is proud of the association. 'I had been offered another product and turned it down, but Schweppes is a Rolls Royce brand. I think I was a pioneer, one of the first recognisable actors to sell himself to commercials; since then everyone, up to Lord Olivier, has followed me.' The association with Schweppes probably harmed his television career at the time, but not his stage work. Now both flourish; he still plays squash regularly with Roger Adams, and continues to regard himself as something of an expert on Schweppes advertising. 'I think they've got to forget about advertising. Schweppes is about re-assuring people, making them feel secure and amused.' In his experience, as soon as the commercials were taken too seriously and became analysed by committees the early sparkle was lost.

But in the late sixties Schweppes television advertising was inexorably wedded to Franklyn, whose sneer was more eloquent than a thousand words. Then Schweppes began to worry that the idea was wearing out, although when the alternative campaigns prepared by the agency were tested they never scored as well as 'Schhh...'. Tubby Pitcher believes that there was still considerable mileage in Franklyn, and the campaign. Indeed the current Schweppes agency, Saatchi & Saatchi, has recently employed his voice, while some of their commercials, especially one in which a young couple on a train switch their mixers in the darkness of a tunnel (each, of course, trying to get the only Schweppes left) carry the early theme up to the present day.

But by 1971 Franklyn was obviously greying and becoming a very strong personality in his own right – was he appropriate for a brand that was anxious to appeal to the growing number of young mixer-drinkers? Was he not a little too sophisticated for a soft drink? Was it becoming the William Franklyn Show? The vote went for a change; but the Franklyn years were not so easily superseded. Research to this day confirms that the company has perhaps not yet come up with anything quite so memorable.

The good thing is that everyone looks back with happy memories of the 'Schhh ... you-know-who' years. For the agency there was a string of prizes; a prestige client who gradually doubled his advertising expenditure to £1m; and assignments in overseas markets because of the success of the British campaign. For Franklyn there was a place as a popular public figure with perpetual appeal.

For Schweppes there was the achievement of most of its marketing objectives – it had come through a decade of rapid change with its brand leadership secure and with a wider spread of loyal consumers. The problems faced in the early 1960s had been overcome – falling market share; a decline in spirit drinking, especially of gin, and campaigns by spirit manufacturers to have their product drunk straight or with water; links between its competitors and the licensed trade; the emergence of the take-home market which attracted new competitors because it was easier to produce disposable bottles than to finance bottle-

cleaning machinery and a distribution network for returned bottles; the danger of reduced consumer interest in the product, coupled with reluctance to specify particular flavours. More to the point, new opportunities – non-returnable bottles; Schweppes Slimline products; drinking Schweppes straight – were seized and built upon. And brand share rose again.

The television commercials were given the highest accolade – David Ogilvy's agency in the US used some of the ideas, including Franklyn, to sell to the American market; Franklyn actually appeared in commercials with Commander Whitehead, a real battle of the heavyweights. But it was not only on film that the 'secret' worked. Press advertisements and posters spread the message – Tubby Pitcher remembers a particularly well-photographed press ad showing a Schweppes tonic lying in a French wine cellar sharing the cobwebs with Premier Cru wines, under the copyline 'Britons be proud – the French are stealing the secret of Schhh...'. The real significance of this era of Schweppes advertising is not only that it safeguarded its market share but that it added value to the image of the product. The company's tradition of humour, style and quality had been extended to the new and sophisticated competition of television advertising and had come out on top again. Now everybody, and not just the original consumers, had an appreciation of what Schweppes stood for, and still represents – quality and taste.

SCHWEPPING INTERNATIONALLY

Schweppes has been exporting its products almost from the start of the operation, even when Jacob Schweppe was still working in Geneva. When in England he was soon exporting to places as far apart as the Antilles, the East Indies and the Cape. Certainly in 1823 Schweppe's were advertising that they could supply at short notice for exportation. Schweppe's products were taken on board sailing ships and soon reached the colonies.

But overseas advertising came much later, and international advertising, in which an effort was made to portray a single Schweppes image throughout the world, has only materialised in the last generation. Schweppes has always allowed its local bottlers and subsidiary companies a great deal of autonomy, encouraging them to appoint local advertising agencies. Even so, with many managers receiving London

An advertisement from an Italian campaign using the Schweppes 'Schhh'

Schhh... non tutti ce l'hanno

Ne parleranno. Ve la chiederanno. Ne berranno parecchia di Schweppes.
E voi, siate dalla parte di chi la versa. Schweppes vi qualifica come barman e
dà tono ai vostri drinks. Che sia Tonic Water, Bitter Lemon, Soda Water
o Ginger Ale, sarà Schweppes che chiederanno. Perché quest'anno Schweppes
è nel vento, cioè in stampa e al cinema, al livello che
si merita, con una campagna pubblicitaria così Schhh...così Schweppes.

Le "drink"
des
Gens
Raffinés

DÉLICIEUSE

BOISSON

PÉTILLANTE,

SE SERT NATURE

AVEC UNE

TRANCHE DE CITRON

OU D'ORANGE

PUBL. EDITIONS - S 16

Schweppes

"INDIAN TONIC"

training, the Schweppes style has pervaded much of the overseas advertising and the advertisements have invariably been influenced from the UK.

The first multi-national advertising campaign for Schweppes was launched in the early 1960s using such magazines as *Life International* and *Time*. It was slightly hesitant, depicting a series of foreign scenes – the Colosseum in Rome, a Spanish bull ring – under the common slogan 'Wherever you go drink Schweppes'. But within a couple of years some of the traditional Schweppes advertising strengths were visible. Attractively photographed scenes of the Colosseum again, the Rock of Gibraltar, Notre Dame in Paris, and more, showed glamorous people enjoying Schweppes in a jigsaw puzzle format, with one piece missing and the caption 'Schweppes completes the picture'.

Very soon the company was playing on the strength of its name. 'Do you speak Schweppes?' ran some advertisements appearing in Switzerland; 'In London they speak Schweppes', proclaimed others, with the copy then reverting to the national language and supporting pictures of Swinging London. The Englishness of the product was regarded as a great strength: in France and in Italy it was portrayed as an essential of English country life, as special as a Rolls Royce or the Derby. The internationalism of Schweppes was also emphasised: one campaign showed it being drunk by groups of young people from Japan, Morocco, Kenya, South America, Norway, etc. And while the company experimented with international campaigns there were national efforts in all the main markets.

But international advertising took on a completely new dimension in 1980 when Schweppes, with a stretch of the imagination which took it far ahead of virtually all the world's mass marketing companies, decided to develop an international advertising campaign which would be as memorable and as effective on a global scale as Schweppervescence, Schweppshire and 'Schhh ... you-know-who' were in British advertising history. The chief executive of Schweppes, Basil Collins, and the international marketing director, Geoff Darby, had had great experience in running Schweppes operations overseas and in international marketing. They were determined that in a shrinking world, with international advertising, through satellites, likely to be an accomplished fact by the mid-1980s, Schweppes should be the leaders in

Left: One of a series of French press advertisements
Facing: Schwepping showcard from the United Kingdom

Schwepping is looking good in glasses.

Above and below: examples of Schwepping advertising from U.S.A.

Schwepping poster from France

Schwepping
is taking
your top off
on a hot day.

Above and below: two more examples of the international Schwepping campaign

advertising to the world market. Collins' basic approach was that only by attracting as many consumers as possible for Schweppes products could the company's assets be worked to the full, and that advertising was the means to maximise sales.

A few other companies have developed international campaigns, notably Coca-Cola, but whereas this company insists on one creative approach for all markets, the Schweppes ideal was to develop a concept, a phrase, a word, that summed up all that was best in Schweppes and then allow the individual countries to build advertising around it that was most appropriate to their national characteristics. In 1980 the advertising agencies from Schweppes' main markets were asked for ideas that would produce a long-term international advertising campaign. The NCK agency came up with the goods – 'Schwepping'.

As NCK pointed out, Schwepping had been there, before the eyes of the company, for years. It had even been used in a fleeting way in the 'How many Schwepping days to Christmas?' campaign devised in the early 1950s. But NCK believed – and succeeded in proving – that Schwepping had tremendous potential for imaginative development. For a start it was a verb, a 'doing' word, and fitted easily into all the major languages of the world. Many of Schweppes' greatest advertising campaigns had been built around the company name: here was another opportunity. Just by imagining a dictionary definition of Schwepping the agency poured out all the words that Schweppes had long sought to identify with – 'enjoyment, fruition, gratification, satisfaction, fulfilment, completion, delectation, zest, gusto, indulgence, wallowing, fun', etc. With creativity the Schweppes advertising agencies could prove to the world that Schweppes, through Schwepping, was all those things and more. NCK even defined Schwepping more prosaically: 'Schwepping is – opening a bottle of Schweppes Tonic (with the inevitable Schhh . . .), pouring it and drinking it. Enjoying the finest tonic water in the world. Knowing how to make the most of one's pleasures – with style, sophistication, and a real sense of humour'.

Some immediate examples showed the flexibility of the word. 'Schwepping is raising the nation's spirits'; 'One sip and you're Schwepping'; 'Schwepping brings out the best in everyone'. Apart from its positive ring and its link with historic advertising, Schwepping had that international appeal that completely chimed with Schweppes' long-term plans. The concept was accepted, and the leading agencies in the main markets were encouraged to build their own advertising around Schwepping. This was making considerable demands

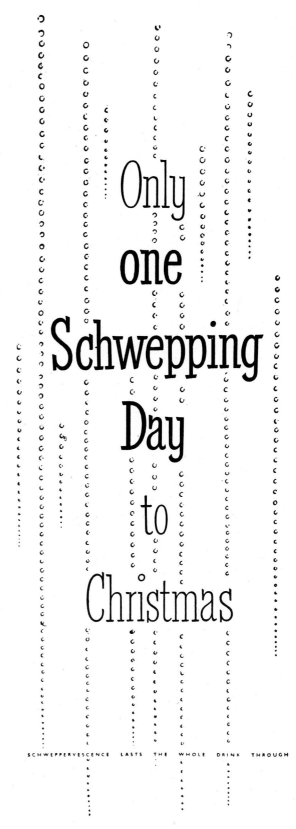

A newspaper advertisement published on Christmas Eve 1953

on them, since few agencies like working to a creative idea designed by a competitor, but within a year Schweppes was examining a rich harvest of imaginative ideas and was even more convinced that the word to represent the company to its international consumers was Schwepping.

The attraction of Schwepping is that it provides a foundation rather than a formula. Schweppes' agencies in its leading markets – in the UK and the US, in France and Italy and West Germany and South Africa and elsewhere – are adapting Schwepping to their individual requirements. By the autumn of 1981 Saatchi & Saatchi in the UK was getting to grips with the idea – 'Schwepping is looking good in glasses' reads one poster, made effective by some brilliant photography of brimming glasses; 'Schwepping is melting the ice at parties' reads another, with a Tonic sparkling on ice cubes. In France, Schwepping has been adapted to television, outdoor and press advertising, using a cartoon format which has direct links with some of the Schweppes cartoon advertising in Britain in the 1940s and 1950s. For extra impact the advertising is in black and white except for the yellow-labelled Schweppes Tonic bottle. Within months the new approach had increased Schweppes' market share in France and the new word had been accepted as the best kind of franglais.

In Italy a sophisticated man instructs an attractive girl in the delights of Schwepping; in Germany a golf player is dragged back to the club-house by the sparkling sound of Schwepping. In the US, commercials have been developed to describe the sophisticated pleasure of choosing Schweppes, in grand surroundings, as 'Schwepping it up'. Not every country has perfected the advertising with the idea yet but Schweppes is pleased with the early progress and is confident that by the time that advertisements are being beamed worldwide by satellite the word will have joined the international language, conveying the idea that Schwepping is a delightful thing to do.

The time, money and mental energy being invested in Schwepping is quite remarkable, but then such a large scale, long-term advertising campaign has never been attempted before. Schweppes had always believed in the power of the extended campaign rather than the brilliant one-off advertisement and in this exercise is taking that belief, a belief in inspired logic rather than the constant re-checking of public response through research, to its furthest limit.

Much attention is being paid to the briefing of agencies. Schweppes' marketing directors and advertising agencies must follow a series of agreed criteria

– that all their advertising is part of a campaign that will last at least five years; that each advertisement is making a positive contribution to the overall campaign; that each advertisement will enhance consumer confidence in the qualities of Schweppes products; that each advertisement is demonstrably part of the international Schwepping campaign; that the advertising should also conform to the established character of Schweppes advertising (confident, adult, stylish); that the Schwepping idea is conveyed through its own qualities and is not dragged in on the back of an older treatment; and, finally, that the Schwepping concept is central to the advertising. And if, by any dread chance, there is a temporary problem in the advertising of a particular country, Schwepping enables the company to have an international campaign ready to plug the gap.

All this planning and preparation of rules suggests that Schwepping might produce regimented advertising. In practice, because all the agencies are making their individual creative contributions and because each of them wants to prove that it is more imaginative than the others, the Schwepping idea is proving to have tremendous potential. The fact that it conveys an active pleasure extends it to the widest possible range of human experience – work and play, travel and home. It also works in all media.

Once the concept of Schwepping has been got across to consumers there is the opportunity to refer to it in a knowing way. The Society of Schweppers, the University of Schwepping (an off-shoot perhaps of the University of Schweppshire), even a Government Department of Schwepping, are some of the suggestions for the mature campaign. By the time international advertising is upon us Schwepping will be as much a common currency word of the western world as 'le weekend' or 'hi fi'.

Schweppes hopes that in the Schwepping campaigns it will present to the international market the same kind of advertising that has served the product so well in the UK in the last fifty years. To begin with Schwepping will be aimed mainly at the UK, the US and Europe, which account for over three-quarters of sales; it can later be adapted easily to other markets. In taking the lead in multi-national advertising Schweppes' management is attempting a positive reaction to the obvious fact that little real growth can be expected from the British market in the future; long term profitability depends on rising overseas sales. Geoff Darby is well aware that the company is breaking new ground; 'The last thing we want is to provide the local management with the excuse that they are doing badly because they have been given a fixed advertising idea. So we will encourage local management to employ the local agency of their choice while receiving creative help and the broad approach from London'. Schweppes is also prepared to back Schwepping with cash. Unlike some major companies it is convinced that advertising is essential for higher sales. This is a company faith that has been passed on from the early days, and certainly from Sir Frederic Hooper to Lord Watkinson to Basil Collins, and it is a faith that becomes a reality in a big budget for Schwepping in 1981, almost doubled in 1982, with the certainty of a further rise in later years as more countries fuel the campaign.

The great achievement of Schweppes advertising in recent years had been its ability to pass on its tradition of quality advertising for a quality market to quality advertising for the mass market. A logical extension is the decision to communicate through one campaign to the mass multi-national market. Its advertising throughout the years has rested, mainly by design, occasionally by chance, on the same firm guidelines – a conspiracy between the company and the consumer as to the quality of the product; gentle humour; a faith in the intelligence of consumers which enables Schweppes to address them with sophistication but without condescension; a sense of the tradition of the Schweppes product, now vindicated by its two centuries of popularity; confidence and style in the advertising and a willingness to pay for the best in the knowledge that the consumer is also prepared to pay for the best; a constant appreciation of the marketable quality of the Schweppes name, a word both intriguing and eminently adaptable; and, finally, the application of intelligence to advertising. Schweppes has also been helped by the fact, which cannot really be a coincidence, that all its chief executives of modern times have taken a great personal interest in advertising and have been convinced of its importance. History has more than justified their confidence, to the gain of both the company and the connoisseur of fine advertising.

Index

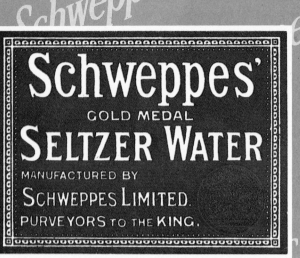

Schweppes'
GOLD MEDAL
SELTZER WATER
MANUFACTURED BY
SCHWEPPES LIMITED.
PURVEYORS TO THE KING.

BY APPOINTMENT

Schweppes
POTASS WATER

SCHWEPPES DRY
Ginger Ale
Dry & Non-Alcoholic
Schweppes Ltd.
ISSUED ONLY BY SCHWEPPES LIMITED.

Schweppes
BY SPECIAL APPOINTMENT
TO H.M. THE KING.
Ginger Beer

SCHWEPPES
SINCE 1783
Schweppes®
Tónica

CONTIENE QUININA. "BEBIDA REFRESCANTE DE EXTRACTOS"
CONTENIDO 180 CC.
EMBOTELLADO EN ESPAÑA POR RIOBLANCO, S.A.
CON LICENCIA DE SCHWEPPES INTERNATIONAL LTD. LONDRES
GB

BY APPOINTMENT TO
HER MAJESTY QUEEN ELIZABETH II
MINERAL WATER MANUFACTURERS
SCHWEPPES LIMITED
LONDON
Schweppes®
GEGR. 1783
BITTER LEMON
200 ml
LIMONENLIMONADE, CHININHALTIG
EIN PRODUKT DER SCHWEPPES LTD., LONDON
HERGESTELLT VON SCHWEPPES GMBH, HAMBURG